SAT® Vocabulary For Dummies®

Cheat

D0521253

Considering Connotation Clusters

Unless you have a photographic memory, you probably don't remember words in alphabetical order, straight off the pages of a dictionary. You need another way to recall not just one word at a time, but groups of words together. The following suggestions can help.

- Group words according to their meanings, such as words about personal appearance, words about intelligence, words about work, and so on.

- Remember words as synonyms (*erudite*, *omniscient* = knowledgeable) and antonyms (*nescient*, *dolt* = ignorant)

- Use three or four words instead of one in conversation and personal writing, such as "She was pulchritudinous, comely, and svelte" or "We suffered from lethargy, torpor, and sluggishness on the weekend."

Benefi... Buildi...

Think of pref... blocks you us............ .... vocabulary. Using these blocks efficiently and effectively helps you maximize your word gain and minimize your brain strain.

- Use prefixes to determine whether a word is positive (*eu*– = good; *pro*– = big or much) or negative (*caco*– = bad; *ex*– = down from, away from, or to put down)

- Use roots to get the gist of the word (*phon* = sound; *culp* = guilt)

- Use suffixes to fine-tune the definition (*–ous* = full of; *–ate* = to make)

- Put everything together to define hard words: *euphonious* = full of good sound (good-sounding, like a pleasant voice); *exculpate* = make away from blame (free from guilt, declare blameless)

Contemplating Contextual Clues

Very rarely in you're life will someone approach you and say, "Quick: What does somnolent mean?" Instead, you encounter words in stories, articles, or speeches. You can remember words by recalling where you read or heard them.

- Review words in the context of stories.

- Remember where you learned a word by recalling the tale.

- Define a word in a way that's close enough by recalling how it was used in an anecdote.

Soaking Up Study Suggestions

After you're introduced to new SAT vocab words, just how are you going to fix them *permanently* in your brain? Here are a few ideas:

- Put prefixes, roots, and suffixes on color-coded flash cards and memorize them.

- Associate words with friends and situations ("Somnolent [sleepy] Sam"; "Vivacious [energetic] Vicky").

- Identify similarities between difficult English words and easier words in another language (facilitate in English; *facil* in Spanish).

- Enlist the help of family and friends to use these words around you as much as possible.

- Keep a card file of groups of words (happy/sad; fun/boring); add new words as you encounter them in your studies.

- Take the practice exams in this book (including the Genius Test in Chapter 27) more than once, repeating them until you get perfect scores.

For Dummies: Bestselling Book Series for Beginners

SAT® *Vocabulary For Dummies*®

Cheat Sheet

Prefixes, Roots, and Suffixes

By mastering these prefixes, roots, and suffixes (along with a few more listed on the front side of this Cheat Sheet), you can determine the meaning of unfamiliar words.

Prefixes

a–, an– = not, without
ab– = away from
ad– = toward, addition
anim– = life, spirit
ante– = before
anti– = opposite
auc–, aug– = increase
aud–, aur– = hear
auto– = self
ben–, bon–, eu– = good
brev– = short
caco–, dys– = bad, abnormal
ceiv–, cept–, capt– = take

circum– = around
co–, con–, col–, cor– = with
contra–, counter– = against
de–, ex– = out of, away from
extra– = beyond, outside
hetero– = other
homo– = same
hyper– = above
hypo– = under
il–, im–, in–, ir–, non– = not
inter– = between
intra– = within
mal–, mis–, ne– = bad

peri– = around
poly– = many
post– = after
pre– = before
pro– = big, much
re–, retro– = back, again
se– = apart
sub–, suc–, suf– = below
super–, sur– = over, above
syn–, sym– = together, with
trans– = across, beyond
ultra–, outr– = beyond
vice– = in place of

Roots

ambu = walk, move
andro = man
anthro = human
bellu, belli = war, fight
carn = flesh
clam, claim = shout
clin = lean, bend
clud, clus, claus = close
cred = trust, belief
demo– = people
dog, dox = thought, idea
duc, duct = to lead, pull
ev = time, age
fac = to do, make
fiss = break, part
flict = strike
fort = strength

fract, frag, frai = break
gnos = knowledge
grad, gress = to go
greg = group, herd
gyn = woman
her, hes = to stick
jac, ject = to throw
loq, log, loc, lix = talk
luc, lum, lus = light, clear
meta, mut = change
morph = shape
narco = sleep
omni = all
oper = work
pac, plac = peace, calm
path = feeling
phon = sound

pug = war, fight
rupt = break
sanct = holy
scien = knowledge
senti = feeling
somn, sop = sleep
son = sound
soph = wise
spec = look
term = end, boundary
terr = earth
theo = God
ven = come
vid, vis = to see
voc, voke = call
vol = roll, turn
xen = stranger

Suffixes

–able, –ible = capable of
–ate, –ify,–efy, –ize, –ise = make
–cess, –cede = to go, yield

–cide = to kill
–cis = cut
–ette, –illo = little

–ist = a person
–logy, –ology = study
–ous = full of

For Dummies: *Bestselling Book Series for Beginners*

SAT* Vocabulary

FOR

DUMMIES®

SAT* Vocabulary FOR DUMMIES®

by Suzee Vlk

Author of *The SAT I For Dummies, The ACT For Dummies,*
The GRE For Dummies, The GMAT For Dummies

WILEY

Wiley Publishing, Inc.

SAT* Vocabulary For Dummies®

Published by
Wiley Publishing, Inc.
909 Third Avenue
New York, NY 10022
www.wiley.com

Copyright © 2003 by Wiley Publishing, Inc., Indianapolis, Indiana

Published by Wiley Publishing, Inc., Indianapolis, Indiana

Published simultaneously in Canada

For general information on our other products and services or to obtain technical support, please contact
our Customer Care Department within the U.S. at 800-762-2974, outside the U.S. at 317-572-3993, or fax
317-572-4002.

Wiley also publishes its books in a variety of electronic formats. Some content that appears in print may
not be available in electronic books.

Library of Congress Control Number: 2002114850

ISBN: 0-7645-2546-8

Manufactured in the United States of America

10 9 8 7 6 5

*SAT is a registered trademark of the College Entrance Examination Board, which is not affiliated with
this book.

WILEY   is a trademark of Wiley Publishing, Inc.

About the Author

While putting the finishing touches on this book, author **Suzee Vlk** passed away when a tree fell on her during a Santa Ana wind-storm near her home in San Diego. At the time of her death, she was gearing up for a busy season of test-prep tutoring and was looking forward to a summer vacation in an exotic locale.

Suzee lived as she died: in an extraordinary way. Born in 1953, Suzee is rumored to have earned a perfect score on the SAT in 1970 — but that could be an urban legend. After passing both the LSAT and GMAT with flying colors, she went on to earn a law degree (J.D.) and business degree (MBA) before turning to full-time test tutoring.

Although her business — Suzee Vlk Test Prep — thrived under her direction, people frequently asked why she chose one-on-one tutoring with high-school and college students over accepting a partnership in a law firm or working in a successful corporation. For Suzee, that choice was simple: She found more joy helping students be successful. And her technique was a proven success: Her students have been accepted at colleges, universities, and graduate schools worldwide, including such dream schools as Harvard, Yale, Stanford, the U.S. Military Academy at West Point, and the Naval Academy at Annapolis.

When Suzee aspired to tutor even more students than those she could work with day to day, she turned to writing a test-prep column that ran in several California high-school newspapers. In 1995, she wrote and published *The SAT I For Dummies,* a successful book that she revised and updated five times and through which she helped tens of thousands of students raise their test scores. Suzee followed that success with other titles, including *The ACT For Dummies, The GRE For Dummies,* and *The GMAT For Dummies. SAT Vocabulary For Dummies* is a book she felt was needed for many years, and she was pleased and excited at the prospect of finally getting it published.

Suzee's chosen profession gave her some down time during the summer and around the holidays, and she traveled with gusto around the world. She visited at least two dozen countries — not just as a tourist, but as an adventurer. She was once hospitalized in Egypt with a camel bite. Suzee lived life to the fullest.

We in the Dummies family at Wiley Publishing will miss Suzee dearly. No one else but Suzee could brighten your day with a bad pun or a silly story, as well as incorporating her wide-ranging knowledge of history, philosophy, mythology, and language.

We proudly publish Suzee's last gift to her students and students everywhere. As long as her books continue to help students achieve their dreams (while having a good laugh, too), Suzee will remain with us, doing what she loved best.

Dedication

Dedicated with thanks to Georgia and Jim McKee, the World's Greatest Travel Agents, who not only got me to my destinations, but are magnanimous enough to allow me to return. I've been grateful to you from China to Peru, Borneo to Bulgaria, Scotland to the Soviet Union, Turkey to Nepal, Hong Kong to Romania, Sicily to Poland, Morocco to Antarctica, Egypt to England, and innumerable points in between. (And we still have half a world to go!)

Author's Acknowledgments

After years of having California and Florida students groan at my puns (they frequently remind me of the Fred Allen joke that "hanging is too good for a person who makes puns; he should be drawn and quoted"), make rude hand gestures in response to my scintillatingly clever quips, and threaten to storm out of the room (as Groucho Marx said, "Don't leave in a huff. Wait a minute and a huff!") if I tell my vocabulary jokes one more time, it's wonderful to get the chance to inflict my dysfunctional sense of humor on a worldwide, unsuspecting audience. The decline of civilization begins here.

Thanks to my agents, Matt Wagner and Bill Gladstone, of Waterside Productions in Cardiff, California, for getting me this opportunity, and to Kathy Cox, acquisitions editor, for securing the project. Approximately 26.2 thanks to my project editor, Tere Drenth, marathoner par excellence who managed to cope with my sprinting style with professionalism, punctiliousness, and patience. Many thanks go also to Thomas La Farge, who reviewed this manuscript for technical accuracy.

It's important for me to acknowledge one of the most underused and underappreciated resources today's students have: high school and university counselors. Thanks to all of you who go out of your way to help students to do their best to prepare for the rites of passage (SAT, GRE, and so on) that use this vocabulary.

And finally, thanks go to my students over the years, those wonderful teens and adults who have had enough faith in me to use my tricks for enhancing their vocabulary and enough kindness to let me share their joy in the good test scores that result. You all keep this fun.

Publisher's Acknowledgments

We're proud of this book; please send us your comments through our Dummies online registration form located at www.dummies.com/register/.

Some of the people who helped bring this book to market include the following:

Acquisitions, Editorial, and Media Development

Project Editor: Tere Drenth

Acquisitions Editor: Kathy Cox

Technical Editor: Thomas La Farge

Editorial Manager: Michelle Hacker

Editorial Assistant: Elizabeth Rea

Cartoons: Rich Tennant, www.the5thwave.com

Production

Project Coordinator: Dale White

Layout and Graphics: Carrie Foster, Michael Kruzil, Jacque Schneider

Proofreaders: Andy Hollandbeck; TECHBOOKS Production Services

Indexer: TECHBOOKS Production Services

Publishing and Editorial for Consumer Dummies

Diane Graves Steele, Vice President and Publisher, Consumer Dummies

Joyce Pepple, Acquisitions Director, Consumer Dummies

Kristin A. Cocks, Product Development Director, Consumer Dummies

Michael Spring, Vice President and Publisher, Travel

Brice Gosnell, Publishing Director, Travel

Suzanne Jannetta, Editorial Director, Travel

Publishing for Technology Dummies

Andy Cummings, Vice President and Publisher, Dummies Technology/General User

Composition Services

Gerry Fahey, Vice President of Production Services

Debbie Stailey, Director of Composition Services

Contents at a Glance

Table of Contents

Introduction

●●●

*W*elcome to *SAT Vocabulary For Dummies*. Don't take the title personally, because you're no dummy. Unfortunately, though, most people don't have the wealth of words, the plethora of prattle, the volumes of vocabulary that enable them to get top scores on the SAT I (the test that most people call "the SAT"), PSAT, GRE, and other exams that expect you to have digested the dictionary and know every seven-syllable word used since Shakespearean times.

As you well know, some people in this world don't simply say "hi" but rather *declaim* (speak in a dramatic way), "*Salutations* (greetings) on this *matutinal* (morning, early) occasion!" Those people, alas, are the ones who write the vocabulary portions of standardized exams. Unless you're the type who can master words by *osmosis,* who can sleep with a dictionary under your head and have the words sink into your brain in the middle of the night, you need some help.

Think of this book as your *cavalier* (knight) in *resplendent* (shining) *carapace* (shell or bony armor). Here, you see billions and billions — well, okay, hundreds and hundreds — of the vocabulary words that are likely to plague and torment you with their presence during the exam. You find out how to *shoehorn* (squeeze) the words into your brain with the least agony and effort, even having a good time in the process.

Bonus: This book can go your White Knight one step better. While *SAT Vocabulary For Dummies* doesn't have the dragon-slaying abilities of the dude in iron Levi's, it has something better: humor. Far too many vocabulary books are dull, dull, dull. You nod off as you read through them. If you can master vocabulary in your sleep, fine. If you prefer to stay awake and get a giggle or two as you go through the words, stick with me. You may become annoyed at my lame jokes ("What kind of furniture do you find in a psychiatrist's office? Overwrought iron!") or distracted by my trivia ("What is the official state sport of Maryland? Jousting!"), but I guarantee you'll never be bored.

Conventions Used in This Book

Sure, you pride yourself in being *un*conventional, but take a minute to read the following list that tells you what conventions are used to help you throughout this book. (A *convention,* in case you're wondering, is a customary practice or usage. In other words, the following paragraphs explain how you'll see the material presented in the following 30 chapters.)

- Vocabulary words are printed in a special font, *like this.* The words are the ones you'll see defined in this book and will likely be tested on college-entrance exams.

- Every word has a pronunciation key following it. These keys may be straightforward, such as "belittled (be *littled*)" or more imaginative, such as "turpitude (rhymes with, *burp* it Dude)". (Note that the emphasized syllable is in italics.)

  While the PSAT, SAT I, GRE, and other exams are nearly always printed, not oral, you want to know how to pronounce the words so that you can use them in the real world. How else will you be able to impress your parents and friends with your incredibly expanded vocabulary if you can't say the words aloud?

- In many definitions and explanations of new vocab words, roots, prefixes and suffixes are given to help break down the words and, therefore, remember them more easily. Chapter 2 gives all of these roots, prefixes, and suffixes in one spot. Even if you like to skip around in a book, you may want to read Chapter 2 first.

- In Part II of this book, words are introduced in groups by categories or cluster, such as words having to do with personal appearance, words having to do with intelligence, words having to do with laziness, and so on. Instead of mastering only one word that describes how smart you are, you can pick up a half dozen or more.

  Contrast this part to Part III of this book, in which vocabulary is introduced in context, used in stories that are — supposedly! — funny and interesting. You can remember the meanings of these words on your exam by recalling how they were used in the story. ("Oh yeah, that was in the part where she told how her student conked her on the head with his SAT book. I remember that.")

- You are given more vocabulary in this book than is apparent at first. Each chapter begins with a word list, detailing the words presented and tested in the chapter. However, that list gives you only the words defined in the main section of each book. In actuality, you're exposed to far more words in each chapter through synonyms given in the definitions, bonus trivia and pathetic jokes, example sentences, exercises, and sidebars. In fact, if a chapter *purports* (gives the appearance of; seems) to present a dozen words, you may, in fact, be introduced to two or even three times that many. Think of these extra words as a *lagniappe* (lan *yap*) or a "gift with purchase."

  The sidebars (gray boxes of text) sprinkled throughout this book are, alone, worth the price of the book. Intentionally written to be amusing, the sidebars in this book give you additional words that are grouped together in some way: terms to use for herds of animals, for example, or words that describe talking trash. Don't skip the sidebars, thinking they are just asides that don't matter. They have a lot of great information in them and are fun to read.

✔ While some of the question styles in this book are identical to the questions you may see on college-entrance exams, others vary from those in the SAT I. The actual SAT I has Analogy questions (although beginning in 2005, Analogies will no longer be on the exam), but this book doesn't. Why would I do this?

I don't include Analogy questions because they can be easy to answer even when you don't know what the words mean (see *The SAT I For Dummies,* written by *moi* and published by Wiley Publishing, Inc., for an entire chapter on tricks and tips for mastering Analogies). So, instead, I focus in this book on Sentence Completion questions (just like those on the SAT I), which require a strong vocabulary. I also include examples that are sort of like Critical Reading questions on the SAT I, but instead of giving your lengthy passage from which you're supposed to understand the meanings of words, I give you sentences only. And then, to keep this book from getting boring, I also include exercises featuring antonyms and matching questions.

Foolish Assumptions

Want some good news? The material in this book doesn't assume that you're starting with a solid Latin or Greek background. You don't have to have mastered any foreign languages (although if you have, you find some tips for remembering words). You don't have to have studied a *googolplex* (the number 10 with a hundred zeros!) of vocabulary lists. You don't have to know more than how to read and have a high tolerance for low humor.

Everyone begins with a different level of vocabulary. You may already know half of the words in here. Or, you may think I'm making these words up. (Honestly, I'm not, but the most fun vocabulary teacher I ever had did just that. On every test, one of the five answer choices was a made-up word. Woe betide you if you chose that answer. You were counted down twice as much as when you chose another wrong, but real word, answer.) Yet, regardless of how strong or how weak your vocabulary currently is, this book helps improve it.

This book focuses exclusively on vocabulary, though. If you're looking for help with math or other subjects, or if you want to see more examples of SAT vocab-type questions, you may want to pick up *The SAT I For Dummies,* published by Wiley Publishing, Inc. and written by Yours Truly (says she with a *stentorian* — loud — toot of her own horn). If you're taking the GRE or the TOEFL, pick up *The GRE For Dummies* (yup, I wrote that one, too) for the same reasons. Both books feature *multifarious* (of great variety, diverse) vocabulary used in the format of the exams, such as in Analogies or Sentence Completion questions.

How This Book Is Organized

This book is organized into five parts that enable you to easily find and work on whatever material is most interesting and relevant to you. You may want to start at Page 1 and work your way through the book, or you may choose to jump from part to part as the mood strikes you.

Part I: Hardwiring Words into Your Brain

This part gives you six *scintillating* suggestions (smart ideas) of ways to master vocabulary words and then turns to a thorough discussion of roots, prefixes, and suffixes, which help you understand enough of a word to answer a test question correctly. If you read nothing else in this book, study Part I.

Part II: Groups and Troops: Essential Vocabulary by Category

The chapters in this part are presented in groups or categories. In these chapters, you discover a set of vocabulary words that are related, such as words about personal appearance, words about age, words of praise and criticism, and so on. Reviewing vocabulary in clusters like these helps you to remember the words "well enough" for the SAT. In other words, you may not recall the exact definition of *comely* (attractive) but you remember it was in the chapter about personal appearance. Knowing even that much about a word can help you to get the right answer to a college entrance–exam question testing that word.

Part III: Story Time: Finding Meaning in Context

Think how you've mastered most of your vocabulary you already know: in context, right, by reading texts, novels, and even comic books. When you see a word you don't know, you probably *don't* immediately put down what you're reading and head for the dictionary (yeah, yeah, your parents and teachers tell you this is what you *should* be doing, but who really does that?) but gather the meaning of the word from the context it's used in.

This part follows the same principle, presenting ten stories that each feature new vocabulary words. Although you should be able to get the meaning of each word from its context in the story, each chapter in this part also provides you with definitions of each word. Each chapter also gives you one exercise (note how carefully I avoid frightening you with the word "test" but used instead the kinder, gentler euphemism, "exercise") that asks you to match the word with the definition.

Part IV: Putting You to the (Practice) Tests

When your brain is so stuffed with knowledge that you absolutely have to download some of it before you explode, you're ready for the sample tests in this part. You get four tests that ask you to complete fill-in-the-blank questions (the same style you see on the SAT, PSAT, and GRE) using the vocabulary you've learned in the previous parts of the book. I *prognosticate* (predict, foretell) that you'll be impressed with yourself when you realize how much test vocabulary you've mastered.

Bonus: In this part, I give you one more exam, aptly named "the Genius Test." This test asks you to recall more complicated words that I weaseled in here and there, some in the sidebars, some in the introductions, some even in the jokes. This test features the worst of the worst, the biggest, longest, hardest, most bizarre words (including some that were introduced just for fun, not for test-prep purposes). Although it may seem like a lesson in humility, I think you'll enjoy this test.

Part V: The Part of Tens

The Part of Tens adds to the good times with lists of ten fun concepts (sometimes nine, sometimes eleven; no sense being *dogmatic,* narrow-mindedly sticking to the rules). One chapter gives you ten ways to use your newfound vocabulary in the real world. Another gives you ten quotations regarding vocabulary. A final chapter gives suggestions to help you if English is a second (or third or fourth) language. This part lets you kick back and enjoy. You don't have to memorize any new vocabulary here, just have fun.

Appendixes

The first appendix in this book gives you additional resources you can use to fine-tune your vocabulary even further, if you choose to put yourself though that.

The other appendix is one you want to bookmark: It's a glossary of all the words defined throughout the book. The glossary is split into two sides: one with the word and pronunciation; the other with the definition. You can use this glossary as a reference tool, sure, but you can also use it as a study guide by covering the side with the meanings and trying to come up with the definitions yourself.

Icons Used in This Book

See those cute little pictures in the margins: the man being hit on the head with an eraser, the mousetrap, the bulls-eye, and the finger tied with string? Those are called *icons,* and their goal is to grab your attention. The following are explanations of what each icon means.

This icon directs you to tips, tricks, and techniques that can make memorizing vocabulary much easier and faster.

This icon encourages you to remember an important point given and not confuse it with a similar concept.

Be wary of the important points that this icon points out. When you see the Dummies Man bonked with the eraser, it's your clue to sit up straight and pay special attention so that it doesn't happen to you.

This icon points out words that are easy to confuse with others (dissemble/disassemble, for example) and shows you how to recognize traps set intentionally by test writers.

Where to Go from Here

Eschew conventionality (avoid normalcy). No one says you have to go through the book front to back, beginning to end, all in order. You can start anywhere you want because this book is not linear. In other words, you don't have to have read Chapter 1 to understand Chapter 2. Find a chapter that appeals to you and start there. Maybe you want to master words about money because you're about to ask for a raise at your part-time job. See Chapter 4. Perhaps you're expecting a bad report card and need some ways to say your brain wasn't working so well: Head for the chapter on intelligence (see Chapter 9).

I have one exception to this advice: the practice exams in Part IV. You want to review the other chapters in the book before taking the exams. Other than that, you can do the chapters backward to forward, inside to outside, upside down, or whatever makes you happy.

Just by reading through this short Introduction, you've already been exposed to 19 vocabulary words. Just imagine how much more you're going to see in the rest of this book!

Part I
Hardwiring Words into Your Brain

The 5th Wave   By Rich Tennant

"I hate the synonyms part of this test. I always get stumped, stymied, puzzled..."

In this part . . .

You have school, sports, chores, maybe a part-time job, family time, and — if you're lucky — some semblance of a social life. How are you going to fit in studying all this vocabulary?

This part can help. Although you're probably eager to get right into the body of this book, take a minute and go through this material first to help you make the best use of your time. Here, you find techniques for making mastering the vocabulary easier and more efficient; you also get a chapter presenting important prefixes, roots, and suffixes. A few minutes invested now can save you a lot of time and brain strain later.

Chapter 1

Mastering Test Vocabulary

● ●

In This Chapter

▶ Coming together for the greater good: connotation clusters

▶ Breaking up is easy to do: roots, prefixes, and suffixes

▶ Name-calling: buddy associations

▶ Getting your money's worth: overusing words

▶ Praising with panache and insulting with impunity

▶ Spreading the wealth: words hard at work

● ●

Does your dictionary serve as a doorstop or a booster seat for your young cousin? Has the verbal portion of your brain grown cobwebs from disuse? Don't worry: Help is at hand. In this chapter, you discover half a dozen fun and easy ways to recognize hundreds of roots without resorting to brain implants.

Giving Kudos to Clusters

Quick: Do you know the difference between a denotation and a connotation?

✓ **Denotation:** Think of D for dictionary: A *denotation* is the dictionary meaning; the legitimate, real meaning of a word — how your English teacher would define it.

✓ **Connotation:** Think of C for *cerebellum* (brain) or cranium. A *connotation* is an association suggested by the word, so it means something in your cerebellum instead of just in the dictionary. Suppose you see two basketball players slap hands on the court and say, "Baaaad shot, man!" They're not using the denotation but the connotation. In their brains, baaaad means gooood.

What're you laughing at?

As you go through this book, you encounter a lot of the jokes I've added to attempt to keep you somewhat sane. Here are several words you can use to describe the laughing you do at my lame humor.

✔ *chortle:* a gleeful chuckling sound. Lewis Carroll, the author of *Alice's Adventures in Wonderland,* invented this word, mixing "chuckle" and "snort."

✔ *guffaw:* a coarse or boisterous laugh. When the other team is talking trash to you on the court and you want to show your contempt for their boasting, you guffaw right in their faces. Guffaw, by the way, is a word described as *echoic,* which means it echoes or imitates the sound itself.

✔ *snicker:* a smothered laugh in a human. It's also, interestingly, a whinny or neigh in a horse. And before you ask how the Snickers bars got that name, I don't know, but if you do, please tell me!

✔ *snigger:* a half-suppressed or secretive laugh. When your history teacher has toilet paper stuck to the bottom of his shoe and parades back and forth in front of the class, dragging his Charmin trail, you and your buddies sit there and snigger quietly.

✔ *snort:* laugh loudly or roughly. If you can't suppress your laugher anymore and have to let it out in a huge burst, you snort.

✔ *titter:* laugh in a nervous manner. When you're having dinner with your sweetie's parents for the first time and Mr. Sweetie cracks a horrible joke, you give a titter — just a tiny, nervous laugh.

Bonus: Anyone can guffaw or give a belly laugh, but the truly pompous person *cachinnates,* which means laughing loudly or too much.

Understanding connotations of words in clusters, categories, or groups is a *scintillatingly* (shiningly) brilliant way of increasing your vocabulary quickly. For example, instead of saying someone is stubborn, why not call him *recalcitrant, obdurate,* and *hidebound?* When you're trying to convince your *dubious* (doubtful) parents that you really are smarter than your *quondam* (former) test score indicates, remind them that you're a *sagacious, erudite polymath.* By clustering words, you can become skilled at three, four, or even a dozen words for the pain and suffering of one. (Part II of this book introduces vocabulary words based on clusters of words.)

Clusters of words aren't always exact synonyms. For example, calling someone *rotund,* meaning plump, is not the same as referring to him or her as *obese,* meaning really overweight. Someone *antediluvian* (very old, literally "before the flood" as in Noah's big watery adventure) isn't necessarily the same as someone *senescent* (growing older by the minute, as everyone is). However, if you group the words together by their general meanings, you can understand them well enough, which is all that's demanded by the exams. No question on the PSAT, SAT, GRE, or other standardized test asks for a precise definition.

You're never given a blank piece of paper and asked to write the meaning of a word. Instead, you use the context to come up with a basic idea of what you want. If you know that you need a word meaning slim, you aren't given both *svelte* (pleasantly, fashionably slim) and *emaciated* (scrawny, overly thin) in the same set of answers. You get one or the other. As long as you know they're both in the "thin" category, you're okay.

When you cluster words, you can also remember them in an *antipodean* (opposite) manner. That is, review all the words that mean thin, and then all the words that mean overweight. Study all the words that mean lucky, then all the words that mean unlucky. You can become a *perambulating* (walking) *prattling* (babbling) thesaurus before you know it!

Reviewing Three Little Words That Mean So Much: Prefixes, Roots, and Suffixes

Prefixes, roots, and suffixes: my three favorite words. Other women thrill to hear, "I love you," but I live for "roots, prefixes, suffixes." If I ever have triplets, I shall call them Prefixes, Roots, and Suffixes (and probably get sued for contributing to the emotional delinquency of minors, but that's another story). The PRS, as I refer to them, are the building blocks of words. If you can memorize just a few basic prefixes, you can remember a lot of vocabulary.

For example, suppose you know that *de* roughly means to put down. By knowing that, you can identify *demean, denounce, defame, decry, deprecate,* and *denigrate,* all of which roughly mean to put down, to criticize, to insult. I denounce, demean, defame, decry, deprecate, and denigrate people who don't take the time to memorize a few basic PRS. If you know that the root *culp* means guilt or blame, you also know *culprit* (a guilty person), *culpable* (blame-able, blameworthy), and *exculpate* (to rid from guilt).

Chapter 2 is dedicated to PRS. I suggest you make flash cards with the PRS and begin studying them immediately. You may be *stupefied* (amazed, astounded, stunned) at how often you see words using PRS in the real world. I once asked a student to memorize the root *salu,* meaning health. He left our tutorial, and not 15 minutes later called me from his cell phone, all excited. He'd seen a billboard on the freeway with a picture of a glass of milk, and the one word caption, "salubrious!" Thanks to his roots, he knew that *salu* meant health, and *–ous* meant full of, so a salubrious beverage, like milk, is healthful.

Playing Mind Games with Your Friends

One of my students' favorite ways to study vocabulary is to associate them in their minds with friends. For example, maybe that new girl at school who is so pretty that she's getting way too much attention (in your miffed opinion!) from all the boys is named Carrie. Think of her as Comely Carrie. Your buddy Ron is tall and thin: *Rangy* Ron. Your physics professor rarely gives more than a one-word answer: He's *Taciturn* Teacher.

Your best friend may be the Queen of *Quibbling,* because she always argues about every little, insignificant thing. The Empress of *Effervescence* is the head cheerleader who is always bubbly and excited. The Monarch of *Moroseness* is the gloomy guy who mopes around school, never smiling. The Princess of *Pulchritude* is the most beautiful girl in school. The Viking of *Virility* is the body-builder who at 16 could probably out-macho Arnold Schwarzenegger.

You can use a little poetical license, as well. "Don't be late, or he'll *vituperate*" (criticize harshly). "When I look lousy, I feel *frowsy*" (ill-groomed, poorly dressed, not looking good that day). The sillier the rhyme or statement, the easier it is to recall. Split up the words with your friends. Brent gets to make associations for the first five words in the chapter; you do the next five; Tiffany does the last five. Making up ridiculous — excuse me, less erudite — rhymes and associations is both fun and challenging.

Having Success with Excess

You know how, when you get a new shirt, you wear it over and over and over again, long after everyone has become sick and tired of seeing it? Do the same thing with a new word. When I discover a cool new word, I use it to amuse and bemuse, confuse and abuse. For example (the following is not a word you're likely to encounter on a standardized exam), I first heard about frass the other day. *Frass* is, uh, the material left behind by bugs . . . in other words, insect poop. I spent the entire day using that word as much as possible. I mentioned that I found frass on the floor of my car and would have to vacuum. I considered the film I had seen that weekend nothing more than a bunch of frass. I pointed at a spider and said he was on his way to create frass. I said that the next boyfriend I had was going to be of a higher quality than my previous one, who had been a crass bit of frass. I probably used that word, no exaggeration, 100 times in one day. Not only will I always remember frass, everyone who was forced to spend time in my company that day will remember it, as well.

Kissing Up and Putting Down

Knowledge is power. Knowledge of vocabulary is power squared. When you have a good vocabulary, you can kiss up to some people and put down others. You like the word *munificent,* meaning generous or attractive? Use it to score some parent points. Tell your mother at allowance time that she is the most munificent mother on the block and don't be surprised if she shares a bit more of her paycheck with you that week. Mention to your father that you've always considered him a *paradigmatic* (example or model) parent and listen to him brag to his buddies about what a good relationship he has with his son. All teachers like to be told that their *lucid* (clear) and *unambiguous* (clear, understandable) explanations really help you.

As you go through this book, keep some index cards handy with titles like, "Mom," "Dad," biology teacher," "boyfriend," or "girlfriend" and jot down on the cards the words you want to use around those people. (And before using them, check out the pronunciation of these words in the glossary.)

The flip side of the coin is that you can use words to insult people without their knowing they've been trashed. With an ever-so-sweet smile, inform the moron who just cut you off in the parking lot that he is certainly the best example of *dross* (waste matter, worthless stuff, rubbish) you've encountered in a while. Use a *saccharine* (sweet) voice to tell your niece who wants to try bandaging you for her Girl Scout First Aid patch that you don't submit to *quacks* (untrained people who practice medicine fraudulently). When the school bully is advancing, ready to *fustigate* (beat with a stick — whatta word!) you for some imagined offense, take the opportunity to compliment him on his *nescience* (ignorance) and hope he confuses the word with *omniscience* (knowledge on all topics, wisdom).

Just one thing: Before using this technique, double-check that said bully hasn't also bought and *perused* (read carefully, studied) this book.

Weaseling Words into Your Work

You have to write reports and essays at school? Fine, include a few of these vocab words, and do yourself a double service. You learn the words from using them, and you impress the teacher/earn a higher grade by your vocabulary erudition (knowledge). When you write that e-mail to your doting grandparents, have handy a few words to weasel into the note. Instead of informing them that you now are dreaming of becoming a doctor, say that your career *aspirations* (desires, ambitions) include practicing medicine. Rather than bore them by mentioning that you want to go into business, impress them with the statement that you hope to be an *entrepreneur* (a businessperson). Don't just say you do charity work. Mention your *eleemosynary* (charitable) pursuits.

Peroration and recapitulation
(that means summary)

In this chapter, you encounter six simple ways to expand your vocabulary. These techniques are as follows:

- Group words by connotations or clusters, such as happy/sad, rich/poor, and so on. See Part II of this book for more.

- Dissect words and use roots, prefixes, and suffixes to acquire "good enough" definitions. See Chapter 2.

- Associate words with your friends, labeling those *kith* (friends) "Affluent Ann" or "Parsimonious Pete."

- Use your new words everywhere, every day, with everyone you meet at every chance you get until they're hardwired into your brain.

- Demean dunces with words beyond their abilities; compliment and impress sages with words they thought were beyond yours.

- Enhance your schoolwork and e-mails with your newfound erudition.

Chapter 2

Digging Out Meaning: Prefixes, Roots, and Suffixes

In This Chapter
▶ Recognizing that everyone has to start somewhere: prefixes
▶ Finding the middle ground: roots
▶ Knowing that the end is near: suffixes

*P*refixes, roots, and suffixes are the ingredients for a great vocabulary. This chapter gives you what you need so that you can use a pinch of prefixes, a ration of roots, and a *soupçon* (tiny amount, bit) of suffixes to create a masterpiece that will impress your teachers and parents and leave your friends asking you for your recipe for success!

Starting Off with Prefixes

Ever hear the saying, "A journey of a thousand miles begins with a single step?" Here's how that applies to vocabulary: "A vocabulary of a thousand words begins with a single prefix." Memorizing the following prefixes (a *prefix* is a syllable or word joined to the beginning of another word that changes the first word's meaning or creates a new word) can help you to expand your vocabulary quickly and painlessly.

For most standardized exams, you don't have to know the precise definition of a term. Often, if you simply know whether the word is good (has a positive feeling to it) or bad (has a negative feeling to it), you can get the right answer to the question. Prefixes help you cure the are-you-sure-that's-English-because-I've-never-seen-that-word-before headache.

a– = **not, without:** Someone *amoral* is without any morals, like the sadists who designed the SAT, GRE and other terrors. Someone *atypical* is not typical, like pocket protector–wearing students who love to take tests. Someone *apathetic* is without feeling, or uncaring, which is like most students by the time they've finished the test and are leaving the test room. ("The world is going to end tomorrow? Fine — that means I can get some sleep tonight.")

ab– = **away from:** Your parents ask you to *abstain* from drinking and driving (stay away from it). What does a queen do when she *abdicates* the throne? She goes away from it. When a thief *absconds* with your valuables, she takes them away from you.

ad– = **toward, addition:** When you *advocate* a point of view, you urge others toward it. Because you are hopelessly *addicted* to the SAT, you are drawn toward it. To *adumbrate* is to foreshadow (to go toward the shade — think of *umbra,* as in umbrella, which shades you) or to suggest beforehand.

am–, ami– = **love, like:** At the pound, you choose a dog that seems *amiable* and *amicable*: friendly, loving, and good-natured. It's not your fault if Bowser later decides to attempt an *amorous* — in love, especially in a physical way — relationship with your grandmother's leg.

an– = **not, without:** An *anaerobic* environment is without oxygen (the way the test room feels when a killer question leaves you gasping for air). *Anarchy* is without rule or government, like a classroom when a substitute teacher is in for the day.

anim– = **life, spirit, anger:** You and your best friend have an *animated* (lively, vigorous, spirited) debate over which singer is the best. Unfortunately, too much debate may lead to *animosity,* a feeling of dislike or hatred. Know the big word *animadversion?* It means hard criticism or disapproval.

ante– = **before:** When the clock tells you that it's 5 a.m., the a.m. stands for *ante meridian,* which means before the middle, or the first half of the day. *Antebellum* means before the war. Tara in *Gone with the Wind* was an antebellum mansion, built before the Civil War. To *antecede* is to precede or go before. Studying algebra usually antecedes taking trig.

anti– = **against, opposite:** If you are *antisocial,* you're a hermit and don't like to be around people. The *antipodes* are any two places directly opposite each other on the earth (sometimes Australia and New Zealand together are referred to as the Antipodes, because they are opposite much of the rest of the world).

auc–, aug– = **to originate, to increase:** You may have to *augment* the meager allowance your folks give you by taking a part-time job. Here's an interesting point: The word *auction* actually means "sales by increasing bids." You augment your allowance and part-time job salary by auctioning off some of your old CDs.

aud–, aur– = **to hear:** An audience sits in an auditorium to hear a speaker who uses a microphone to make sure her words are *audible* (loud enough to be heard) even to those way in the back. Something *auricular* is spoken — whispered — directly into the ear, such as those sweet nothings from your boyfriend or girlfriend.

auto– = **self:** Your *autobiography* is the story of your life. An *autonomous* person is independent, self-governing (as, in, you can't wait to get away from your parents and finally be autonomous). Something *autochthonous* (don't worry, that jaw-breaker won't be on your exam; it's just a word you can toss into a conversation to look intelligent) is indigenous, native: "No, even though I'm a tall blue-eyed, blond surfer-dude, I'm not autochthonous to Southern California, but was actually born and raised in Brooklyn."

ben–, bon– = **good:** A benefit is something that has a good result, an advantage. Someone *benevolent* is good and kind; a benevolent father lets you take his new car rather than your old junker on a date. *Bon voyage* means have a good voyage; a *bon vivant* is a person who lives the good life.

bi– = **two:** A bicycle has two wheels. A bimonthly meeting occurs every two months (don't confuse *bimonthly* — every two months — with *semimonthly,* which means every half month). *Bicameral* means having two legislatures. You may have heard this word in your government class, because the United States has a bicameral Congress.

bibli– = **book:** A *bibliography* is a list of all the books and resource materials you use to write a paper. If you are a *bibliophile,* you love books. If you're obsessed with books and collect them constantly, you suffer from *bibliomania.*

brev– = **short:** You may have heard that "brevity is the soul of wit," an expression that may be translated as, "Keep it short and fool everyone into thinking you're smart." To *abbreviate* is to shorten a word. Here's something to toss at your English teacher: A *breve* is the squiggly mark placed over a short vowel or a short syllable.

caco–, dys– = **bad, abnormal:** Something *cacophonous* is bad-sounding, such as nails scratching on a chalkboard. A *dysfunctional* family doesn't function normally. *Muscular dystrophy* occurs when the muscles are faulty.

ceiv–, cept–, capt– = **to take, to hold:** You receive an excellent score on your test and exclaim, "I'll accept (take) it!" You struggle at the gym to look your best so that you can *captivate* (take or hold the attention of) that cute new student in your economics class.

circum– = **around:** The *circumference* of a circle goes around the circle. If you *circumnavigate* the globe, you go around the world. When you come home late for curfew, you are *circumspect* as you enter the house, looking all around, judging the situation carefully and cautiously.

co–, con–, col–, cor– = **with, together:** You work together with coworkers. When you put together all the notes you've taken over the semester, you *correlate* them. Then you may *collaborate* with your coworkers and study together for the exam. A school *convocation* is an assembly, a coming together of students for a meeting.

contra–, counter– = **opposite, against:** To *contradict* is to assert the opposite. A classy, fun way to say "to the contrary" is to use the word *contrariwise.* The *counterculture* is a culture opposite to the norm, such as the hippies of the '60s.

de– = **down from, away from (to put down):** To descend or depart is to go down from or away from. To *denounce* is to put down or to speak badly of; to expose the crimes of, as in denouncing those hogs who chow down on all the pizza before you get to the party.

eu– = **good:** A *eulogy* is a good speech, usually given for the dearly departed at a funeral. A *euphemism* is a polite expression, like saying that someone has passed away instead of calling him worm meat.

ex– = **out of, away from:** An exit is literally out of or away from it — *ex*-it. (Exit is probably one of the most logical words around.) To *extricate* is to get out of something. You can extricate yourself from an argument by pretending to faint, basking in all the sympathy as you're carried away. To *exculpate* is to get off the hook — literally to make away from guilt. (*Culp* means guilt.) If the dean of students wants to know who egged his house last weekend, you can claim that you and your friends are not *culpable.*

extra– = **beyond, outside:** Something *extraneous* is beyond what you need, not essential. To *extradite* a criminal is to send a criminal outside of his current location, back to where he committed the crime. You've probably heard of ESP, but did you know it stands for *extra sensory perception?* That's the ability to go beyond your normal senses to perceive something. Your ESP tells you when it's time to duck down in the seat as a car passes because it may be your parents.

hetero– = **other, different:** *Heterogeneous* means dissimilar, unlike, or unrelated. A heterogeneous society has many different types of people from many different backgrounds. A *heterosexual* is attracted to people of the opposite sex. Here's a fun word you can probably relate to: *heterography,* which is spelling that differs from current standard usage. When the teacher calls you to task for errors in spelling, you can say that you're a practicing *heterographologist.*

homo– = **same:** *Homogeneous* means similar, uniform. If a club is made up of all the kids who look and dress and act the same, it's homogeneous. A *homosexual* is attracted to people of the same sex. *Homochromatic* is a fancy word meaning of a single color. When your father shows up for a golf game wearing plaid pants, tell him to go change into some more homochromatic trousers and not embarrass you.

hyper– = **above:** A hyperactive person can't sit still for more than five minutes. Someone who hasn't had the benefit of learning all the words in this book may *hyperventilate* (breathe too fast) and pass out from anxiety during the test. A *hyperbole* is an exaggeration to make a point, as when you tell your friends you've learned a million words in this book.

hypo– = **under, less than:** A *hypodermic* needle goes under your skin. Did you know that a *hypotenuse,* the bane of your geometry class, comes from a word meaning "to stretch under?" The hypotenuse is the longest side, "stretching under" the triangle.

il–, ir– = **not:** If you're irresponsible, you are not responsible. If something is illegal, it's not legal. An *irrefutable* argument can't be disproved. You have irrefutable proof that studying vocabulary reverses brain damage caused by having too much fun.

im– = **not:** Something impossible is not possible. Someone immortal isn't going to die, but will live forever. Someone *implacable* is not able to be calmed down; is stubborn. Notice that *im–* can also mean "inside" (*immerse* means to put into), but that meaning is not as common on standardized tests. First think of *im–* as meaning "not;" if that doesn't seem appropriate, switch to plan B and see whether it can mean "inside" in the context of the question.

in– = **not:** Something inappropriate is not appropriate. Someone *inept* is not adept, not skillful. Someone *insolvent* has no money, is bankrupt, like most students after the prom. *In–* can also mean "inside" (*innate* means something born inside of you) or "beginning" (the initial letters of your name are the beginning letters) or into (you insert a coin when you put it into the vending machine). However, its most common meaning is "not." Think of that one first; if it doesn't seem to work, try the others.

inter– = **between:** An intermission comes between the acts of a play. The interstate highway goes between the states. *Interstices* are crevices, small or narrow spaces between things or parts. When you *interpolate,* you insert something new, such as interpolating words in a vocabulary book.

intra– = **within:** An intrastate highway is within one state, not between several states. If you play intramural sports in college, you stay within your own college; that is, you don't go to play against other schools. Here's a fun word: intrapreneur. You've probably heard of an *entrepreneur,* one who takes a risk organizing a business for profit. An *intrapreneur* is a person *within* a corporation who is encouraged to initiate products and business ventures.

micro– = **small:** A microscope lets you look at very small items. A *microcosm* is a small universe, a world unto itself. High school is the microcosm in which teenagers function. In the sixties, very, very short skirts were called *microminis.*

mis– = **bad:** A mistake is bad to make on a test. A *misnomer* is a wrong name, such as calling me Floozie instead of Suzee. A *miscreant* is a bad, evil person; a criminal.

mono– = **one, alone:** A *monocle* is one lens. (Ever see reruns of the TV show *Hogan's Heroes?* Colonel Klink wears a monocle.) A *monopoly* is an exclusive control or privilege. If you have a monopoly on headache remedies the day of a big exam, you'll make a killing!

ne–, mal– = **bad:** Something negative is bad, like a negative attitude. Someone *nefarious* is "full of bad," or wicked and evil, like a nefarious wizard in a science-fiction novel. Something *malicious* is also "full of bad," or wicked and harmful, like a malicious rumor that you're really a 30-year-old narc in disguise. A *malapropism* is a ridiculous use of words. I heard my favorite malapropism on a television show: "Lincoln freed the slaves with the Emasculation Proclamation." Ouch.

non– = **not:** Something that's nonsensical makes no sense. If you're nonproductive, you are not producing anything. A *nonpareil* is a person who is not equaled or unrivalled, such as the best-ever student at your school. If you're *nonplussed,* you aren't able to speak or act further, but are totally *flummoxed* and bewildered (snuck another vocab word in on you there!).

peri– = **around:** A *periscope* lets you look around (think of a submarine). The *perimeter* goes around a figure. If you are *peripatetic,* you walk around, not staying in one place. A *peripatetic* teacher doesn't sit at his desk but wanders up and down the classroom aisles.

poly– = **many:** A *polygon* has many angles. *Polygamy* was the practice of being married to two or more people at the same time. If you're a *polymath,* you're a person of great and diversified learning; you know many things.

post– = **after:** When the clock tells you that it's 5 p.m., the p.m. stands for *post meridian.* It means after the middle, or the second half of the day. Something *postmortem* occurs after death. A postmortem exam is an autopsy.

pre– = **before:** A preview is given before the movie is put in wide distribution. Your *predecessor* is the person who came before you. If you *preclude* something, you prevent it, make it impossible in advance. Your getting a hole-in-one on a golf course precludes your taking a second shot. Your getting a 1600 on the SAT precludes your taking the test again.

pro– = **big, much:** *Profuse* apologies are big — in essence, a lot of apologies. A *prolific* writer produces a great deal of written material.

Pro has two additional meanings that are less commonly used on exams. It can mean before, as in "A *prologue* comes before a play." Similarly, to *prognosticate* is to make known before or to predict. A *prognosticator* is a fortune teller. *Pro* can also mean for. Someone who is pro freedom of speech is in favor of it. Someone with a *proclivity* toward a certain activity is for that activity or has a natural tendency toward it.

re–, retro– = **back, backward, again:** When you review your demand for an hourly pay, you go back and view them again. You ask your boss whether you can have a *retroactive* raise, one going back to the beginning of your work history. Your boss *retorts* — answers back at you — that he's thinking about a retroactive decrease, given your poor work performance. You beat a hasty *retreat* (going back, withdrawal).

se– = **apart:** An ill person may be *segregated* (separated) from her friends so she doesn't infect them. A jury may be *sequestered* (separated) from the public while making its decision. The decision to *sever* (break apart from) your relationship with your boyfriend is never easy.

sub–, suc–, suf– = **below, under, beneath:** If you are in a subway, you are in the *subterranean* (below earth) depths of the city. You may *succumb* (give way to, yield to) a slight bout of claustrophobia, that fear of enclosed spaces. You're strong enough to bear the suffering (undergoing something painful) until you're above ground again. Interesting point: *suc–* and *suf–* are just variations of *sub–,* used before certain letters. For example, you don't have a subfix, but a suffix at the end of a word.

super–, sur– = **over, above, upon:** Superman is above the ordinary man. Something *superfluous* is above what you need; extra; unnecessary. A *superannuated* person is very old. A *surcharge* is an extra charge, over and above the standard fee. A *surfeit* is a surplus, an amount over the norm. A patient who has several doctors all show up the day of the operation has a surfeit of surgeons.

syn–, sym– = **together, with:** If you feel sympathy, you feel the same way with someone; you're together emotionally. Things that are in *symmetry* are together; the same. *Synonyms* have the same meanings, can be used together to make the same point.

tele– = **distant:** A telephone sends sounds across distances. A television allows you to see things sent from a distance. On television, you may see an exhibit of *telekinesis,* during which a person supposedly is able to move an object across distances by means of psychic force, using his mind to pick an algebra book up off the table and move it to the garbage can.

trans– = **across, beyond, on the other side:** You transport something when you move it across distances. To *transcribe* is to write out in full, such as going home and transcribing the scribbles you took in class into full-length, readable notes. A *transgression* is an overstepping of the law or duty; a sin.

ultra–, outr– = **excessive, beyond:** You may call your father *ultraconservative* if he won't let you wear a belly tee. Someone *ultramontane* is beyond the mountains, living on the other side of the mountains. If you're outrageous, you're beyond belief; really out of control.

vice– = **in place of:** The vice-president is in place of the president, standing in for him at official functions. A *viceroy* is the person ruling in the name of the king (*roy* = king, as in royalty).

There's another *vice,* meaning twenty. Something *vicennial* lasts twenty years or happens every twenty years. If you speak Spanish, you know *veinte,* meaning twenty, from the same root.

Getting to the Root of the Matter

Think of this section as a gymnasium for brain body-building. Roots are the body, muscle, and sinews of any word. Working out in this section gives you the mental muscle necessary to overcome any vocabulary bullies you may encounter on an exam.

Vocabulary by the numbers

Okay, so you probably know that *mono* means one (as in monocle and monopoly) and *bi* means two (as in bicycle or bisect). But how many of the more sophisticated number roots can you identify? (And just to make this a thorough sidebar, I've included definitions of *mono* and *bi.)*

✔ *kilo, mill:* thousand. A *kiloliter* is one thousand liters. A *millennium* is a period of a thousand years. A million, logically enough, is a thousand thousands.

✔ *milli:* thousandth. A *milliwatt* is one-thousandth of a watt.

✔ *mega:* million. A *megabyte* holds a million bytes. *Note:* Mega can also simply mean large or great. A *megalopolis* is a very large or great city, like New York.

✔ *micro:* millionth. A *microvolt* is a millionth of a volt.

✔ *giga:* billion. A *gigabyte* holds one billion bytes of information. (Don't confuse giga, billion, with nano, billionth. You want to make sure your education nets you billions of dollars, not a billionth of a dollar!)

✔ *nano:* billionth. One second divided by a billion equals one nanosecond.

✔ *tera:* trillion. A *teraflop,* in computerese, is equivalent to one trillion flops. Now there's a word a Hollywood producer needs to know!

✔ *pico:* trillionth. A *picogram* is one trillionth of a gram. I wish I'd known this word when I was younger and accusing my parents of favoring my brother over me: "You gave him a picogram more candy than you gave me!"

✔ *femto:* quadrillionth. A *femtosecond* is one quadrillionth of a second (how long it seems you have for each question on a test).

Too big? Okay, let's try some more common, smaller numbers.

✔ *mono:* one. For a while in the '60s, one-piece swimsuits were called monokinis.

✔ *uni:* one. A *unicycle* has one wheel. A *unicorn* has one horn.

✔ *bi:* two. A *bilateral* trade agreement affects two countries.

✔ *tri:* three. A gambler tries to win a *trifecta,* in which she correctly bets the first-, second- and third-place finishers.

✔ *quad:* four. Your *quadriceps* are muscles that have four heads or points of origin; the large muscle at the front of the thigh.

✔ *quint:* five. Ever hear the word, *quintessence,* meaning the most nearly perfect manifestation of a quality or thing, and wonder what it had to do with five? Ancient philosophers believed the world was composed of four elements: air, fire, water, and earth. The fifth element, or quintessence, comprised the heavenly bodies.

✔ *pent:* five. Every high school student in geometry class becomes painfully familiar with the five-sided figure, the *pentagon.* You may eventually join the military and go to work in the Pentagon, the five-sided building in Washington, D.C.

✔ *hex:* six. *Hexagons* have six sides. The *hexadecimal* system, used with some computers, is based on the number 16 (hex = 6, dec = 10).

✔ *hept:* seven. A *heptagon* has seven sides. If a monarchy is a government by one leader, what do you suppose a heptarchy is? It's rule by seven leaders (a system of government found in the Anglo-Saxon kingdoms).

✔ *sept:* seven. Question: Why isn't September the seventh month? It originally was, but two additional months, July and August, were added to the calendar at a later point, pushing all the months from September on back two months.

✔ *oct:* eight. All drivers know the familiar *octagon,* the stop sign.

✔ *non:* nine. A *nonagon* has nine sides. A *nonagenarian* is someone in his 90s.

✔ *dec:* ten. The *decimal* system is based on units of ten. A *decade* has ten years.

***ambu* = walk, move:** In a hospital, patients are either bedridden (they can't move) or *ambulatory* (they can walk and move about). A *somnambulist* is a sleepwalker. (*Somn–* means sleep; *–ist* is a person).

***andro* = man:** Commander Data on *Star Trek: The Next Generation* is an *android;* he's a robot that's shaped like a man. Someone *androgynous* exhibits both male (*andro*) and female (*gyn*) characteristics (literally, he/she is full of man and woman) — for example, the character Pat on the TV show *Saturday Night Live* was androgynous.

***anthro* = human, mankind:** *Anthropology* is the study of humans (not just men and not just women but humans in general). A *misanthrope* hates humans (an equal-opportunity hater: He or she hates both men and women).

bellu, belli = **war, fight:** If you're *belligerent,* you're ready to fight — in fact, you're downright hostile. A *postbellum* mansion is one that was created after the Civil War.

carn = **flesh:** If you're a *carnivore,* you eat flesh (meat). *Incarnation* is appearance in human (flesh) form, such as the incarnation of a god who appears as a human (you see that all the time on TV shows). *Carnal* means of the flesh; bodily. Carnal pleasures are sensual or sexual pleasures.

clam, claim = **shout:** When you proclaim your good scores, you shout them from the rooftops. To *acclaim* someone is to greet her with loud applause or approval. *Clamor* is a loud outcry or an uproar.

clin = **lean, bend:** If you're inclined to take chances, you lean toward the dangerous side of life. When you politely decline to go skydiving with your friend, you lean away from, or refuse, his kind offer. One of my favorite jokes (puns) uses this root: Why is there a clock in the Leaning Tower of Pisa? What good's the inclination if you don't have the time? (Get it? You may have the inclination to go see the latest movie, but you just don't have the time, what with all this vocabulary you're studying.)

clud, clus, claus: **to close, shut:** When you exclude someone from your club, you deny him entrance or shut him out. A *recluse* is a hermit, someone who shuts himself away from the world. If you have claustrophobia, you have a fear of being shut into small, enclosed places.

cred = **trust, belief:** Something incredible is unbelievable, such as the excuse: "I was abducted by aliens over the weekend and didn't have time to finish my homework." If you're *credulous,* you are trusting and naive (literally, full of trust). In fact, if you're credulous, you probably actually believe I was beamed up to a flying saucer.

Be careful not to confuse credible with credulous. Something *credible* is trustable or believable. A credible excuse can get you out of trouble if you come home after your curfew. *Credulous,* on the other hand, means full of trust, naive, or gullible. The more credulous your parents are, the less credible that excuse needs to be.

demo = **people:** Democracy is rule by the people. An epidemic spreads rapidly among many people. A *demagogue* is a would-be leader who tries to stir up the people with emotion or prejudice in order to win them over. For example, if your school has an election and someone runs on a "Let's fire all the teachers!" platform, he may be a demagogue.

dog, dox = **thought, idea:** If you are *orthodox,* you conform to the usual beliefs and ideas. A *paradox* is an idea or statement that seems contradictory but may be true. A *dogma* is a doctrine or belief. If you are *dogmatic,* you state your beliefs in a positive, even arrogant, manner.

duc, duct = **to lead, pull:** A *duct* is a tube through which gas or liquid moves (duct tape was originally created to seal up a duct). A *viaduct* is a long bridge to carry a road or railroad over a valley. An *aqueduct* is a pipe made to lead water from a distant source. Some of the aqueducts the Romans made throughout the world are *extant* (still in existence). As a fraternity prank, you may abduct or take away a rival fraternity's front-lawn statue.

ev = **time, age:** A *medieval* costume party requires that everyone come dressed as a character from the Middle Ages. A *primeval* forest has been around since the earliest times. You and your best friend are *coeval*. That doesn't mean that you're both rotten scoundrels, but that you are of the same age or period; contemporaries.

fac = **to do or make:** Something *facile* is easy to do. A facile job is easy, requiring little effort. To *facilitate* is to make easy. Recognizing roots facilitates learning vocabulary. In Spanish, facil means easy. To *manufacture* is to make something.

fiss = **break, part:** A *fissure* is a break in the earth's surface. Nuclear *fission* occurs when the nucleus is broken.

flict = **strike:** You *inflict* a blow when you pounce on your buddy. An *affliction* is pain or suffering, a strike to your health and well-being.

fort = **strength:** To *fortify* something is to strengthen it. *Fortitude* is the strength to bear misfortune. When you have a test today that you forgot to study for, you have to summon up your fortitude. Your *forte* is your strong point, something you do exceptionally well. After going through this book, of course, you'll consider vocabulary your forte.

fract, frag, frai = **break:** If you fracture your leg, you break it. A sentence fragment is a broken or incomplete sentence. Something frail or fragile is easy to break. Someone *refractory* is hard to control. Refractory comes from refract, as when light is refracted (bent).

gnos = **knowledge:** A doctor shows his or her knowledge by making a *diagnosis* (analysis of the situation) or a *prognosis* (prediction about the future of the illness). An *agnostic* is a person who doesn't know (is without knowledge about) whether God exists. Differentiate an agnostic from an *atheist,* who is literally "without God," a person who believes that there is no god.

grad, gress = **to go:** When you exchange rings with your beloved, your relationship progresses (goes forward). When Beloved gets second thoughts and asks for the ring back, the relationship *regresses* (goes backward). When you two are in the middle of arguing over your future and Beloved suddenly is distracted by the game on TV and begins discussing a good three-pointer, the conversation *digresses* (goes in a different direction). Finally, your conversation becomes *retrograde* (going back to an earlier state), and you call it a night.

greg = **group, herd:** A *congregation* is a group or herd of people. A *gregarious* person likes to be part of a group — is sociable. To *segregate* is literally to make away from the group. *Egregious* means remarkably bad. An egregious act makes you stand out from the group and be distinguished by the horrible thing you did.

gyn = **woman:** A *gynecologist* is a physician who treats women. A *misogynist* is a person who hates women.

her, hes = **to stick:** Adhesive tape sticks to your leg, resulting in acute pain when you yank it and most of your leg hair comes off. A *coherent* argument sticks together; is logically consistent. *Cohesion* is the tendency to stick together. If you hesitate, you pause or delay (stick for a minute) before going forward.

jac, ject = **to throw:** An *ejector* seat in a spy's car can throw a passenger out of the vehicle. To *project* your voice in a theater is to throw it way, way back to the last row of seating. The *trajectory* of a ball is the curved path it takes after being thrown. A *dejected* person is thrown down in spirit, sad, depressed.

loq, log, loc, lix = **speech, talk:** Someone *loquacious* talks a lot. (That person is literally full of talk.) A *dialogue* is talk or conversation between two people. *Elocution* is proper speech. A *prolix* person is very talkative.

luc, lum, lus = **light, clear:** Something *luminous* is shiny and full of light. Ask the teacher to *elucidate* something you don't understand (literally, to make clear). *Lustrous* hair reflects the light and is sleek and glossy.

meta = **change, transformation:** A *metamorphosis* is a change of shape. *Metastasis* is a spread of disease from one part of the body to another; a changing of the location. For example, if cancer metastasizes, it spreads throughout the body.

morph = **shape:** Something *amorphous* is without shape. *Morphology* is the study of shape. ("Hey, Mom, I'm going to the beach to work on morphology. . . .")

mut = **change:** The Teenage Mutant Ninja Turtles *mutated,* or changed, from mild-mannered turtles to pizza-gobbling crime fighters. Something *immutable* is not changeable but remains constant.

narco = **sleep:** A *narcotic* puts you to sleep. If you have *narcolepsy,* you have a frequent and uncontrollable desire for sleep.

omni = **all:** An *omnipotent* person is all-powerful, like the parents in most families. An *omniscient* person knows everything, like the teenagers in most families. An *omnivorous* person eats everything, like the preteens in most families.

oper = **work:** Something *inoperable* doesn't work any longer. An *opus* is a work or a composition.

Here's something I bet even your teachers don't know: The word opera comes from the same root. An opera originally was simply a work, a musical play. Opera is the plural of opus. You don't have opuses, you have opera.

pac = **peace, calm:** Why do you give a baby a *pacifier?* To calm him or her down. To get its name, the Pacific Ocean must have appeared calm at the time it was discovered.

path = **feeling:** Something *pathetic* arouses sympathy or a feeling of pity. To *sympathize* is to share the feelings (literally, to make the same feeling). *Antipathy* is a dislike — literally, a feeling against, as in: No matter how much the moron apologizes, you still may harbor antipathy toward the jerk who backed his car into yours, denting the fender and raising your insurance rates.

phon = **sound:** *Phonics* helps you to sound out words. *Cacophony* is bad sound; *euphony* is good sound. *Antiphony* is the opposition of sounds. For example, one person may sing or chant part of a song, and the rest of the choir will respond with a second part.

plac = **peace; calm; soothe:** To *placate* someone is to soothe him or her or to make peace with that person. You placate your irate sweetheart, for example, by sending a dozen roses (hint, hint). Someone *implacable* is someone you're not able to calm down — or someone really stubborn. If those roses don't do the trick, for example, your sweetheart is too *implacable* to placate.

pug = **war, fight:** Someone *pugnacious* is ready to fight. A *pugilist* is a person who likes to fight — such as a professional boxer. (Did you ever see those big sticks that the American Gladiators use — the ones that look like cotton swabs with a thyroid condition? Those are called *pugil* sticks.)

rupt = **break:** When a pipe *ruptures,* it breaks. A volcano *erupts* when the lava bursts forth. When you *corrupt* a person such as a judge, you make him morally unsound, dishonest. *Corruption* of the body occurs in the grave as the body breaks down and decomposes.

Don't confuse *erupt* (to break) with eruct. To *eruct* is to burp!

sanct = **holy:** To *sanctify* is to make holy. A *sanctuary* is a holy place, such as a church. If you are *sanctimonious,* you are holier-than-thou, pretending to be holy. Something *sacrosanct* is very holy, sacred, inviolable. To some teenagers, the weekend is a sacrosanct time of fun and sleep and shouldn't be defiled and polluted with homework.

scien = **knowledge:** A scientist is a person with knowledge. Someone *prescient* has forethought or knowledge ahead of time — for example, a *prognosticator* (a fortune teller). After you learn these roots, you'll be closer to being *omniscient* — all-knowing.

senti = **feeling:** If you are *sentimental,* you have strong feelings. If you're *insentient,* like a robot, you have no feelings at all. I bet you wouldn't have guessed that the word *sentinel,* meaning a guard or sentry, comes from this same root. A sentinel senses or feels what's going on around him.

somn = **sleep:** Take Sominex to get to sleep. If you have *insomnia,* you can't sleep. (The prefix *in–* means not.)

son = **sound:** A *sonic* boom breaks the sound barrier. *Dissonance* is clashing sounds. (My singing, quite frankly, is so bad that the governor declared my last opera a disaster aria!)

sop = **sleep:** A glass of warm milk is a *soporific.* So is a boring teacher.

soph = **wise:** A sophomore is a second-year student, and thus (supposedly) wiser than a first-year student. (Interestingly, the *mor* part of sophomore comes from the same root as moron!) *Philosophy* is the love of wisdom, a theory of the principles of knowledge. A *sophisticated* person is wise in the ways of the world; not naïve.

spec = **look:** You can inspect something by looking through your spectacles. If you are *circumspect,* you look all around, checking things out carefully.

term = **end, boundary, limit:** A bus terminal is the end of the bus line. To *terminate* is to end; to *exterminate* is to kill or wipe out completely, bringing it to an end. An *interminable* lecture seems as if it will never end.

terr = **earth:** You change your aquarium to a *terrarium* by taking out the water and fish and putting in dirt and lizards. Someone *extraterrestrial* isn't from earth, but from outside the limits of the planet. Someone *interred* is put into the earth, buried. When you're all done with your exams, you may want to have a ceremonial *interment,* tossing your books into a hole in the ground and saying a few words.

theo = **God:** *Theology* is the study of gods and religion. An *atheist* believes there is no god. A *polytheist* believes in many gods. If you know the word *autonomous,* meaning self-governing, can you deduce what *theonomous* means? It means controlled by God. If you're crossing your fingers that the weather will be nice for your Homecoming Parade with all those tissue-paper floats, you may say, "Oh well, it's out of my control; the weather is theonomous."

ven = **come:** During a *convention,* people come together. Something *conventional* is normal because it has become common from all the people who came together to do the same thing. For example, it's conventional to wear blue jeans to a picnic; everyone does so. To *intervene* is to come between. You *intervene* between two friends who are fighting, shoving them apart. Ever take Latin? The famous saying, "*Veni, vidi, vici*" means, "I came, I saw, I conquered."

vid, vis = **to see:** Your *visage* (face) is visible on the hidden video taken to prevent shoplifting. A *vista* is a view or outlook. A *visor* on a suit of armor is the part that the knight sees or looks through. A *videophone* lets you see the person on the other end of the line.

voc, voke = **call:** When you *vocalize* your demand for better food in the cafeteria, you call for a change. To *provoke* is to excite or call forth some action or feeling, such as provoking the principal into changing the lunch menu. If the principal *equivocates,* he hedges or misleads; is intentionally ambiguous. (You see the prefix *equi,* meaning equal? Someone who equivocates gives equal voice to both sides of the issue without stating something definitively.)

volv, volt, vol = **roll, turn:** You turn around and around in a revolving door. When the peasants revolt, they turn against the landowners. The *evolution* of a species is its unrolling, how it develops or works out.

Know anyone who drives a Volvo? She or he may be interested to know that the term simply means "I roll."

xen = **stranger, foreigner:** If you're *xenophobic,* you have a fear of strangers. If you are a *xenophile,* you love strange and foreign things. In chemistry class, you may have studied xenon gas. It was named xenon because it was a previously unknown inert gas.

Ending with a Bang: Suffixes

Are you the type of person who reads the last chapter of a book first? Do you want to know the ending of a movie before you go to see it? If so, *suffixes* — letters or syllables added at the end of a word — are for you. Memorizing a few of these basic endings can help you to define and remember many different words.

–able, –ible = **capable of, worthy of:** Someone huggable is worthy of being hugged. Something legible is capable of being read. A *navigable* waterway can be navigated or sailed on. A *risible* cartoon makes you laugh.

–ate = **to make:** To duplicate is to make double. To *renovate* is to make new again (*nov–* means new). To *placate* is to make peaceful or calm (*plac–* means peace or calm).

–cess, –cede = **to go, to yield:** When you *precede,* you go before. When your hairline *recedes* (you have a few years before you have to worry about that, right?), it goes backward. When you *accede* to a request, you agree with it; go along with it; yield to it. *Secession* is formal withdrawal, going away from (the southern states seceded from the Union just before the Civil War).

–cide = **killing, to kill:** Pesticide kills pests or insects. *Genocide* is a killing of a race or group of people. Here's a word that I learned in law school: uxoricide. *Uxoricide* is the murder of a wife by her husband. Many TV shows feature uxoricide episodes that are neatly solved by the detective in just 60 minutes.

–cis = **cut:** An *incision* is a cut. To *excise* is to cut out, like excising a tumor. You use scissors to cut. Interestingly, the word precise comes from this same root. A precise comment is exact, has cut off all excess and gotten right to the point.

–ette = **little:** A cigarette is a little cigar. A dinette table is a little dining table. A *coquette* is a little flirt (literally, a little chicken).

–ify (also *–efy*) = **to make:** To beautify is to make beautiful. To *ossify* is to make bone. (If you break your wrist, it takes weeks to ossify again; for the bone to regenerate.) To *deify* is to make into a deity, a god.

–illo = **little:** An armadillo is a little armored animal. A *peccadillo* is a little sin. (Do you speak Spanish? *Pecar* is to sin.)

–ist = **a person:** A typist is a person who types. A *pugilist* is a person who fights (*pug*– means war or fight), a boxer. A *pacifist* is a person who believes in peace, a noncombatant (*pac*– means peace or calm).

–ity = **a noun suffix that doesn't actually mean anything; it just turns a word into a noun:** *Jollity* is the noun form of jolly. *Serenity* is the noun form of serene. *Timidity* is the noun form of timid.

–ize, –ise (British) = **to make:** To alphabetize is to make alphabetical. To *immunize* is to make immune. To *ostracize* is to make separate from the group; to shun. If you walk around chirping merrily, "C'mon over to my house tonight, and we can all study suffixes," expect to find yourself ostracized.

–logy, –ology = **study:** Biology is the study of life. Geology is the study of the earth. Any idea what *phrenology* is? It's the study of the bumps on your head! In the 1800s, it was popular to try to determine what type of person you were by feeling the shape of your skull.

–ous = **full of (very):** Someone joyous is full of joy. Someone *amorous* is full of amor, or love, and is very loving. Something *capacious* is full of capacity or has a very large capacity. You shop for a capacious backpack that can hold your books, phone, laptop, calculator, and lunch.

Part II
Groups and Troops: Essential Vocabulary by Category

The 5th Wave   By Rich Tennant

"I went around to all the businesses in town collecting new words for the vocabulary part of the SAT. I learned a lot of new words related to not being annoying."

In this part . . .

Where do you fit in at your school: Are you an intellectual? An athlete? A counterculture musician? Chances are, you identify yourself as part of a group. When someone mentions another student, you probably say, "Oh yeah, Dennis; he's the computer whiz."

Just as you remember people in groups, you can more easily remember vocabulary words when they're grouped into categories. In this part, you discover words in categories based on their definitions: words having to do with appearance, words having to do with money, words having to do with speaking, and so on.

Chapter 3

Mirror, Mirror on the Wall: Words about Personal Appearance

• •

Words in This Chapter

- ▶ attenuated
- ▶ comely
- ▶ corpulent
- ▶ dandy
- ▶ dapper
- ▶ emaciated
- ▶ fop
- ▶ frowzy
- ▶ gaunt
- ▶ homely
- ▶ lanky
- ▶ obese
- ▶ pallid

- ▶ pulchritudinous
- ▶ rangy
- ▶ rotund
- ▶ sartorial
- ▶ slattern
- ▶ slovenly
- ▶ soignée
- ▶ stout
- ▶ svelte
- ▶ swarthy
- ▶ unkempt
- ▶ wan

• •

*Y*our assignment is to write a personal ad about your physical appearance, using ten words or less. What would you say? Would you call yourself soignée or frowzy? Swarthy or wan? A dandy or someone unkempt?

If you want to get "the outer you" across (allowing the person who answers the ad to discover "the inner you" in due time), you need to find just the right word. This chapter can help.

Keeping Up Appearances with New Vocabulary Words

The words in this section help you say just the right thing the next time you find yourself talking to the image in the mirror.

attenuated (at *ten* you waited): slender, thin.

> *After spending a month hiking in the Himalayas, Nestor came back so attenuated that we changed his soubriquet from Santa Claus to Ichabod Crane.*

To attenuate can also mean to draw out and make long and thin. For example, when you pull your bubble gum out of your mouth, drawing it out into a long line before stuffing it back in, you're attenuating the gum. An attenuated person looks as if he has been drawn out — long and thin.

Bonus trivia: What's your sobriquet? Bubbles? FuzzBall? Rapmaster? A *sobriquet* is a nickname. (This word has an interesting origin. Some word experts believe it's from the French for "chuck under the chin," meaning to sort of tap under the chin.)

comely (rhymes with, *some* he): attractive.

> *Answering the ad for "comely wenches," the young women found out they were auditioning to be singing serving girls at a medieval-themed restaurant noted for its attractive waitresses.*

corpulent (*corp* you lent): fat, fleshy.

> *The corpulent kindergartner thought a lot about food, so his teacher wasn't surprised when he answered the test question, "Name the four seasons" with "salt, pepper, mustard, and vinegar."*

What's a corpse? It's a body. Someone corpulent has a lot of body.

dandy (rhymes with, *can*dy): a man whose style of dress is ostentatiously elegant or fashionable.

> *When the man showed up for a picnic wearing the latest fancy jeans and highly polished boots when everyone else was in ripped shorts and flip-flops, he gained the label Dandy Don.*

Of course you've heard the song "Yankee Doodle Dandy." Ever wonder why Yankee Doodle was such a dandy? Think about what he did: He stuck a feather in his cap. A man who is so concerned with appearances that he walks around with a feather in his cap is definitely a dandy.

Bonus trivia: While I'm on the subject, whence the term Yankee? Many believe it came from the habit of calling the early Dutch settlers Jan Cheese, or John Cheese, in reference to their habit of making and eating much cheese. The Dutch were in the Northeast; eventually all people in that region were referred to as Jan Cheese, or Yankees.

dapper (rhymes with, *tap* her): neat, trim, smart in dress or appearance.

> *One requirement of working for the Secret Service is a dapper appearance because the agents are often shown on television and are seen by many as representative of U.S. citizens.*

Bonus joke: Speaking of Secret Service agents, have you heard about the adult *libation* (beverage, drink) called the Secret Service Martini? One shot, and you're on the floor!

emaciated (rhymes with, he *may* she waited): abnormally thin or wasted.

> *The students began crying after seeing pictures of the emaciated prisoners from the World War II concentration camps, wondering how anyone could be so thin and still survive.*

Emaciated is a strong word. Someone who has dropped ten pounds on a diet isn't emaciated, but someone wasting away from a serious illness may be.

fop (rhymes with, *cop*): a dandy, someone who is excessively concerned with being fashionable.

> *The school counselor found that the student was flunking classes because he was spending time at the mall buying clothes instead of studying.*

A fop is also a foolish person. If someone is acting ridiculously, you can call him a fop.

frowzy (rhymes with, *lou*sy): dirty, untidy, neglected in appearance.

> *I visited my brother in Europe after backpacking around for weeks and taking few showers. Ron told me later that at first he couldn't figure out who this frowzy woman was on his doorstep.*

gaunt (rhymes with, *haunt*): abnormally slim, especially from lack of nourishment.

> *After riding his bicycle across the country to raise funds for charity, Paul was so gaunt that we couldn't wait to take him to dinner and try to put some weight back on him.*

Some twig-like models with hollow cheeks can be described as gaunt. When a friend of mine appeared to be dieting way too much, I used to greet her by saying, "Going . . . going . . . gaunt!"

homely (rhymes with, *Rome* Lee): plain or unattractive in appearance.

> *The television show used the standard ploy of having a homely woman let down her hair, take off her glasses, and suddenly became a gorgeous siren.*

A homely person doesn't remind you of someplace exotic or sophisticated, but of home, of a plain place. Somehow over the years, the word has evolved to mean not just plain but unattractive.

And what's a siren? A *siren* is an attractive woman, one who uses her beauty to trap men. The origin of this word is interesting. Siren comes from seira, meaning cord or rope. A siren entangles or snares (today we may say lassoes) her man. If you've read any mythology, you may remember the beautiful women, called sirens, who lured sailors to their deaths with seductive songs.

lanky (rhymes with, *cranky*): awkwardly or ungracefully lean or long.

> *The lanky teenage boy, unaccustomed to the five inches he put on in his growth spurt, constantly knocked over items and bumped into the furniture.*

obese (rhymes with, go *peace*): very overweight.

> *Because dachshunds will eat anything and everything, they often become dangerously obese.*

Obese is a word often used in Analogies. If you see the question: OBESE: CORPULENT::, you can make a sentence, "Obese is very, very corpulent."

Bonus trivia: Do you know what the word "dachshund" means? It's German for badger hound. Dachshunds were originally bred as hunters, to go down in the holes after the badgers and bring them back. Alas, an obese dachshund would likely get stuck in one of those holes.

pallid (rhymes with, *gal* hid): pale, especially from illness or shock.

> *Upon hearing the news that he would have to have brain surgery to remove a tumor that was causing hearing and vision problems, Mr. Arkekan became pallid and said he would look for some alternative therapy.*

Pallid pale, and it means pretty much the same thing.

Bonus joke: Short of surgery, know how to get rid of ringing in the ears? Get an unlisted head!

pulchritudinous (rhymes with, hulk bit *two* din us): beautiful.

> *The would-be Romeo at the bar leered at the pulchritudinous woman and said, "You're such a lovely chick, truly poultry in motion!"*

Have you studied Latin? *Pulcher* is Latin for beautiful; *–ous* means full of. If I were writing a novel with a lovely heroine, I'd make her last name Pulcher and see whether any of my readers got the reference. (One of my students told me one time, "You know, with the strange names you come up with, it's a good thing you don't have children. They'd be in therapy for years!)

rangy (rhymes with, *strange* he): tall and thin.

> *The casting director stated that he wanted a "Clint Eastwood type: tall, rangy, masculine" to be the male lead in his next picture.*

Think of a rangy person as someone like a cowboy, a Clint Eastwood type, riding tall in the saddle. I remember this word because a cowboy is home, home on the range; so, rangy.

Bonus trivia: Have you seen the movie or read *The Lord of the Rings?* The character Strider (Lord Aragorn), who is tall and thin, is known as a Ranger.

rotund (rhymes with, so *punned*): round, plump.

> *The couple who had met at a weight management class changed their wedding vows to read that they would be in love, "for better or for worse, for thin or for rotund, till death do us part."*

Ever been to Washington, D.C.? Did you visit the Capitol and stand in the Rotunda? That's the round or "plump" part of the building. A rotund person is round in the middle, like Santa Claus or Homer Simpson.

sartorial (rhymes with, car *story* ull): pertaining to clothing or to tailors.

> *The second banana on the TV talk show often wore something outrageous like a lime green tuxedo so that the host could tease him about being sartorially resplendent.*

Bonus trivia: Okay, so now you know that sartorial means pertaining to clothing. What do you think tonsorial means? Nope, it has nothing to do with tonsils. *Tonsorial* means pertaining to hair or haircutting. After you visit the sartorial shops to buy clothing, you stop at the tonsorial establishment for a wash and cut.

slattern (rhymes with, *pattern*): an untidy and slovenly woman.

> *Worried about being typecast as the girl next door, the actress turned herself into a slattern for her next audition by not bathing or grooming for over two weeks.*

As you may expect from the definition, the term has a secondary meaning of a, well, a promiscuous woman. A slattern is also a slut.

slovenly (rhymes with, *glove* hen lee): untidy, dirty.

> *When the young couple entered the expensive restaurant only to be greeted by a slovenly maitre de whose hands had enough dirt on them to grow truffles, they decided to change their plans and instead grab a hot dog from the cart outside.*

Bonus joke: What did the Zen master say to the hot dog vendor? Make me one with everything!

soignée (for women); *soigné* (for men) (pronounced swan *yea*): meticulously dressed, well-groomed.

> *French women who won't go outside the door to pick up a newspaper without having their hair and nails done perfectly are often referred to as soignée.*

stout (rhymes with, *out*): fat, corpulent.

> *The kindergartner sang the verse, "I'm a little teapot, short and stout," making motions to indicate she had a big tummy.*

Stout can also mean brave, courageous, undaunted. Children in school learn many a song with the chorus that goes something like, "Give me some men who are stouthearted men who can fight with the might we adore . . . ."

svelte (rhymes with, *felt*): slender, willowy, elegant, graceful.

> *When pushed to take a stage name, the tall, slender actress decided to go with a one-word moniker and call herself Svelte.*

swarthy (*swore* thee): dark-complexioned.

> *Asked to describe her ideal mate, the giggling girl said he would be short, swarthy, and look like an Hispanic Danny de Vito.*

If you know someone who is Hispanic or Italian, his complexion is probably more swarthy than that of someone from Sweden.

Monikers for mutts

Oh sure, you can name your dog Blackie, Prince, or Rover. Or you can think of something more apt. Here are a few good suggestions for names that will better befit your bowser.

- **Amiable** (*aim* he uh bull): Labrador retriever. Ever met a Lab that didn't love everyone?

- **Brawny** (rhymes with, *scrawny*): bulldog. A bulldog usually is well-muscled and looks like the Schwarzenegger of the doggie world, terminating all opposition.

- **Brobdingnagian** (brob ding *nag* ee un): great Dane. They aren't called Great for nothing; some of these dogs can stand shoulder-high to a human.

- **Effervescent** (eff fur *vess* cent): Jack Russell terrier. A Jack Russell will run around for hours and hours, never wearing out.

- **Enervated** (*en* nerve ate ed): bloodhound. Have you ever seen a bloodhound that didn't look totally tuckered out?

- **Glutton** (rhymes, with *button*): dachshund. Dachshunds chew anything that isn't nailed down — and some things that are. I once saw a Doxie actually chew up a corner of the linoleum tile on a kitchen floor and systematically chomp her way through it.

- **Hirsute** (*here* suit): Pomeranian. A Pomeranian is so hairy it looks like a fuzzy little pom-pom ball.

- **Lassitude** (rhymes with, *pass* it Dude): an exhausted collie.

- **Lilliputian** (*lily* pyoo shun): Chihuahua. I've baked muffins that weighed more than most Chihuahuas.

- **Lithe** (*lie*-th): whippet. Whippets are so lithe, limber, and flexible that they seem to stretch in all directions at once when they jump up and grab a Frisbee.

- **Lugubrious** (loo *gyoo* bree us): basset hound. Bassets have those long, sad faces; even when they're happy, they look woebegone.

- **Pied** (rhymes with, *fried*): Dalmatian. Did you know the Pied Piper was called that because he was covered with spots (okay, he probably wore a polka-dotted outfit)? Now that's a fellow who should have owned a Dalmatian.

- **Soignée** (swan *yea*): French poodle. Most poodles are elegantly groomed, even to the point of sporting toenail polish.

- **Svelte** (rhymes with, *felt*): greyhound. Greyhounds tend to be fashionably thin.

---

unkempt (rhymes with, fun *them*'t): untidy, having a neglected appearance.

> *During the '90s, grunge was popular, and band members worked hard at sporting an unkempt look with torn jeans and filthy, matted hair.*

Unkempt sounds somewhat like un-kept, or uncombed, as in, not kept up or not kept looking nice. An unkempt person has not kept herself clean and neat.

wan (rhymes with, *on*): unhealthily pale, of a grayish, sickly color.

> *After spending most of his vacation in Borneo exploring the caves and rarely venturing out into the light, Armando finally emerged, wan and exhausted.*

More than Skin Deep: Beautiful Practice Exercises

No, no, don't bend down and touch your toes; I'm not asking you to complete those kinds of exercises! These exercises are for your brain, recalling the words you've mastered to this point. Note that the answers to these questions can be found — logically enough — in the "Answers to the Exercises" section, later in this chapter.

Exercise one

Directions: Select the appropriate word to complete the sentence.

1. Claiming she looked too (frowzy/pulchritudinous), the actress refused to let the reporter film her for an interview.

2. When asked how she was going to spend her winnings, the young lottery winner announced she was going to the nearest (sartorial/attenuated) establishment to buy everything that fit.

3. When our buddy showed up for school wearing the latest new fashion his girlfriend had bought him, we hassled him for being a (fop/slattern) and threatened to send his picture into *GQ Magazine*.

4. Stacy was always (unkempt/soignée), even on her trip to Alaska, when she had her nails done even though her hands would never be out of their gloves.

5. The man refused to buy an economy car, saying it didn't have enough legroom for his two (wan/lanky) teenage sons.

6. When asked to describe her beau, the girl said he was tall, (wan/swarthy), and handsome, with the dark, brooding looks of a film star like Ben Affleck.

7. We decided to adopt the most (comely/homely) puppy at the pound, reasoning that the cute ones could easily get homes, but the ugly ones needed our love.

8. The cat's belly brushed the ground as she waddled along, but from the way she begged at the dinner table, you'd think she was starved and (emaciated/pulchritudinous).

9. Realizing that writing a truthful personal ad, such as, "superannuated man with beer belly seeks female without" wouldn't get him many dates, Skip chose instead to describe himself as (stout/pallid).

10. Bruce went to his fraternity's Halloween party as a (fop/slattern), with ripped nylons, a skirt with the hem coming down, a stuffed and padded sweater with sweat stains under the arms, and greasy hair in curlers.

Exercise two

Directions: Choose the antonym (opposite) of each word.

1. unkempt: (wan/soignée)
2. pallid: (stout/swarthy)
3. comely: (frowzy/pulchritudinous)
4. fop: (slattern/dandy)
5. gaunt: (rotund/emaciated)
6. pulchritudinous: (slatternly/comely)
7. attenuated: (sartorial/rotund)
8. homely: (comely/attenuated)
9. lanky: (rangy/obese)
10. svelte: (corpulent/rangy)

Exercise three

Directions: Choose the most appropriate word to complete the sentence.

1. The candidate hired a wardrobe manager to enable her to present a more - - - - appearance for her on-camera debate.

    (A) frowzy

    (B) lanky

    (C) soignée

    (D) swarthy

    (E) wan

2. The - - - - man was surprised when he got sunburned, because he thought only fair-skinned people had to wear sunscreen.

    (A) swarthy

    (B) dapper

    (C) comely

    (D) attenuated

    (E) pallid

Beastly words

Animals play a role in your life and your vocabulary. How many of these beastly words do you know? *Hint:* Most of them don't mean what you think!

- ✔ *carp* (rhymes with, *harp*): While a carp is a fish, to carp is to complain or find fault in a petty, nagging way (think of some fish-faced old grump carping at you). When your parents carp at you, they are on your case about things you consider insignificant.

- ✔ *cow* (rhymes with, *now*): To cow is to intimidate. Don't let vocabulary words cow you; with a little practice you too can be a *sesquipedalian* (one who uses big words).

- ✔ *fawn* (rhymes with, *yawn*): To fawn is to act *servilely*, to cringe and flatter. A groupie fawns over a rock star; an employee may fawn over the boss.

- ✔ *sheepish* (rhymes with, *creep* fish): Someone sheepish is embarrassed; awkwardly shy or bashful. A young man asking out a girl for the first time may be a little sheepish.

- ✔ *toady* (rhymes with, *road* he): A toady is a yes-man, one who flatters to excess; a sycophant. This word came from the expression "toad eater." In the traveling medicine shows, the "doctor" selling the medications would plant his assistant in the audience. This "stranger" would pretend to eat a toad (thought to be poisonous) and then be cured by the very medicine the doctor happened to be selling.

3. Upon seeing a documentary showing the - - - - shipwreck survivors, some of whom weighed only 80 pounds, the class became quiet and upset.

   (A) obese

   (B) foppish

   (C) pulchritudinous

   (D) emaciated

   (E) rotund

4. Randall, who owned only two shirts and one pair of jeans, said that he had no reason to be - - - - because he lived alone in the woods.

   (A) homely

   (B) gaunt

   (C) rangy

   (D) a dandy

   (E) a slattern

5. When a bear emerges from hibernation, it is - - - -, having used up all its stored fat, and so must immediately begin looking for food.

   (A) stout

   (B) corpulent

   (C) comely

   (D) dapper

   (E) gaunt

6. The colorblind man took little interest in - - - - matters, wearing the same navy-blue clothing every day.

   (A) frowzy

   (B) slovenly

   (C) dapper

   (D) homely

   (E) sartorial

7. Concerned with presenting a - - - - appearance at the job interview, the woman shined her shoes and pressed her suit.

   (A) lanky

   (B) rangy

   (C) svelte

   (D) attenuated

   (E) dapper

It's just a pigment of your imagination: Colorful words

Think of how often you use colorful vocabulary. You talk about having the blues, feeling in the pink, or being green with envy. Here are a few more terms to add to your speech:

✔ *blanch* (rhymes with, *ranch*): to make white, to take the color out.

✔ *blench* (rhymes with, *wrench*): to whiten, to bleach, to become pale.

✔ *pallid* (*pal* lid): pale.

✔ *ruddy* (rhymes with, *buddy*): red or reddish.

✔ *tinge* (rhymes with, *hinge*): to color slightly, to give a tint to.

✔ *verdant* (rhymes with, *fur* dent): green.

✔ *xanthous* (*zan* thuss): yellow, yellowish.

Bonus joke: Did you ever wonder whether Smurfs get the blues?

8. The photographer suggested that the - - - - woman would be even more attractive if she went to a professional makeover artist.

    (A) homely

    (B) gaunt

    (C) comely

    (D) unkempt

    (E) pallid

9. The nutritionist warned that while a - - - - body looks good, some children, even some as young as ten, are going on crash diets to lose weight, becoming not just slender but emaciated.

    (A) unkempt

    (B) stout

    (C) slatternly

    (D) svelte

    (E) pallid

10. The military recruit was given demerits for presenting a - - - - appearance, with his uniform wrinkled and his hair in need of a trim.

    (A) pulchritudinous

    (B) frowzy

    (C) attenuated

    (D) soignée

    (E) lanky

Answers to the Exercises

So, how well do you believe you did? Are you thinking you got a perfect score? Check the answers in this section to confirm your guess.

Exercise one

1. **frowzy.** Frowzy means dirty, untidy, neglected in appearance.

2. **sartorial.** Sartorial means pertaining to clothes or tailors. A sartorial establishment is a clothing store.

3. **fop.** A fop is a clothes horse, a dandy, someone excessively concerned with being fashionable.

4. **soignée.** Someone soignée is meticulously dressed, well-groomed.

5. **lanky.** Someone lanky is awkwardly or ungracefully lean or long. When my brother was a teenager and grew very quickly, he liked to tell people who hadn't seen him in a while, "Yes, I had leg extensions this year!"

6. **swarthy.** Someone swarthy is dark-complexioned.

7. **homely.** A homely puppy is plain or unattractive in appearance, just the kind of animal that needs a good home.

   When my boyfriend — make that former boyfriend for a reason you see later in this sentence — and I went to the pound, I insisted on adopting a homely puppy, saying she had stolen my heart. My boyfriend responded, "Mine too, but I have three more at home in the freezer!"

8. **emaciated.** An emaciated animal is abnormally thin or wasted. That term is definitely not appropriate for a cat whose belly touches the ground as she walks!

9. **stout.** Had Skip told the truth and said he was old and fat or corpulent, he may not have gotten too many responses.

   Bonus trivia: Superannuated is a logical word. *Super–* means above, over, extra. You know that annual means yearly. Someone *superannuated* has extra years, is old. The word is also used to mean old-fashioned. A pair of jeans that's only a few months old but has already gone out of style is superannuated.

10. **slattern.** A slattern is an unkempt, not neatly groomed woman. The word can also refer to a woman whose virtue is in doubt.

    Bonus joke: What's green and hops from bed to bed? A prostitoad!

Exercise two

1. **soignée.** Someone unkempt doesn't care about her appearance; someone soignée is always perfectly groomed.

2. **swarthy.** A swarthy person has a dark complexion. A wan person is pale and sickly-looking.

3. **frowzy.** A frowzy person looks unkempt and poorly groomed. Someone comely is attractive. Think of Mae West's famous line, purred to a handsome man, "Come up 'n' see me sometime." Given how comely she was, the man was most eager to take her up on her invitation!

4. **slattern.** A slattern is a person who isn't best friends with her mirror, usually a woman who has let herself go. A fop is a clothes horse, someone obsessed with grooming. Fop would make a lovely name for a cat that never stops licking and grooming.

5. **rotund.** Someone gaunt is abnormally thin. A rotund person is overweight, pudgy, and round.

6. **slatternly.** A pulchritudinous woman is beautiful, gorgeous, the woman you see staring at you from the screen during the Miss Universe pageant. A slatternly woman is dirty, unkempt, poorly groomed, the woman who is in fuzzy pink slippers and yesterday's T-shirt, sitting on the couch watching the game show.

7. **rotund.** Someone attenuated is thin, looking drawn-out. Someone rotund is heavyset, rounded.

   Ever see the painting "American Gothic," by Grant Wood? That's the one of the male and female farmers, with a pitchfork? Those are a couple of attenuated folks.

8. **comely.** Homely means unattractive; comely means attractive.

9. **obese.** Someone lanky is tall and thin, rather on the rangy side. Someone obese is very overweight.

10. **corpulent.** A svelte person is thin, willowy, and shapely. A corpulent person is overweight.

Exercise three

1. **C.** Someone soignée is well-groomed and dressed in an appropriate manner.

2. **A.** A swarthy person is dark-skinned. While someone with dark skin may be less prone to sunburn because of a darker skin pigmentation than someone with fair skin, he or she can still burn if not protected.

3. **D.** Someone emaciated is overly thin, like an 80-pound shipwreck survivor.

   Bonus trivia: Who's Alexander Selkirk? He's probably the most famous shipwreck survivor of all time. The fictional character, Robinson Crusoe, was based on Alexander Selkirk.

4. **D.** A dandy is someone excessively concerned with clothing and appearance. Someone who lives alone in the woods probably doesn't care too much whether he's wearing the latest styles.

5. **E.** A bear that hasn't been eating all winter is thin from lack of nourishment — or gaunt.

6. **E.** The man, wearing the same clothes all the time, takes little interest in his dressing or clothing, in sartorial matters.

7. **E.** A dapper appearance is a well-groomed, well-dressed appearance.

8. **C.** By saying the woman would be "even more attractive," the sentence implies that the woman is already attractive — or comely — now.

9. **D.** A svelte body is slender, trim, thin, willowy. Being svelte is usually seen as a good thing. Being emaciated is too much of a good thing, being overly svelte to the point of becoming malnourished.

10. **B.** A frowzy recruit doesn't put much effort into his appearance and is not well-groomed.

Chapter 4

For Richer or for Poorer: Words about Money

Words in This Chapter

- affluent
- avarice
- cupidity
- destitute
- fiscal
- frugal
- impecunious
- indigent
- mendicant
- mercenary

- miserly
- munificent
- opulent
- parsimonious
- parvenu
- plutocrat
- prodigal
- profligate
- solvent
- squander

Smart planner that you are, you wait until your dad is in a good mood before you spring it on him that you need a new outfit for the big party next weekend. He looks you in the eye and informs you he is impecunious.

Should you grab the keys and get ready to hit the mall, knowing you're about to get dear old dad's credit card, or should you skulk back to your closet and dig in its subterraneous depths, hoping to find something you can wear without humiliating yourself entirely because there's no way you're getting any more money this month?

When you master the words in this chapter, you know that it's the closet, not the mall, for you. *Impecunious* means poor, penniless. Your father is telling you he's broke, and you're on your own.

Showing You the Money: New Vocabulary Words

The words in this chapter have to do with ~~money,~~ words that describe being rich and poor, generous and stingy.

affluent (rhymes with, *laugh* you gent): wealthy, having an abundance of money.

> *We laughed at our teacher's statement that she was fluent in French and affluent in China, where the U.S. dollar can buy a lot.*

avarice (rhymes with, *have* a hiss): greed, desire to get something.

> *Donald Duck's uncle, Scrooge McDuck, is noted for his avarice and is always scheming to get even more bags and bags of bucks.*

You've probably heard of the seven deadly sins. Avarice (greed) is one of them. The others are pride, envy, gluttony (overindulging), lust, anger, and sloth (laziness).

cupidity (rhymes with, stu*pid*ity): greed for gain, inordinate desire to appropriate another's wealth or possessions.

> *We were astounded by the cupidity of the woman who compromised her integrity and reputation just for the sake of getting more money.*

You know Cupid is the god of love. Think of cupidity as the "love of money." One of my students told me she thinks of *cup*idity as a desire to fill one's *cup* with cash.

destitute (rhymes with, *yes* bit toot): without resources, in poverty.

> *The treasure hunter bemoaned the fact that the sunken ship he spent millions to find had been transporting musical instruments, and the only gold aboard was the flaking paint on the trumpets and tubas, leaving the searcher more destitute than he was before he began his quest.*

Bonus joke: How do you clean a tuba? With a tuba toothpaste!

fiscal (rhymes with, *this* gull): pertaining to money.

> *The accountants thought they were hysterically funny when they showed up at the meeting in workout clothes and claimed they were "fiscal fitness buffs!"*

You may have heard of the fiscal year, which goes from July 1 to June 30. That's simply the accountant's or bookkeeper's year, as opposed to a calendar year.

frugal (rhymes with, *who* gull): economical, careful in the use of goods.

> *"I'm not cheap, but I am frugal," said Andrew, "and I refuse to waste money on renting videos repeatedly when I can buy them for almost the same cost."*

Frugal is the politically correct way of calling someone cheap. If you like Andrew, you call him frugal; if you dislike Andrew, you call him cheap. (Wouldn't Fru-Gal make a good name for a brand of young girl's inexpensive clothing?)

impecunious (im peck *you* knee us): poor, penniless.

> *The impecunious student was not able to afford a math tutor and flunked Calculus class.*

Bonus joke: My Calculus teacher, whenever passing out tests on which we didn't do well, would always make the same joke: "It's not the math that gets you into trouble . . . it's the aftermath!"

indigent (rhymes with, *in* smidge gent): poor, needy

> *Realizing that there were many indigent people downtown, the charity opened up a branch soup kitchen and emergency shelter.*

 Be careful not to confuse indigent, meaning poor, with *indignant,* meaning angry at unjust action. If you are fired and then go broke from the lack of a job, you may be indignant over being fired and indigent as a result, but the words are different.

mendicant (*men* duh can't): a beggar.

> *Every day when he passed the mendicant on the sidewalk, Mr. Weise would give the man a dollar and ask him how he was doing that day.*

mercenary (rhymes with, *purse* in dairy): serving merely for pay.

> *Timothy was so mercenary that he would do anything for a dollar, even betray his buddies by telling the gossip reporter which football players had broken curfew the night before the match.*

Bonus trivia: You've probably had a curfew all your life, times you had to return home or face the wrath of your parents. But do you know the origin of the term curfew? It's from the Norman-French *couvre-le-feu,* meaning cover (douse) the fire. The curfew was the hour at which the cities extinguished their candles and fires for the night.

miserly (rhymes with, *wiser* Lee): stingy, hoarding wealth.

> *When you read the novel* Silas Marner, *you observe one of the most miserly men in fiction, a man who never shared any of his money until he learned to love a child.*

If your parent is miserly when it comes to your allowance (if he's cheap and stingy), you're miserable because you don't have enough money.

munificent (rhymes with, spoon *if* is sent): splendidly generous.

> *"Sure, I like his munificent gifts," sighed the young woman married to the rich older man, "but this relationship is like a split-level house: It has two stories, and the other one isn't pretty."*

Even though *muni* doesn't mean money per se, thinking of the words together can be helpful. Muni sounds rather like money; remember that when you are munificent, you are money-magnificent, giving out cash.

Even though the words are different, munificent can be thought of as financially magnificent. If you are magnificently generous, you are munificent.

opulent (rhymes with, *pop* you lent): rich, wealthy, affluent.

> *The opulent lifestyle of the yuppie couple showed they didn't mind spending their money on themselves, spoiling themselves with expensive cars and clothes.*

Bonus joke: Where do yuppies buy their computers? Answer: At Nerdstroms!

parsimonious (pars im *moan* he us): stingy, sparing.

> *When I was young and my folks refused to give me money, I threatened to grow up and write an expose of their cheapness and title it "The Parsimonious Parents."*

parvenu (rhymes with, *far* when you): a person of humble origins who has gained wealth and position and risen in society, especially one considered unfit for the position (an upstart).

> *The elderly professor scoffed at the parvenu in plaid pants and a beanie, telling him that even though he had made millions designing computer games, he was not going to be welcomed into their sedate golf club.*

My parents still talk about the time I was a little girl and came home all proud of myself from the golf course. I grandly announced, "I almost got a hole in one! I missed by only five strokes!" (No self-esteem problems in that child!)

plutocrat (rhymes with, *you* toe brat): a person exercising power or influence over others by right of wealth or position.

> *We recognized that the club was controlled by a few plutocrats who had been in charge for years and whom no mere* nouveau riche *member ever challenged.*

If you speak French, you know that *nouveau riche* means "new rich." It has a connotation (idea, impression) of someone who is a parvenu, a social climber, not old money. Usually, calling someone *nouveau riche* is meant to be an insult.

prodigal (rhymes with, *odd* dig gull): recklessly wasteful, extravagant.

> *The prodigal son in the Bible spent all his money and had to go home to his father because he was broke.*

profligate (rhymes with, *off* fig late): recklessly extravagant (this word also refers to someone who has abandoned himself/herself to vice or indulgence).

> *Knowing how profligate Emira is, her parents don't put more than a few dollars in her checking account at any time.*

Think of someone profligate as a "pro" at spending money.

solvent (rhymes with, *doll* vent): able to pay one's debts, financially sound.

> *After my grandfather gave me a hundred dollars as a graduation gift, I was solvent and finally able to pay back all the friends who had loaned me money.*

If you are solvent, you have enough money to solve your problems. You aren't rich, just not bankrupt. Don't confuse *affluent* (having a lot of money) with solvent (having just enough money).

The opposite of solvent is *insolvent*: unable to pay one's bills; bankrupt. An insolvent person cannot solve his money problems. Many of my international students seem to think of insolvent as not able to be dissolved. The correct word for that is *insoluble.* A rock is nearly insoluble. If you have hit rock bottom financially, you are insolvent.

squander (rhymes with, *w*ander): spend recklessly, use in a wasteful manner.

> *If I had a million dollars, I would squander it all on fishing trips, even if I did nothing but sit on deck and talk about the big ones that got away.*

Bonus joke: What kind of musician makes the best fisherman? The one with the castanets!

The Buck Stops Here: Practice Exercises

There you sit, all that knowledge swirling around in your brain, begging for relief. Won't it feel good when you've let it out, doing the exercises in this section? Check your responses in the "Answers to the Exercises" section, later in this chapter.

Exercise one

Directions: Select the appropriate word to complete the sentence.

1. Heather, known for her (cupidity/munificence), was so greedy she almost knocked over a little old lady in her rush to pick up a coin she saw on the sidewalk.

2. My grandfather is so (miserly/affluent) that when he gave me a dollar for my birthday, he asked me to give him back seventy-five cents in change.

3. The (avarice/prodigality) of the bank robber was his downfall; he spent so much time digging every last cent out of the bank drawers that the police had time to capture him.

4. My excuse to my father when I spent all my allowance on a new sweater was that unless I were completely (indigent/solvent), I wouldn't qualify for the scholarship, so actually, my shopping was saving him money in the long run.

5. "The way you go through my money, I'll be (profligate/destitute) in no time," grumbled my mother as she opened her purse.

6. The school club had a (mendicant/parvenu) Monday, in which everyone went around begging for money for charity.

7. Thanks to the company's (miserly/munificent) contribution, we were able to update our school's office, buying new computers, fax machines, and printers.

8. "I'll forgive you for calling me a (plutocrat/mendicant)," said Garfield, "but unlike dogs, cats don't have to beg; my charming cat personality makes people do exactly what I want them to do and feed me lasagna without my even asking."

9. Claiming that his unit was (impecunious/mercenary), General Patton petitioned Congress for additional funds.

10. The television show about the (opulent/frugal) lifestyle of the people in their Beverly Hills mansions made me wonder why anyone really needed a 20-car garage.

The *–ine* line

Rootmeister that you are, you know that the suffix *–ine* means similar to, or in the manner of. For example, feline means like a cat. Here are some other *–ine* words you may find useful. (See Chapter 2 for more on roots.)

✔ **aquiline** (*aqua* line): like an eagle. A person may be spoken of as having an aquiline nose, which means hooked like an eagle's beak.

✔ **bovine** (*bow* vine): like an ox. Ah, you thought bovine meant like a cow? The first meaning of the word is ox-like; rather slow; dull and stupid.

✔ **canine** (*kay* nine): like a dog. This one is easy.

✔ **equine** (*eek* wine): like a horse. You've probably heard this one, too.

✔ **lupine** (*lou* pine): like a wolf. If that gorgeous gal has made you so interested that you forget for a minute to be a gentleman, she may label you lupine (and possibly even knock you supine, which means lying on the back, face upward!).

✔ **ovine** (*oh* vine): like a sheep. Little Bo Peep hung around with some pretty ovine types.

✔ **ursine** (*er* sign): like a bear. You've probably seen the constellation called the Great Bear. The more formal name for it is Ursa Major.

✔ **vulpine** (*vuhl* pine): no, it doesn't mean like a vulture; that word, logically enough, is *vulturine*. Vulpine means like a fox, foxy. A cunning person may be described as vulpine.

Exercise two

Directions: Choose the antonym (opposite) of each word.

1. profligate: (frugal/wasteful)
2. opulent: (poor/rich)
3. parvenu: (person who inherited family money/person who created his or her own wealth)
4. squander: (waste/spend wisely)
5. destitute: (poverty-stricken/financially sound)
6. munificent: (open-handed/tightfisted)
7. cupidity: (unselfishness/greed)
8. affluent: (poor/generous)
9. parsimonious: (stingy/open-handed)
10. insolvent: (rich/poor)

Handy words to know

Give yourself a big hand after you've finished learning the following vocabulary.

✔ *closefisted* (rhymes with, nose *twisted*): same thing as tightfisted, stingy, closing your hand on money.

✔ *highhanded* (rhymes with, fly *branded*): overbearing, arbitrary. Your boss may high-handedly tell you to come in to work over the weekend, even though he knows you had a family event scheduled. Think of a highhanded person as having the upper hand.

✔ *ironhanded* (*eye* urn handed): in a rigorous, severely controlling manner. An ironhanded coach slams down her fist and tells you in no uncertain terms that two-a-day practices will be the norm for the next month.

✔ *openhanded* (*oh* pen handed): generous, giving or sharing freely.

✔ *tightfisted* (rhymes with, bite *twisted*): stingy, holding tight to money.

✔ *underhanded* (rhymes with, *blunder* handed): secret, sly, deceitful. An under-handed spy might steal a secret, then hand it under the table to the Bad Guys.

Exercise three

Directions: Select the best answer to each question.

1. After scrutinizing the books, the director realized that unless he became more - - - - with the charity's monies, the charity would soon be - - - -.

    (A) frugal .. insolvent

    (B) prodigal .. bankrupt

    (C) miserly .. solvent

    (D) opulent .. broke

    (E) munificent .. indigent

2. Many motivational speakers discuss how they were - - - - at one point in their lives, but through hard work and sacrifice, managed to become wealthy and successful.

    (A) mercenary

    (B) munificent

    (C) destitute

    (D) opulent

    (E) frugal

3. The corporation's security director warned that the vice-president's - - - - had in the past caused him to steal and sell corporate secrets and that the company should take steps to keep him under observance.

   (A) parsimony

   (B) cupidity

   (C) opulence

   (D) impecuniousness

   (E) prodigality

4. Having grown up surrounded by wealth and power, Mr. Martinez had the self-confidence of a - - - -, able to remain poised in any situation.

   (A) parvenu

   (B) mercenary

   (C) miser

   (D) mendicant

   (E) plutocrat

5. When it was obvious that the symphony would have to shut down unless a - - - - gift was offered, all of the musicians, who could never be accused of being - - - -, offered to give up their salaries for six months.

   (A) frugal .. plutocrats

   (B) miniscule .. destitute

   (C) generous .. opulent

   (D) sizeable .. prodigal

   (E) munificent .. mercenary

6. The - - - - of the novel's main character — already a millionaire — led him to compromise his principles and live in a loveless marriage in order to obtain yet more money.

   (A) indigence

   (B) avarice

   (C) destitution

   (D) affluence

   (E) solvency

7. When the father informed his son that it was time the two men had a discussion about ---- matters, the son knew that his father realized the money had been ---- on unimportant items and not saved for college expenses.

    (A) fiscal .. squandered on

    (B) pecuniary .. hoarded for

    (C) monetary .. husbanded for

    (D) financial .. safeguarded for

    (E) academic .. wasted

8. The bankrupt zoo failed in its attempts to purchase a rare California condor and bemoaned the fact that its ---- forced the seller to offer the animal to a competitor.

    (A) avarice

    (B) affluence

    (C) insolvency

    (D) prodigality

    (E) miserliness

9. Bob Hope used to joke that Bing Crosby was so ---- that he never paid taxes, he simply asked the government how much it needed!

    (A) affluent

    (B) miserly

    (C) insolvent

    (D) impecunious

    (E) mercenary

10. Although customarily ----, Dennis was delighted to be ---- when it came time to purchase a thank-you present for his mentor who was retiring from the firm.

    (A) insolvent .. mercenary

    (B) frugal .. munificent

    (C) destitute .. poor

    (D) stingy .. avaricious

    (E) magnanimous .. affluent

Answers to the Exercises

Are you getting so many new words entered into your brain that you are not sure you're processing them all correctly? The following answers to the exercises in the preceding section let you know how you're doing.

Exercise one

1. **cupidity.** Cupidity is the love of money, greed for gain. Someone willing to knock over a little old lady for a coin is definitely suffering from cupidity . . . not to mention stupidity!

2. **miserly.** A miser is a cheapskate, someone penny pinching and extremely stingy. Someone who is so cheap he'd put slugs in his penny loafers is a miser.

3. **avarice.** Avarice is greed. The robber's lack of sense about his lack of cents got him caught when he wasted time picking up the pennies.

4. **indigent.** Someone indigent is poor, needy. The student was trying to say that unless she could prove she was broke, she wouldn't be able to qualify for a scholarship. Not a bad argument, come to think of it!

5. **destitute.** Destitute means broke, in poverty. The mother carped (complained) — as mothers can do — that her daughter was driving her to the poorhouse.

6. **mendicant.** A mendicant is a beggar. I got voted best/worst punster at my high school because of this word. We had a mendicant day, and I said no gum would be allowed on that day because "beggars can't be chew-sers!"

7. **munificent.** Munificent means generous. The contribution must have been generous, not cheap (miserly) for the school to get all the new equipment.

   Bonus trivia: Did you know that the fax machine was invented almost 30 years before the telephone? An "image-facsimile transmitter," meant be used to transmit a document over telegraph wires, was patented way back in 1842. Alas, because Morse code was faster, the early fax never really caught on.

8. **mendicant.** A mendicant is a beggar. Garfield is proudly making the point that cats don't beg; they just sit there and wait for the world to do their bidding.

9. **impecunious.** If the general needed more money, he must have been broke (impecunious).

   Bonus joke: Where did General Patton keep his armies? Answer: Up his sleevies!

10. **opulent.** Opulent means rich, wealthy, affluent. People who live in Beverly Hills and have 20-car garages have opulent lifestyles.

Exercise two

1. **frugal.** Someone profligate wastes money, is recklessly extravagant. Someone frugal is careful with money, uses it wisely.

2. **poor.** Opulent means rich, wealthy.

3. **a person who inherited wealth.** A parvenu made his own money, like someone who got rich in a dot-con scheme.

4. **spend wisely.** You squander your allowance when you spend it all on junk food; you spend it wisely when you buy running shoes to run and work off all those junk food pounds you put on.

   Bonus joke: Did you hear about the runner who ran backward and gained ten pounds?

5. **financially sound.** I always associate destitute with desperate; if you are totally broke, you are both destitute and desperate. (My financial situation is so bad that I can't save up for a rainy day; one good drizzle would wipe me out!)

6. **tightfisted.** Someone who is tightfisted (cheap) grabs a bill and squeezes so hard that poor George's powdered wig falls off. If you are munificent, open-handed, you leave your hands open so that anyone can help himself to your money.

7. **unselfishness.** Someone with cupidity is greedy and selfish, wanting all the money and not sharing any with you. If you are the opposite type — a generous soul who would share your last cent with someone else — you are unselfish.

8. **poor.** Someone affluent is wealthy. In the future, affluent people may be able to go to the moon on vacation instead of merely the French Riviera.

   Bonus joke: Speaking of the moon, did you hear about the new restaurant there? Great food, but no atmosphere.

9. **open-handed.** Someone open-handed is generous; someone parsimonious is cheap and stingy.

10. **rich.** Insolvent means poor, not having enough money to meet the bills. The opposite is rich.

Exercise three

1. **A.** Frugal means economical, careful with money. If the director kept giving away too much money, the charity would soon be insolvent, which means bankrupt, unable to pay the bills.

   Bonus word: Are you familiar with the term ***eleemosynary***? It means "pertaining to charity." If you're teasing a friend of yours who hasn't had a date in some time, you may say to him, "Try to find a girl in an eleemosynary frame of mind so she'll go out with you as an act of charity!"

2. **C.** Destitute means bankrupt, poverty-stricken. A motivational speaker may discuss how he used to be poor, but now is rich . . . and then, perhaps, try to sell the listeners a "guaranteed three-step plan that can make you a millionaire, too!" Suckers, uh, I mean, people, who fall for these speeches and give their money often become not affluent (rich) but destitute (poor).

3. **B.** This question is difficult. Cupidity means greed for gain, inappropriate desire for another's wealth or possessions. You may have been tempted to choose A, parsimony. But parsimony is not so much being greedy as being stingy. A parsimonious person wants to keep what he already has, not give any away. A person with cupidity wants to take what someone else has.

4. **E.** The key here was that Mr. Martinez grew up with wealth, didn't acquire it just recently. A plutocrat is someone who exercises power over others by right of wealth. A parvenu is also wealthy, but recently acquired the wealth, and is seen by others as somewhat of an upstart, someone who doesn't really deserve the money.

5. **E.** You can predict that the symphony needs a big, generous gift. Eliminate choices A (frugal means economic, spending money carefully and sparingly) and B (minuscule means small). The second word should mean that the musicians are not selfish, or playing only for the money. Mercenary means working solely for money or material gain.

   If you know your roots (see Chapter 2), you can easily dissect a symphony. *Sym* means with or together; *phon* means sound. A symphony is many instruments joining their sounds together, blending with each other. It does not have clashing sounds.

6. **B.** The key here is that the character is already a millionaire. He already has money, isn't broke, but is greedy for even more money. Avarice is greed, desire to get something. (I've always thought Avarice would make an excellent name for a character in a soap opera, a grasping gold digger who goes after all the rich old coots and takes out large insurance policies on them.)

7. **A.** Any of the answers work for the first blank. Fiscal, pecuniary, monetary, and financial all mean relating to money. The conversation could be about money, or it could be (choice E) about other important matters. The key to this question is the second blank. If the money had been spent on things that were unimportant, it was wasted or squandered.

8. **C.** If the zoo that hoped to buy the rare bird couldn't afford it, the zoo was insolvent, unable to meet its bills.

Note that choice E is a trap. A miserly (cheap) zoo might choose not to spend the required money to get the bird, but the sentence specifically says the zoo was bankrupt, not that it was too cheap to put a crowbar in its wallet and hand over the cash.

9. **A.** The joke is that Bing Crosby is so rich, he can afford to give the government whatever it needs. Affluent means wealthy, rich.

10. **B.** The "Although customarily . . ." tells you that the two parts of the sentences contradict each other, that the two blanks will have words that are nearly opposites. Frugal means economical, spending as little money as possible. Munificent means extravagantly generous.

The original Mentor, with a capital M, was the friend and advisor of the Greek hero Odysseus and the teacher of his son, Telemachus. A *mentor* today is anyone who teaches, coaches, takes you under his or her wing.

Chapter 5

Look Who's Talking: Words about Speaking

*W*hen you finally agree to a blind date, your friend nods, then *diffidently* (timidly, shyly) says, "Uh, one more thing. He (or she) is rather on the *taciturn* side."

You have to make a decision: Does this mean you go out and buy earplugs because your date shouts, or should you buy an ear trumpet because he or she is so soft-spoken? Maybe you need to have prepared several topics of conversation in case you have to do all the talking. Or should you *surreptitiously* (stealthily, sneakily, on the sly) pack your Walkman and headphones, knowing that a taciturn type won't let you get a word in edgewise?

Knowing the words in this chapter can help you make the right decision.

Talking Up a Blue Streak with New Vocabulary Words

How many times in your life have you said, "The word is right on the tip of my tongue; I'll get it in a minute" and been frustrated because you couldn't come up with exactly what you wanted to say? The words in this chapter will have you talking in no time.

bombastic (bomb *bass* tick): using high-sounding language, pompous.

> *The bombastic movie agent leered at the blonde starlet and said, "Let's cogitate on appropriate machinations to ensure your pulchritude turns you into the biggest star Hollywood has ever seen!"*

Bombastic is an interesting word. It comes from *bombast,* a type of cotton padding. Someone bombastic is full of verbal padding, having an extravagant style but very little substance.

To *cogitate* is to think seriously and deeply about. *Machinations* are an artful or skillful plot or scheme. *Pulchritude* means beauty. In other words, the agent, in his bombastic way, was saying, "Let's think up a plan to use your beauty to make you a big star."

chatterbox (rhymes with, *fatter* fox): a person who talks incessantly.

> *Samantha was such a chatterbox that she once won an award for talking nonstop from Los Angeles to New York on a flight.*

Bonus trivia: Okay, you chatter with your friends, and your teeth chatter when you're cold. What animals are said to chatter? Dogs bark. Cats meow. Cows low . . . and squirrels chatter.

declaim (rhymes with, re*claim*): to speak in a dramatic, pompous way.

> *Nine-year-old Juan amused his parents when he asked for an allowance increase by declaiming, "The undervaluation of my contributions to this family have led to a serious underfunding of my weekly income."*

The *claim* part of declaim comes from the same root as *clamor,* meaning shouting or noise. When you *declaim,* you grandly shout your message for all to hear.

diatribe (rhymes with, *try* a bribe): a lengthy bitter, abusive criticism.

> *The police officer tried to calm down the man who had just gotten a ticket for putting his car in front of a fire hydrant by the coffee shop, saying, "There's no need for a diatribe; you know you're in a No Perking zone!"*

Okay, if you want to go into a diatribe about my lame jokes and horrible puns, go ahead. You won't be the first!

discursive (rhymes with, this *purse* give): rambling, wandering from one topic to another.

> *When the old Air Force buddies got together once a year, their discursive conversation jumped from their families to sports to their latest flights.*

Bonus trivia: Did you know that most economy seats on airplanes are tilted at 35 degrees — the same angle favored by interrogators wishing to deprive their subjects of sleep?

Don't confuse discursive with discourse. **Discourse** is conversation. Both words, however, have the same Latin root, *discurre,* that means "to run to and fro."

garrulous (rhymes with, *barre*l us): talking too much.

> *Charles Dickens and many other authors of his time were paid by the word for their writing, and thus made their characters garrulous to earn more money for themselves.*

Don't confuse this word with **gregarious,** meaning sociable. The root *greg* means group or herd; *–ous* means full of. While an outgoing person may be talkative, the two words are not the same.

glib (rhymes with, *bib*): speaking in a smooth, easy manner.

> *The shipboard Romeo earned his living by using his glib speech, polished appearance, and smooth manners to romance elderly women.*

Bonus joke: Speaking of ships, did you hear what happened when the red cruise ship crashed into the blue one? The passengers were marooned.

grandiloquent (rhymes with, hand *brillo* went): using pompous, bombastic words.

> *The grandiloquent speaker got the nickname "Pompous Pete" for his habit of using seven-syllable words when two-syllable ones would suffice.*

Grand means big; *loq* means speech. Someone grandiloquent has "big speech," is a big talker. Politicians often make grandiloquent promises.

harangue (ha *rang*): a loud, noisy, or scolding speech; a tirade.

> *We were so used to the harangues of the wrestling coach who was always after us to make weight, that we at first didn't get his joke when he said, "If I asked you to haul butt, it'd take two trips!"*

hector (rhymes with, *vector*): to bully or browbeat.

> *When the rowdy teens at the amusement park hectored their buddy who was making a little extra cash by dressing up as a rodent for a children's play, he turned tail and sighed, "I thought I was a man, but I'm just a mouse."*

Have you heard the word *browbeat* before? It means to intimidate with harsh, stern looks and words. If your father sees a long scratch on the side of his new car after you've been driving it, he can browbeat you by furrowing his brown and scowling at you, then letting loose a few choice comments that leave you vowing to give up cars and just ride your bike for the rest of your life.

inaudible (rhymes with, in *clawed* drib bowl): not loud enough to be heard.

> *The class clown made sure his voice was inaudible when he responded to the biology teacher's question of "What is a seizure?" by saying, "A seizure is a Roman emperor."*

A lot of words are based on the Latin *audibilis,* meaning able to be heard. An audience listens to a speaker in an auditorium. A quarterback calls an audible on the field. An audio-visual presentation is both heard and watched. An *audiologist* evaluates your hearing. In college, you may *audit* a class, which means you sit in the class and listen to the professor, but you get no credit for the course.

laconic (la *con* nick): using few words, terse.

> *When the beautiful woman was asked whether she was a model, she responded laconically, "No. Full size."*

As a 5'9" woman, I've used this line myself. I am just waiting for a clothing store to sell products in size 14 and up and call it "Not models, but full size!" just for laughs.

loquacious (rhymes with, no *play* she us): very talkative.

> *The comedian complained about his loquacious wife, saying he wouldn't mind her having the last word — if only she'd get to it!*

Loq is a root meaning talk or speech (you may know this root in a more familiar word, *eloquent,* meaning fluid, vivid, and persuasive in speech); *–ous* means full of. Someone loquacious is full of speech; chatty.

mellifluous (rhymes with, sell *if* flu us): sounding sweet and smooth, honeyed.

> *The school Romeo approached the girl and asked her in a mellifluous voice whether she was e-mailed from heaven.*

The Latin word *mellis* means honey. Interestingly enough, the word mildew is from the same root, because mildew originally meant honeydew, the fungus that could grow on a fruit.

Bonus joke: Why is a mushroom always welcome at a party? Because he's a fungi (fun guy)!

pithy (rhymes with, *with* he): concise, terse, and full of meaning.

> *The doctor, asked to name a disease associated with cigarettes, gave the pithy response, "Death."*

The ***pith*** is the center or core of such things as plants, bones, and even feathers. When you make a pithy comment, you get to the center of the matter quickly.

These are not dirty words!

The following words are quite tame and harmless, not dirty at all. But they are just the type of naughty-sounding words that you can say in a whisper and accompany with a wink to make others think you're saying things you shouldn't. Having a good vocabulary can be a lot of fun!

- ✔ ***dastard*** (rhymes with, class *nerd*): tsk, tsk. What did you think this word was? You should be ashamed. A dastard is a sneaky, cowardly evildoer. You can call your teacher, who springs a pop quiz on you, a dirty dastard and get away with it, as long as you pronounce the word very, very clearly!

- ✔ ***hoary*** (rhymes with, *four* he): If you pictured ladies in fishnet stockings, think again . . . unless those ladies are very old, with gray hair. Hoary has two meanings. One is grayish white, or having gray hair. The other meaning (logically enough) is old. A hoary man may be very old with a long gray beard.

- ✔ ***horology*** (rhymes with, four *all* oh gee): It's not the study of what you think. Horology is

the art or science of making timepieces. If you craft a clock in shop class, you're a horologist.

- ✔ ***opisthenar*** (oh *piss* then are): No, an opisthenar is not something that's used in a bathroom. Your opisthenar is where you wrote the answers to the quizzes when you were in grade school: the back of your hand.

- ✔ ***titivate*** (rhymes with, *bit* give ate): Don't even go there. To titivate is to dress up or spruce up. You titivate yourself before having your picture taken.

- ✔ ***tittup*** (rhymes with, *bit* up): To tittup is to move in a frolicsome or prancing way. Interestingly, this word is believed to be an imitation of the sound of horses' hoof beats.

- ✔ ***turdine*** (rhymes with, *nerd* wine): No, wrong again. Turdine means of, like, or pertaining to a robin or a bluebird. Isn't that much prettier than what you were thinking?

pontificate (pahn *tiff* fi kate): to speak in a pompous or dogmatic way.

> *The principal chose to pontificate to his students, stating that only education could help them accomplish their goals.*

prolix (rhymes with, *go* licks): wordy, long-winded.

> *The humorous character on the TV series was noted for being a prolix telephone addict who could talk for hours on any topic.*

rail (rhymes with, *sail*): to speak bitterly, to complain against.

> *Jeremiah railed against the media specialist who was shushing him; he called her Conan the Librarian.*

Do you see the inside joke in the example sentence? It has to do with the name, Jeremiah. A *jeremiad* is a long lamentation or complaint (referring to the Lamentations of Jeremiah, a Hebrew prophet). Jeremiah railed at the woman, then went back to school and inflicted a jeremiad on his friends, griping about the librarian.

stentorian (rhymes with, when *story* un): very loud.

> *The children could hear their mother's stentorian voice throughout the neighborhood, calling them home from play.*

In Homer's *The Iliad*, Stentor is a Greek herald "with the voice of 50 men." In other words, he shouted.

succinct (rhymes with, the *pinked*): clearly and briefly stated; terse.

> *The teacher always asked us to be succinct, saying, "If you must cry over spilt milk, try to condense it."*

taciturn (rhymes with, *acid* turn): not liking to talk, almost always silent.

> *Calvin Coolidge, reputedly the most taciturn president, upon being told by a woman that she had bet money she could make him say three words, said simply, "You lose."*

terse (rhymes with, *verse*): brief, concise, succinct, free of superfluous words.

> *The comedian Henny Youngman, was a terse man, noted for his one-liners, such as, "Take my wife — please!"*

Many attorneys advise their clients that if they absolutely must answer questions from the press, they should limit themselves to terse responses, such as "No comment" or "Speak to my attorney." You've probably heard the saying, "Least said, soonest mended." That's the epitome of terse.

verbose (rhymes with, sir *gross*): wordy, long-winded.

> *The verbose comedian got laughs by going on and on about his girlfriend's obsession with candy, saying that she went to the doctor and tested positive for chocolate!*

The suffix *–ose* means full of or having the qualities of. If you eat a lot of sugar, you may be consuming foods with glucose, sucrose, and dextrose — just to mention a few of the ingredients listed on the side of the junk-food wrappers.

vociferous (rhymes with, go *differ* us): loud, noisy, vehement.

> *The grandmother complained vociferously about the length of time it took to fill out the paperwork, saying she'd like to finish while she still had her original hips.*

The root *voc* means voice (think of vocal or vocalize). The suffix *–ous* means full of. A vociferous person is full of voice.

voluble (rhymes with, *doll* you pull): talkative.

> *Easily the most voluble student in the class, Flint turned a ten-minute book report into a full hour's entertainment, acting out the book and doing the character's voices.*

Voluble is often confused with two other words, *valuable* (meaning having value, worth something) and *volatile* (meaning unpredictable, unstable, explosive).

Letting Your Actions Speak Louder than Words: Practice Exercises

Even with all the words about speaking you've reviewed in this chapter, there's no way you can talk your way out of taking a little test. This section gives you three exercises that help you assess just how much you've improved your vocabulary. The answers are in the "Answers to the Exercises" section at the end of the chapter.

Phobias

Everyone is afraid of something. Some people have *claustrophobia* (fear of closed spaces, like elevators). Some people have *agoraphobia* (fear of open spaces; these people hate to leave the cozy confines of their own houses). You may have *cynophobia* (fear of dogs) or *ailurophobia* (fear of cats). How many of the following phobias can you identify?

✔ *brontophobia* (*brahn* toe phobia): fear of thunder. If your cat hears one thunderclap and scurries to hide under the bed, he is a brontophobe. Where have you heard this prefix, *bronto,* meaning thunder, before? In the word brontosaurus, or thunder lizard. The brontosaurus was one loud lizard.

✔ *hydrophobia* (*high* droe phobia): fear of water. The Wicked Witch of the West from the *Wizard of Oz* movie had every right to be hydrophobic, because water caused her to melt into nothingness.

✔ *pogophobia* (*poe* go phobia): fear of beards. Did you think this was a fear of pogo sticks? Nope. A pogophobic child may bounce merrily on a pogo stick for hours, but scream at her first sight of a man (or woman, for that matter) with a *hirsute* (hairy) face.

✔ *xenophobia* (*zee* no phobia): fear of strangers. *Xeno* means foreign or strange. If you don't like going to parties because you are afraid of people whom you don't know, you're a xenophobe. On the other hand, if you're like Will Rogers, who said he never met a man he didn't like, you are a xenophile (*–phil* means love).

✔ *xerophobia* (*zero* phobia): fear of dryness and dry places. Don't like the desert? Afraid it'll make you shrivel up? You're a xerophobe. *Xero* means dry. If you live in the West with all the droughts, you're asked to plant a *xeriscape,* which is landscaping with drought-tolerant plants, like cacti.

Exercise one

Directions: Select the appropriate word to complete the sentence.

1. The friends laughed at comedienne Lily Tomlin's (diatribe/grandiloquence), agreeing with her statement that, "Humans invented language because of our deep-seated need to complain."

2. The quiet girl's voice was nearly (inaudible/prolix) when she said she was depressed because she got an F in Spanish.

3. It was extremely difficult for the television reporter to interview the (voluble/taciturn) woman who responded to all his questions with a simple yes or no answer.

4. The criminal complained (succinctly/vociferously) to the judge that no one understood him, going on and on at length about his deprived childhood and his inability to fit into society, demanding that he be given a psychiatric examination and allowed to plead not guilty by reason of insanity.

5. In her most (stentorian/mellifluous) voice, Snow White cooed to the camera shop owner, "Someday, my prints will come."

6. The racetrack gambler treated us all to a (pontification/ harangue) on his bad luck, saying he bet on a horse at ten to one . . . and it didn't come in until half past five.

7. The (chatterbox/terse), who served as a butler to a wealthy family, amused his friends by telling everything about his employer, including the fact that "he's so rich, the bags under his eyes are Gucci!"

8. Juan lost no opportunity to (pontificate/rail), even informing us at lunch that the peaches we were eating were originally called Persian apples, because the word "peaches" is Latin for Persia.

9. The student applying for admission to the university had a (pithy/glib) response to every question, annoying the interviewer, who felt that the applicant wasn't taking the process seriously.

10. When asked what the newly fired worker produced, the manager's (loquacious/laconic) response was, "Carbon dioxide."

If you could talk to the animals

What is chattering? To you, the word probably means talking fast and foolishly, as in the chattering of overexcited five-year-olds at a birthday party. But to a biologist, chattering has a different meaning. A *chattering* is a group of starlings (birds).

Here are some other interesting terms for animal groups, with the "people meanings" next to them:

- ✔ **A convocation of eagles:** A *convocation* is a group, especially an academic assembly. When everyone assembles or is convoked in the school's auditorium to hear a speaker, that's a convocation.

- ✔ **An exaltation of larks:** *Exaltation* is a feeling of great joy and pride. When you master the words in this book, you'll feel exaltation.

- ✔ **A muster of peacocks:** To *muster* is to summon, to collect, and to gather together.

The cliché "to muster up the courage" means to summon up your bravery. You muster the courage to confront the school bully.

Bonus: Peacock gatherings have more than one term; you may also hear of an ostentation of peacocks. To be *ostentatious* is to be flamboyant, showy, pretentious — like a peacock spreading his tail feathers to attract attention.

- ✔ **A parliament of owls:** A *parliament* is a council or legislative body, something like a Congress. Wise people are in the parliament; owls are stereotyped as wise animals.

- ✔ **A skulk of foxes:** To *skulk* is to slink, to move in a stealthy or sinister manner. You would skulk around the neighborhood if you were spying on your sweetie, trying to see whether he or she is seeing anyone else.

Exercise two

Directions: Choose the antonym (opposite) of each word.

1. inaudible: (stentorian/bombastic)
2. voluble: (discursive/taciturn)
3. diatribe: (compliment/confusion)
4. grandiloquent: (glib/laconic)
5. garrulous: (pithy/verbose)
6. declaim: (accept/suggest)
7. rail: (complain/praise)
8. bombastic: (self-effacing/pompous)
9. pontificate: (speak arrogantly/speak diffidently)
10. verbose: (voluble/taciturn)

Exercise three

Directions: Select the best answer to each question.

1. The psychiatrist sat patiently, listening to the man - - - - everyone he hated, from his parents to his employer to his neighbors.

    (A) rail at

    (B) declaim

    (C) discourse with

    (D) be inaudible about

    (E) be pithy about

2. The - - - - voices of the choir delighted the picnickers who hadn't realized there was a singing group joining their activities at the top of Pike's Peak.

    (A) haranguing

    (B) mellifluous

    (C) bombastic

    (D) pontificating

    (E) stentorian

3. The politician, speaking to the United Nations, slammed his hand down on the lectern and bellowed in a(n) ---- voice that his country, small though it was, would not be intimidated by the superpowers.

   (A) pithy

   (B) inaudible

   (C) loquacious

   (D) stentorian

   (E) terse

4. The chemist on a project that was overbudget, behind schedule, and — according to rumor — having no success accomplishing its goals, gave only ---- answers to the reporter's questions, usually not going beyond a simple yes or no.

   (A) glib

   (B) verbose

   (C) garrulous

   (D) vociferous

   (E) terse

5. The usually ---- woman, realizing that anything she said at the costume party could not be heard over the din of the crowd, said nothing and instead gestured with her fan to communicate with her date.

   (A) succinct

   (B) loquacious

   (C) pithy

   (D) terse

   (E) mellifluous

6. After Dr. Martin had spoken for ten minutes without stopping to take a breath or let anyone else get a word in, his wife jokingly told him not to be so ---- the next time, but to feel free to talk a bit more.

   (A) pithy

   (B) glib

   (C) mellifluous

   (D) discursive

   (E) grandiloquent

7. When the drill instructor continued to - - - - the recruit to do more repetitions of the exercise, the recruit lost his temper, shouted at the sergeant, and stormed off the field, an event that had unfortunate repercussions shortly thereafter.

    (A) pontificate

    (B) declaim

    (C) verbose

    (D) hector

    (E) prolix

8. The politician was able to have breakfast with one group of people and explain in a grand and - - - - manner how he was supporting their goals and causes. He then did a repeat performance at lunch with a second group whose goals were exactly the opposite of those of the first group.

    (A) succinct

    (B) terse

    (C) taciturn

    (D) pithy

    (E) bombastic

9. The neighborhood coalition staged a - - - - protest against having the nuclear waste dump located in its area, chanting loudly and ringing a bell called The Death Knell.

    (A) verbose

    (B) vociferous

    (C) pontifical

    (D) garrulous

    (E) prolix

10. The - - - - teacher talked so much during class that she invariably ran out of time before she could assign homework, making her very popular with students.

    (A) railing

    (B) haranguing

    (C) chatterbox

    (D) grandiloquent

    (E) glib

Answers to the Exercises

After the mental exercise of taking the exams, you're ready for the physical exercise of patting yourself on the back after you see the excellent results. Check your answers with those in this section.

Exercise one

1. **diatribe.** A diatribe is a bitter, abusive criticism, just the type of statement from someone who complains a lot.

2. **inaudible.** Someone who is quiet and depressed would have an inaudible voice, one not (*in*– means not) loud enough to be heard.

3. **taciturn.** A taciturn person doesn't talk much, is habitually silent.

   Bonus: Ever hear of a tacit agreement or a tacit understanding? Those are unspoken agreements and understandings. For example, you and a friend may have a tacit or unspoken understanding that you'll let each other share clothes or borrow books. You don't have to ask specifically each and every time.

4. **vociferously.** Someone vociferous is loud, noisy, vehement.

   Bonus joke: Speaking of psychiatrists, know what kind of furniture they have in their offices? Overwrought iron!

5. **mellifluous.** A mellifluous voice is honeyed, sweet, and smooth-sounding. If you're going to harass me about my lame jokes, please be so kind as to do so in a mellifluous voice.

6. **harangue.** A harangue is a long, noisy, or scolding speech, a temper tantrum, a hissy fit, just what someone who has lost money would indulge in.

   While of course not all "h" words are bad, it's surprising how many of them generally mean to yell at: harass, harangue, hector, hassle.

7. **chatterbox.** A chatterbox is someone who talks all the time, someone who makes your ears ache.

8. **pontificate.** To pontificate is to speak in a pompous or dogmatic way, to sound highfalutin and bombastic. Someone who can't resist the opportunity to talk about fruit origins with his friends is a pontificator.

9. **glib.** Someone glib speaks in a smooth, easy, almost too-slick manner. Think of a fast-talking used car salesman or a telemarketer as glib.

10. **laconic.** Laconic is using few words, terse. The manager got his message across about the uselessness of the erstwhile (former) employee in just two words.

Bonus trivia: You may know the word *Spartan,* meaning plain, simple, austere. Sparta was actually a city in Laconia, Greece. Laconic people were plain and simple and austere in speech as well, using few words.

Exercise two

1. **stentorian.** An inaudible person can barely be heard; someone stentorian is extremely loud.

2. **taciturn.** Someone voluble is talkative; someone taciturn uses few words, doesn't talk much.

   Think of someone voluble as having a "large volume of words," a lot of words.

3. **compliment.** A diatribe is a bitter, abusive criticism. You reserve a diatribe for the idiot who backs into your car in the parking lot and doesn't leave a note.

4. **laconic.** Someone grandiloquent speaks in a very pompous, big-shot sort of way. A laconic speaker says as little as possible. (No, the words aren't exact opposites, but they are much more opposite than are grandiloquent and glib.)

5. **pithy.** A garrulous person talks too much; a pithy person makes sure her speech is terse and concise.

   You've probably heard the urban legend popular in college about the Philosophy class final. The professor, after making his students study the entire book, gave a one-word test: "Why?" The only student to get an A gave the pithy response, "Because."

6. **suggest.** This question was rather difficult. To declaim does not mean "to unclaim" (if you chose "accept," pack your bags; you're going on a guilt trip). To declaim is to speak in a dramatic, pompous way. Someone who is rather hesitant and not dramatic would suggest, rather than declaim.

7. **praise.** To rail is to speak bitterly of, to complain against. An accomplice rails at his partner who leaves behind a clue that gets the two of them convicted and sent to prison for life.

   Bonus trivia: Do you know the origin of the word "clue"? It used to be spelled clew, and meant a ball of yarn or thread. According to Greek mythology, Ariadne, the Princess of Crete, fell in love with the hero Theseus and gave him a clew of thread that would help him find his way out of the labyrinth, after he had slain the monster inside.

8. **self-effacing.** You could get this question correct even if you didn't know that self-effacing meant modest, retiring, keeping in the background. (A self-effacing person is self-erasing, trying to keep out of view.) You know

that pompous means arrogant, big-talking, very close to bombastic. A **bombastic** person uses high-sounding language. Charlotte, of *Charlotte's Web* fame (my favorite book when I was a child) said, "Salutations!" to Wilbur the first time they met. (Incidentally, Wilbur's response was, "Salu-what?")

9. **speak modestly.** When you pontificate, you speak in a pompous or dogmatic way. When you speak diffidently, you speak in a timid or shy manner, unsure of what you're saying. One who pontificates is usually very close-minded; someone diffident is open-minded (as my dad used to say, "Don't be so open-minded that your brains fall out!").

10. **taciturn.** A verbose person is very verbal, quite talkative. Someone taciturn talks very little.

Exercise three

1. **A.** To rail at is to speak bitterly about, to complain against. If the man were talking to his psychiatrist about people he hated, he would be railing.

Choice B was a trap. Even though *de-* means down from, and even though many *de–* words (such as **denounce, defame, decry, deprecate**) mean "to put down," declaim does not mean to criticize or complain about or put down. To declaim is to speak in a dramatic, pompous way.

Choice C is a variation of one of the words in this unit: discursive. When you're discursive, you are rambling, wandering from one topic to another. However, discourse is simply conversation. I tell my students, "You and I are having discourse during this course."

2. **B.** Mellifluous means sounding sweet and smooth, honeyed. If the picnickers were delighted, the choir must have sounded good.

Bonus trivia: What famous song was inspired by Pike's Peak? When you ask this question of your friends, most of them will probably guess, "She'll be comin' round the mountain when she comes," but that's not it. The song is *America the Beautiful.* The view from the summit inspired Katherine Lee Bates to write the song in 1893.

3. **D.** Stentorian means very loud. If someone bellows (shouts), he is using a stentorian voice.

4. **E.** A terse response is brief, concise, succinct and to the point. The scientist didn't say anything more than simple syllables.

Bonus joke: Speaking of science, did you hear about the neutron that went into a bar and asked the bartender how much for a drink? Said the bartender, "For you, no charge!"

5. **B.** Loquacious means talkative. The woman was usually talkative, but realized conversation would be futile in the din (noise, clamor) and used the language of the fan.

Bonus trivia: Everything sends a message. Did you know that the way a lady holds or move her fan is meant to communicate? For example, resting the fan on the right cheek means, "Do you love me?" Tapping the fan on the left ear means, "I want to get rid of you." The next time you see a movie with a Southern belle flirting with a Rhett Butler type, check out what she's really saying. (There are some interesting Web sites that give all sorts of interpretation of "fan language.")

6. **A.** The doctor went on and on and on, not stopping to take a breath, not letting anyone else talk, which meant he was extremely talkative or discursive. If his wife facetiously (jokingly) told him not to hold back, she was saying he didn't need to be so terse, or brief and concise.

   Bonus trivia: What's special about the word facetiously? It contains all the vowels in alphabetical order, even the "sometimes y."

7. **D.** To hector is to bully or browbeat. The job of a drill instructor is to hector the recruits, to get in their faces and make men and women out of boys and girls. *Repercussions,* later in the sentence, means a reaction to an event. You can bet that if a recruit mouthed off to a drill instructor, there would, in fact, be unfortunate (that's an understatement!) repercussions.

8. **E.** Bombastic means using high-sounding language, pompous. For some reason, the word is often associated with politicians.

   Bonus word: Another word often associated with politicians is funambulism. You may read that, "The senator put on a show of funambulism when he was being interviewed that impressed friend and foe alike." *Funambulism* literally is tightrope walking, but figuratively, it means a show of mental agility. If you can weasel and worm and twist and squirm your way out of something, you are a funambulist.

9. **B.** Vociferous means loud, noisy, vehement. If the protestors are chanting and ringing bells, they are definitely loud.

10. **C.** A teacher who talks so much she doesn't have time to assign homework is a chatterbox. Note that choice D was a trap. A grandiloquent teacher doesn't necessary talk a lot, just grandly or pompously.

    Bonus joke: The chatterbox teacher above was popular, but know who in history was the most *un*popular teacher? Cyclops: He had only one pupil!

Chapter 6

Never Trust Anyone Over Thirty: Words about Age

*W*hen you look in the mirror, do you see someone sleek and snazzy, the type of young go-getter who would drive a black Jaguar . . . or do you see a gray panther? The words in this chapter help you select the *mot juste* (French for "exactly the right word") to describe yourself.

Growing Older, Growing Wiser with New Vocabulary Words

Younger than springtime. Older than dirt. You've probably heard a lot of cliché describing how youthful or ancient someone is or appears to be. With the words in this section, you can avoid using a too-common expression and come up with a more precise, classier description.

antediluvian (ant tea dill *loo* vee un): very old, old-fashioned, primitive.

> *When my father jokingly introduced my Auntie Delilah as Auntie-Diluvian, she reminded him that she may be old, but she would always be his baby sister.*

Ante means before. Something antediluvian literally means before The Flood . . . the one in the Bible. You call someone antediluvian, you're saying she makes Noah look young.

antiquated (*ant* tick waited): old-fashioned, out of date, obsolete, old.

> *The antiquated car was quite dilapidated and sported a bumper sticker saying, "Honk if anything falls off!"*

Logically enough, antiquated and antique come from the same Latin term.

archaic (ark *hay* ick): ancient, antiquated, old-fashioned.

> *I don't want to say my old car is archaic, but the license-plate holder reads, "Bedrock Motors, Fred Flintstone, Proprietor."*

The root *arch* means old or original. **Archeology** is the study of the past, of the older, original people and places.

They call it puppy love

Humans give special names for youngsters. We call a baby dog, a puppy; a baby cat, a kitten; a baby sheep, a lamb. How many of the following unusual baby names can you identify?

✔ *cygnet* (rhymes with, *pig* net): young swan. If you know a little girl in a ballet costume who is graceful as a swan, you can call her a cygnet.

✔ *fledgling* (rhymes with, *pledge* wing): young bird. The term is also used to describe a novice, anyone new and inexperienced. A six-year-old just learning to read is a fledgling scholar.

✔ *joey* (rhymes with, *showy*): Do you have any friends named Joey? If so, he may be surprised to learn that a joey is a baby kangaroo!

✔ *poult* (rhymes with, *bolt*): You've probably heard of poultry, but did you know that a poult is any young fowl, like a turkey? I love to use this word as a classy way to call someone a turkey, "You poult, you don't have a clue, do you?"

✔ *whelp* (rhymes with, *help*): young dog — or a young lion, tiger, leopard, bear, or wolf. (You may have heard of a whelping box. That's the special box in which a dog gives birth to her puppies.)

One final fascinating fact: What do you call a baby dragon? You're probably thinking of all sorts of exotic terms, but in fact, a baby dragon is called simply a pup.

callow (rhymes with, *shallow*): young and inexperienced, immature.

> *The blind date had a callow sense of humor, ending every evening with the sick joke, "You've stolen my heart, but I have another at home in the freezer."*

This word has an interesting background. Originally, callow meant bald or naked and referred to a bird that lacked the feathers needed for flying. Because the bald birds were young birds, the word developed the secondary meaning of young and immature.

hoary (rhymes with, *story*): very old, ancient.

> *The speaker, who was obviously fond of hoary jokes, trotted out the aged line, "I don't mind getting older, 'cause after the Middle Ages come the Renaissance!"*

Hoary has a second meaning of gray or white, or having gray hair from age. You can call your grandfather the Silver Fox, or you can call him hoary.

immature (rhymes with, *him* that sure): not completely grown, not finished.

> *Derek apologized to his girlfriend for his immature behavior, saying he was genetically incapable of growing up.*

ingénue (*on* gin oooh): an innocent, inexperienced, unworldly young woman.

> *The starlet said she didn't mind playing an ingénue as she knew she looked young for her age, but she was tired of always playing the dumb blonde IQ donor.*

The word *ingenuous* is related to an ingénue. If you're ingenuous, you are simple, naïve, without guile. A young girl asking a pregnant lady, "Why are you so fat?" is ingenuous.

Don't confuse ingenuous, meaning naïve, with *ingenious,* meaning intelligent, like a genius. Confusing these two words is an easy mistake to make, especially under time pressure on the exam.

jejune (rhymes with, duh *spoon*): not mature, childish.

> *The speaker was popular with elementary schoolchildren because his jejune humor was on their level, with jokes along the lines of, "What are goose bumps for? To keep geese from speeding!"*

This word actually got its definition by mistake. Jejune originally came from the Latin term meaning empty. Jejune usually meant barren, not interesting, dull. But over the years, confusion with the term juvenile has resulted in a third meaning for jejune: childish.

In French, the term *jeune* means young, as in *jeune enfant* (young child).

juvenescent (rhymes with, you've an *ess* sent): becoming young, growing youthful.

> *The cosmetic company called its new brand Juvenescence, because it said the product would turn back the hands of time to make a younger you.*

My mother always used to joke about being old. Whenever she made a comment about something from the past, she'd say, "Am I dating myself? I probably am, but at least when I date myself, I don't have to dress up!"

neophyte (rhymes with, *see* oh fight): beginner, novice.

> *The new legal secretary was such a neophyte that she thought Roe vs. Wade were two ways to cross a river!*

You probably know the root *neo* means new (think of the **neonatal** care unit for newborn babies in the hospital). If you've had biology (or better yet, botany), you know that **phytos** means to grow. A neophyte is new at growing; a beginner, or a new growth, like a fresh sprout on a plant.

newfangled (rhymes with, too *tangled*): new, novel.

> *The curmudgeonly old cowpoke called the computer a "confuser," and said he wasn't going to use such a newfangled device.*

Newfangled has a slightly derogatory **connotation** (mental meaning). Use the word newfangled when you're being funny and a little bit insulting.

novice (*nah* viss): a beginner, an apprentice.

> *The more experienced nurses teased the novice, saying she had to carry her supplies with her at all times or she could be fired for "being absent without gauze."*

The root *nov* means new. A **novel** idea is a new idea. Ever hear of the province of Nova Scotia in Canada? The name simply means New Scotland.

precocious (pre *coe* shuss): developed or matured beyond what is normal for the age, prematurely developed.

> *The fifth grader was so precocious that he was able to do tenth-grade math without breaking into a cerebral sweat.*

Pre– means before; *–ous* means full of. Think of precocious as being "full of before," or advanced for one's age.

puerile (rhymes with, *sure* while): childish, silly, immature.

> *It was obvious he was fond of puerile humor from the license plate on his black jeep that said "baa baa." (Get it? Remember hearing when you were a kid the nursery rhyme that began, "Baa baa, black sheep, have you any wool?" Black sheep, black jeep? Trust me, it's funny!)*

Think of puerile as "pure child." The term is *pejorative* (critical) and means immature. Being *childlike* (innocent, naïve) is nice and sweet; being *childish* means you are pouting and throwing temper tantrums like a toddler.

Poodles, toast, vocabulary: French things you love

You don't have to speak French to have a French vocabulary. Following are some of the common French terms you use in everyday life without realizing their origins.

✔ **ambience** (*ahm* bee unce) (also spelled ambiance): The environment, the atmosphere, the milieu are the ambience. You go to a restaurant with horrible food because you like the ambiance: the décor, people, and style of the place.

✔ **bete noire** (bet no *wah*): A person or thing that's disliked or feared, and thus avoided, is a *bete noire* (literally "black beast"). When I was in school, chemistry was my bete noire.

✔ **bon mot** (bone *moe*): A bon mot is an apt, clever, or witty remark . . . just the sort of thing you think of at 2:00 in the morning, slapping your head and going, "Man, *that's* what I shoulda said!" Bon mot is French for good word.

✔ **bourgeoisie** (boor zwah *zee*): The bourgeoisie are the middle class. To call someone bourgeois (the adjective form of bourgeoisie; someone from the bourgeoisie is bourgeois) is to say he is conventional . . . and rather smug and materialistic. It's not a compliment.

✔ **ennui** (on *we*): The French word for boredom. Interestingly, the word shares a root with the word "annoy."

✔ **fait accompli** (fate ah comb *plea*): A fait accompli is something already done or in effect, making opposition or argument useless. For example, if you come home and your parents have cut down that big tree outside your bedroom window that you used to climb down to sneak out of the house, the slaughter of the oak tree is a fait accompli. Gripe all you want, the tree won't come back. The term is French for "an accomplished fact."

✔ **mot juste** (rhymes with, go *shoes*): The mot juste is exactly the right word, just what you wanted to say. If you actually manage to utter exactly the right insult at the right minute (instead of thinking of it at 2:00 a.m. as mentioned previously in this sidebar), that's the *mot juste*.

✔ **rendezvous** (rhymes with, *pond* they you): A rendezvous is a designated meeting place. The term comes from the French *rendez-vous,* meaning present yourself.

✔ **self effacing** (rhymes with, elf *erase* sing): The French term *efface* means to erase. To be self-effacing is to "erase your face," or to be inconspicuous and withdraw yourself from notice. When you don't know the answer to the question, you become self-effacing, leaning down to tie your shoelace, hiding your face from the teacher's view.

senescence (rhymes with, when *yes* sense): growing old, aging.

> *When Amy, thinking she was clever, called into school saying she wouldn't be in that day because she was suffering from senescence, the savvy principal responded, "We're all getting older every day, so get yourself in here pronto!"*

Actually, Amy *needed* to go to school to learn how to use senescence correctly. The term actually means "growing old," not "growing older." In other words, you rarely use the term about someone young, like a high schooler.

You had juvenescence earlier, meaning growing younger. Senescence is the flip side of that coin. Don't confuse senescence with senility. Everyone is senescent; we're all growing older. But not everyone turns senile (see the following word in this list).

Bonus: Do you know the word ***savvy,*** used to describe the principal in the preceding example? It means shrewd, understanding, discerning — knowing what's going on.

senile (rhymes with, *she* while): showing deterioration from old age, especially mental impairment and confusion.

Although senility is usually associated with the elderly, not all old people are senile, and not all senile people are elderly. A type of premature senility can afflict young people.

superannuated (super *ann* you ated): too old or worn for further work; old-fashioned, outdated.

> *The man finally agreed to take a pension, claiming that he realized he was superannuated when all he wanted to do was sleep late, have breakfast, take a nap, have lunch, take a nap, have dinner, and go to bed early.*

The root *super* means extra or above; *annus* is Latin for year. If you have "extra years," you are old.

Bonus word: Do you know the word ***clinomania***? It means an overwhelming desire to stay in bed. If you're in the middle of a snowstorm and just want to pull the covers over your head and sleep in all day, you are in the throes of clinomania.

tyro (rhymes with, *why* bro): a novice, a beginner.

> *The tyro psychiatrist was so naïve he believed it when the bartender told him, "Sorry buddy, we can't serve you a drink — you're too Jung!" (If you're not laughing hysterically at my joke, you may not know that Jung was a famous psychiatrist.)*

venerable (rhymes with, *when* her able): worthy of respect by reason of age and dignity.

> *We were pleased to meet the venerable patriarch, who said he became wealthy by following John D. Rockefeller's advice: 1. Go to work early. 2. Stay at work late. 3. Find oil.*

To *venerate* someone is to revere or respect him, but venerable also carries the connotation of respect earned over the years. You venerate an 80-year-old, not an eight-year-old.

No, don't confuse venerable with *venereal,* as in the disease. The term venereal has a much prettier derivation than you would think: It comes from Venus, the goddess of love.

veteran (*vet* er un): experienced, practiced.

> *The veteran tour guide, anticipating the question, told his group of tourists visiting the prison that Alcatraz meant "pelican" and that the island was named after the large bird colony there.*

If veteran means experienced, what do you suppose *inveterate* means? It means habitual, long-standing, deep-rooted. This word shows one example in which the prefix *in–* means "inside" instead of "not" (see Chapter 2 for more on roots).

Coming of Age with These Practice Exercises

Now that you are no longer a novice, but a veteran and have mastered all the words in this section, you're ready to go through the practice exercises. The answers to these sections are at the end of this chapter in the "Answers to the Exercises" section.

Exercise one

Directions: Choose the most appropriate word to complete the sentence.

1. The - - - - man was forced to retire, even though he had started the company himself and swore that people would be allowed to work well into their 80s.

    (A) jejune

    (B) senile

    (C) callow

    (D) superannuated

    (E) puerile

2. The band members all behaved as if they were five-year-olds, making - - - - jokes and comments about the tuba player every time he blew a note.

    (A) veteran

    (B) neophyte

    (C) puerile

    (D) antediluvian

    (E) tyro

3. Every - - - - ball player was asked the first day at practice to tell the real name of Cy Young and was judged by the veterans on whether or not he could do so.

    (A) veteran

    (B) novice

    (C) antiquated

    (D) senescent

    (E) senile

4. The math teacher won the admiration of his class when he played straight man for all the - - - - jokes the children told him, even though he had known the punch lines for decades.

    (A) ingenuous

    (B) precocious

    (C) newfangled

    (D) antediluvian

    (E) tyro

5. The ---- child entered college at age 10 and graduated with a Ph.D. just before his 16th birthday.

    (A) archaic

    (B) precocious

    (C) hoary

    (D) neophyte

    (E) veteran

6. Beginning a romance at age 80 after having been a widow for more than a decade seemed to spark a ---- in Pearl, who looked and acted like a giddy young woman in love.

    (A) puerility

    (B) senescence

    (C) immaturity

    (D) juvenescence

    (E) superannuation

7. Realizing that while he was considered a ---- member of Congress, the senator was often dismissed as a relic and sidelined in favor of the newer Congressmen. For that reason, the senator hired a public relations firm to update his image.

    (A) venerable

    (B) ingenuous

    (C) tyro

    (D) neophyte

    (E) juvenescent

8. The ---- professor understood that it was common for the newest teachers to get the worst assignments, so he resigned himself to teaching the 7:00 a.m. classes his first year.

    (A) hoary

    (B) venerable

    (C) tyro

    (D) antediluvian

    (E) immature

9. The fraternity was known for playing childish and - - - - pranks on people, such as short-sheeting their beds, dressing in sheets and pretending to be ghosts, and loosening the tops of the salt and pepper shakers.

 (A) immature

 (B) precocious

 (C) superannuated

 (D) senescent

 (E) neophyte

10. The elderly lady appeared to be - - - -, calling everyone by the name of her deceased husband and not being quite sure where she was.

 (A) callow

 (B) venerable

 (C) venerable

 (D) archaic

 (E) senile

Exercise two

Directions: Choose the best word to complete each sentence.

1. The (puerile/hoary) worker was so inexperienced that he believed his coworkers, who told him that the boss liked people who dressed formally; he reported for work on the construction crew in a three-piece suit.

2. The teen magazine accused the TV networks of having (antediluvian/ newfangled) ideas about what teenagers wanted to see, simply recycling the same comedies and dramas that had been popular a generation or two ago.

3. The (juvenescence/senility) club met every Friday to exchange stories and secrets on how to remain youthful both physically and mentally.

4. My Apache grandfather loved to pull out the (puerile/venerable) scrapbook he had been given by his own grandfather and show newspaper clippings of the lives of his warrior ancestors who had fought with Geronimo.

5. Fed up with his daughter's (immature/antediluvian) attitude toward her responsibilities, Mr. Chin took away her car until she began acting in a more adult manner.

The wizard of OS

One day during a tutoring session, I noticed that my student, who had told me he was up until past midnight the evening before, was politely trying to stifle a yawn. I told him to go ahead and oscitate, which he correctly deduced meant to yawn. Then he commented that "oscitate must be the only "os" word around; I don't think I've ever heard any others." That was my cue to inundate the poor guy with the words below.

✔ *oscillate* (rhymes with, *ahs* till late): To oscillate is to move back and forth. You may have seen a machine called an oscillator in a physics lab. If you yourself oscillate, you are indecisive, vacillating, and changing your mind all the time. You oscillate over whether to spend the weekend playing volleyball at the beach with your friends or studying your vocabulary.

✔ *osculate* (rhymes with, *ahs* que late): Ah, don't confuse oscillate with osculate. To osculate is, in my humble opinion, much more fun. To osculate is to kiss.

✔ *ossify* (rhymes with, *ahs* if try): Literally, to ossify is to develop into bone. For example, a baby's head has cartilage that later ossifies, or hardens into bone. However, ossify is often used figuratively to mean "to fix rigidly into a position." When your parents tell you that the only way you're getting that trip to Europe is to get a job and earn the money for it yourself, no ifs, ands, or buts, they are ossified in their position.

✔ *ossuary* (rhymes with, *ahs* you airy): An ossuary is a container, like an urn, for the bones of the dead. When you visit a history or anthropology museum, you may see several ossuaries.

✔ *ostensibly* (rhymes with, ahs *ten* sib lee): Ostensibly means seemingly, apparently (with the strong implication that the truth is otherwise). Ostensibly, you had a desire to learn Calculus, which is why you registered for the class, but in fact, you really just wanted to be in any class with that cute new student.

✔ *ostentatious* (rhymes with, ahs ten *played* us): If you are ostentatious, you like to make a showy display of your wealth; you are pretentious. A peacock is often described as "making an ostentatious show of his tail feathers to impress a potential mate."

✔ *osteopath* (rhymes with, *ahs* we oh path): An osteopath is a bone doctor, a physician who primarily works with the skeletal system. As a former ice skater, I visited my share of osteopaths.

✔ *ostracize* (rhymes with, *ahs* duh size): To ostracize is to banish, bar, and exclude. More than once in my life, I have been ostracized from polite company because of my weak jokes.

One more: The suffix *–osis* (oh sis) means a state, condition or action. Think tuberculosis, sclerosis . . . halitosis. *Halitosis* (bad breath) prevents osculation (now there's a good bumper sticker for a dentist's car!).

6. An elderly man complained as he walked up and down the aisles of the hardware store that there were entirely too many (newfangled/antiquated) products and that he would stick with the tried-'n'-true sprays he had used since he was a lad.

7. The (veteran/jejune) car salesmen hazed a colleague his first day on the job by hiding his salesbook, unplugging his telephone, and telling him their best seller was the Ford Amnesia, which never gets recalled.

8. The office was so (antediluvian/precocious) that it had typewriters instead of computers, and sported black dial telephones from the 1960s and '70s.

9. The experienced model's agent told the (veteran/tyro) during her very first interview that she would never make it as a model because she had a Supreme Court figure . . . no appeal.

10. The university agreed to accept the (hoary/precocious) 12-year-old into its summer school program to do research into earthquakes, citing the child's earlier empirical studies.

Exercise three

Directions: Choose the most appropriate word to complete the sentence.

1. The casting agent said he understood that the girl was - - - - with no screen work done yet and that he didn't mind her inexperience but he was unhappy with the fact that she was so dull she could be the poster child for brown.

   (A) an ingenue

   (B) superannuated

   (C) antediluvian

   (D) antiquated

   (E) senescent

2. The businessman, wanting to present a modern, hip image, pulled out a yo-yo to play with at the meeting, and succeeded only in looking - - - -.

   (A) senescent

   (B) antiquated

   (C) immature

   (D) precocious

   (E) archaic

3. On his very first day in class, the - - - - actor was asked to portray a mime trying to get out of a box.

   (A) juvenescent

   (B) neophyte

   (C) newfangled

   (D) senile

   (E) veteran

4. The new computer teacher was so - - - - that his students quickly sensed his inability to control the class and began looking at computer sites that the previous teacher had forbidden them to open.

   (A) precocious

   (B) hoary

   (C) antediluvian

   (D) callow

   (E) newfangled

5. The long-term worker was made to feel - - - - by his younger colleagues who used technical terms he didn't understand, talked about programs he'd never heard of, and discussed topics that were never taught in his day.

   (A) ingenue

   (B) puerile

   (C) novice

   (D) superannuated

   (E) newfangled

6. Although his wife believed that the Gilligan's Island Fan Fest Convention was too - - - - for a man in his 50s, Beau stated that he was a child at heart and loved everything about the show.

   (A) archaic

   (B) tyro

   (C) senile

   (D) puerile

   (E) antiquated

7. The man's furniture was so ---- that the money he found under his mattress was Confederate dollars.

   (A) precocious

   (B) immature

   (C) callow

   (D) jejune

   (E) archaic

8. The man's attitude was so ---- that his wife said their two toddlers had more maturity and self-control than their father did.

   (A) jejune

   (B) senile

   (C) antediluvian

   (D) newfangled

   (E) senescent

9. Dr. Harmon's ---- office still featured the same furniture and even the same magazines it had over 100 years ago when the doctor's great-great-grandfather began the practice.

   (A) neophyte

   (B) antediluvian

   (C) juvenescent

   (D) newfangled

   (E) jejune

10. The ---- child, when asked where her bellybutton came from, responded, "That's where the angels poke you to see if you're done."

    (A) hoary

    (B) venerable

    (C) ingenuous

    (D) superannuated

    (E) novice

Answers to the Exercises

Time for you to find out just how smart you really are by checking your answers with those below.

Exercise one

1. **D.** Superannuated means too old or worn out to use. You may try to con your parents into buying you a new car by claiming your current one is superannuated.

2. **C.** Puerile jokes are childish jokes, the kind a five-year-old would make. My favorite tuba joke (which makes more sense spoken than read): What's a tuba for? Oh, about eight inches (2×4).

3. **B.** A novice ball player is new, one at his first day of practice and is judged by the veterans, or more experienced, players.

   By the way, were you yourself able to answer the question? Cy Young's real name was Denton True.

4. **D.** Antediluvian means very, very old; older than The Flood of Biblical times.

   Bonus joke: Here's one of those antediluvian jokes you have probably known since your first-grade math teacher told it to you: How many three-cent stamps in a dozen? (If you said four, you fell for the trap. Think about it: There are twelve of anything in a dozen!)

5. **B.** A student who begins college at age ten is advanced for his age, prematurely developed.

   As for me, I took it easy going through school, doing it by degrees.

6. **D.** Juvenescence is becoming young, growing youthful. If an 80-year-old woman is acting younger, she's juvenescent.

7. **A.** Venerable means worthy of respect by reason of age.

   Did you know the extra vocabulary word in the sentence: relic? A *relic* is something that has survived from the past, something kept as a keepsake of the past. The Congressman felt he was kept around merely for his history, not for anything he could contribute in the future.

   Cynical question to ponder: If pro is the opposite of con, is progress the opposite of Congress?

8. **C.** A tyro is a novice, a beginner. The new kid on the block, the newest teacher in the school, got the worst assignments.

   Bonus trivia: Speaking of professors and universities, do you know why the Ivy League schools are called that? It has nothing to do with ivy, the plant that may grow on the walls of the buildings at those schools. The original term was the IV League, because there were four — IV in Roman numerals — schools in the League: Columbia, Yale, Princeton and Harvard.

9. **A.** It's pretty immature to short-sheet the bed or take the sheets off and wear them, pretending to be ghosts.

   Bonus joke: What's the first thing a ghost does when he gets into a car? He fastens his sheet belt.

10. **E.** Someone senile is showing deterioration from old age, especially mental confusion.

    The words senile and Senate have the same root, interestingly enough: *Senatus* means old. Originally, the Senate was a council of elders.

Exercise two

1. **puerile.** A person who is puerile is young and inexperienced, immature.

2. **antediluvian.** Antediluvian means old or old-fashioned.

3. **juvenescent.** Juvenescent means growing young, becoming more youthful. A club that meets to swap tales of how to look, feel, and act younger is full of juvenescent types.

4. **venerable.** Venerable means worthy of respect by reason of age. If the grandfather's grandfather had the scrapbook of times with Geronimo, the book was pretty old.

5. **immature.** Someone immature is not mature, not acting in a grown-up or adult manner.

6. **newfangled.** A newfangled product is not just new, but new in a slightly derogatory sense. A person who doesn't like something new would call it newfangled.

   Bonus trivia: Speaking of sprays in hardware stores brings to mind WD-40, the lubricant many people use. Know how it got its name? The WD comes from "water displacer," and the 40 refers to the fact that the product was perfected on the 40th attempt.

7. **jejune.** Someone jejune is childish and immature, like the salesmen who pull these types of pranks.

8. **antediluvian.** Antediluvian means very old, old-fashioned, like the rotary telephone and the typewriter.

9. **tyro.** A tyro is a novice, a beginner.

10. **precocious.** A precocious child is advanced for his age, prematurely developed. A 12-year-old going to college is definitely precocious.

Speaking of earthquakes, do you know why Dr. Richter quit the earthquake biz? He was tired of working for scale!

Exercise three

1. **A.** An ingenue is an inexperienced, innocent, unworldly young woman.

2. **C.** It's immature — not grown-up, not fully developed — to take a yo-yo to a business meeting.

   Bonus trivia: Do you know where the yo-yo was first created? It came from the Philippines, where it was used as a weapon to kill snakes in the fields.

3. **B.** A neophyte is a beginner, a novice (remember that *neo–* means new).

   Bonus joke: If you have to shoot a mime, should you use a silencer?

4. **D.** A callow person is young and inexperienced, immature. A callow teacher wouldn't be able to keep the class under control.

   Bonus joke: If a Russian gets convicted of committing an Internet crime, where is she sent? To Cyberia!

5. **D.** Someone superannuated is too old or worn out for further work, old-fashioned, outdated.

6. **D.** Puerile means childish, silly, immature. If you've ever seen the TV comedy, you know it's not something PBS is likely to carry.

   Bonus trivia: The name of the ship on *Gilligan's Island* was the Minnow. You probably thought it was named that after the small fish, right? Wrong. The ship was named after the former chairman of the Federal Communications Committee, Newton Minnow, who called television "a vast cultural wasteland."

7. **E.** If the man's furniture is old enough to have Confederate dollars under the mattress, it is archaic, ancient, antiquated.

   Bonus joke: Speaking of beds brings to mind my favorite Stephen Wright quote. When someone asks him, "Did you sleep well?" he responds, "Well? No, I made one or two mistakes."

8. **A.** A jejune attitude is childish, immature.

9. **B.** Something antediluvian is very old or old-fashioned.

10. **C.** Someone ingenuous is naïve, innocent, unworldly, inexperienced, like a child.

Chapter 7

Hip, Hip, Hurray! Words of Praise and Criticism

. . . .

Words in This Chapter

- ▶ acclaim
- ▶ accolade
- ▶ belittle
- ▶ castigate
- ▶ censure
- ▶ demean
- ▶ denigrate
- ▶ denounce
- ▶ disparage
- ▶ encomium
- ▶ eulogy
- ▶ extol
- ▶ fawning

- ▶ kudos
- ▶ laud
- ▶ malign
- ▶ paean
- ▶ panegyric
- ▶ plaudits
- ▶ rebuke
- ▶ sycophant
- ▶ toady
- ▶ upbraid
- ▶ vilify
- ▶ vituperate

. . . .

*Q*uick — if a teacher hands you back a paper and says "I expressed my panegyric to your parents over the work you put into this project," should you go home grinning or grab your backpack and run away to become a roadie for a Ska band? Did the teacher just praise you or trash you? After reading this chapter and mastering the words in here, you'll know that it's safe to go home! (A *panegyric* is high praise.)

Singing the Praises of New Vocabulary Words

The words in this chapter express praise and criticism. These are words you're likely to use when you try to impress (or thoroughly depress) your date's parents or ace the biggest test of your life (I refuse to think you could do otherwise).

acclaim (a *claim*): approval, praise (also as a verb meaning, to approve, to praise).

> *Paul received national acclaim for his science fair experiment about conditions on the moon.*

Paul's parents chose to acclaim his work in front of the neighbors, making sure everyone knew what an excellent job their son had done on his project.

Bonus joke: Did you hear about the restaurant on the moon? Great food, but no atmosphere.

The prefix *ac–* means to or forward. Think of yourself going forward to "claim your fame" and receive the praise you deserve.

Note that acclaim can be a noun or a verb. You acclaim the performance of someone who's doing a good job. You may also have heard the phrase, "the critically acclaimed film." This expression means that the film critics liked the picture (even though the public may have thought it stank).

accolade (rhymes with, *back* coal aid): a sign of approval.

> *During the dog obedience trials, Tessie and Jake were so nervous that they never knew whether they had performed correctly until they heard the cheers and accolades of the crowd.*

As noted in the preceding vocab word, the prefix *ac–* means to or forward. Picture yourself going forward, progressing, and receiving a cola (a-cola-lade) as a reward for your good performance.

belittle (be *little*): speak slightingly of.

> *Never satisfied, Troy belittled every birthday gift he was given and complained he never got what he really wanted.*

Be careful not to confuse *de–,* meaning to put down, with *be–.* (It's very easy to misread these prefixes during the rush and stress of the test.) The prefix *be–* means thoroughly and completely. To belittle is to make something thoroughly little; to make it seem like nothing; to complain about it.

Bonus joke: The comedienne and actress Lily Tomlin made a statement about belittling that I've adopted as my own: "I personally believe we developed language because of our deep need to complain."

castigate (rhymes with, *pass* the gate): punish by giving public criticism.

> *When the building superintendent began speaking on the PA system, I had a premonition he was going to castigate me for putting the skunk in the air conditioning system.*

Don't confuse castigate, meaning to punish, with ***castrate,*** meaning to neuter; to cut off the genitalia. You castrate a bull, not a prankster who has polluted the AC system (talk about overdoing the punishment!).

censure (rhymes with, *then* sure): strong disapproval; a formal expression of disapproval.

> *When the congressman was suspected of accepting bribes, he was aware of the censure of his fellow politicians.*

Be sure not to confuse censure with censor. To ***censor*** is to remove the offensive portions, like censoring a book to get rid of the dirty parts. Just remember that a censor eliminates the parts (think of the "o" in censor standing for "out") because of your censure of their content. (You are upset by the dirty parts and cut them out.)

demean (rhymes with, see *teen*): treat badly.

> *At the roast, we all got up to demean the guest of honor, saying things about him like, "He's so dumb, it takes him two hours to watch* 60 Minutes!"

The prefix *de–* means to put down. When you demean someone, you "put him down," treat him badly, or criticize him. Note that demean and denounce both mean "to put down."

denigrate (rhymes with, *then* pig great): blacken the reputation of someone; defame, decry.

> *Although I didn't want to denigrate my friend, I had to admit that she had told me about cheating on her tax returns last year.*

This word put the prefix *de*– with *niger,* which is Latin for "black." When you blacken someone's reputation, you put him down or criticize him.

denounce (rhymes with, the *ounce*): condemn strongly.

> *The students denounced the increase in parking fees, saying that charging over a hundred dollars a year to park on campus was ridiculous.*

Don't confuse announce with denounce. When you **announce** something, you talk about it; introduce it. The prefix *de*– means down. When you denounce, you put something down, talk down about it, and criticize it.

disparage (rhymes with, this *carriage*): show disrespect for.

> *The ten-year-old boy was near tears because the teacher disparaged the art project on which he had spent so much time.*

The prefix *dis*– means not. You do not show any respect for something when you disparage it.

Think of the song, "Home on the Range." There's a line in it that goes, "Where seldom is heard, a discouraging word." You could change that to "Where seldom is heard, a disparaging word" to help you remember that disparage is negative.

encomium (in *comb* he um): a formal expression of praise.

> *At the end-of-the-year banquet, the Chess Club honored Larry, who had not lost a game the entire year, with a long scroll full of encomium.*

Bonus trivia: According to some mathematicians, the number of possible moves in a chess game is 10 followed by 43 zeros! No wonder computers have such difficulty anticipating all possibilities.

eulogy (rhymes with, *you* low gee): high praise.

> *At the funeral, Blair delivered a eulogy for his grandmother, talking about all the good she had done for her family and friends.*

The prefix *eu*– means good, and the root *log* means word. When you have a good word for someone — when you praise her — you give a eulogy.

extol (rhymes with, necks *pole*): to praise highly.

> *Television commercials extol the virtues of the latest style of overpriced blue jeans.*

Ever hear of Toll House cookies (chocolate chip cookies)? Do you like them? Of course! Nearly everyone likes chocolate chip cookies, so you ex*tol* or praise, *Toll* House cookies.

fawning (rhymes with, *yaw*ning): flattering, showing servile deference.

> *The psychiatrist quickly deduced that his new patient had an obsessive desire to be liked, because she was fawning all over everyone, even people she didn't like.*

When you want to be popular sooooo badly that you will kiss up to the "in" crowd at school, you are fawning.

Bonus joke: What did the psychiatrist say when the patient yelled into his office, "Doctor! Help, help! I'm shrinking!" Answer: "I'm busy now. You'll just have to be a little patient."

kudos (rhymes with, *you* doze): praise, glory, fame.

> *Tim received kudos for his excellent detective work at the firehouse, discovering who put the captain's jockey shorts up the flagpole.*

The manufacturer of the candy bar called Kudos hopes you think the taste of the candy is worth praising. (When I praise my students during a tutorial, I often make the wisecrack, "Kudos to youdos, you got that one right!")

laud (rhymes with, *clawed*): to praise.

> *The coach lauded me for making the difficult three-point shot just as the buzzer sounded, winning the game for our team and sending us to the State finals.*

Notice how similar the word laud is to the word applaud? When you laud someone's performance, you are applauding him for doing so well.

You may see different forms of this word, including ***laudable,*** meaning worthy of praise *(joining the Peace Corps is a laudable thing to do)* and ***laudatory,*** meaning expressing praise *(my boss's laudatory comments on the good job I did on the project made me feel great all day long).*

malign (rhymes with, the *sign*): speak evil of.

> *Even though the newspaper editorials are always criticizing the ambassador to Spain, I think he's doing a good job and refuse to malign him.*

Mal means bad. If you speak Spanish, you know the expression, *muy malo,* meaning very bad. To malign is to say something bad.

You may have heard about a *malignant* tumor. That's a cancerous tumor, one that is considered bad. (The opposite is a *benign* tumor, one that isn't cancerous or harmful. *Ben* is a root meaning good.)

paean (*pi* uhn): a song of praise.

> When Alice wondered what her blind date looked like, Anne broke into a paean about his dark hair and blue eyes.

panegyric (pan uh *jeer* ick): speech expressing high praise.

> When Alice returned from her blind date, she called Anne and went into a panegyric about the wonderful time she had.

plaudits (rhymes with, *clawed* its): expressions of praise.

> Deidre's law exam had plaudits written all over it, with a huge A+ in red ink at the top.

The word plaudits may remind you of applaud. When you applaud, you offer plaudits.

rebuke (rhymes with, see *duke*): scold.

> Rich rebuked me when I spent my money on candy bars rather than books, saying I needed to feed my mind more than my body.

My friend Rich really did say this to me, adding that I was so mentally challenged that a mind-reader would charge me half price!

sycophant (*sick* oh fant): a flatterer.

> The movie star had difficulty knowing whom to trust, because most of the people around him were groupies and sycophants who told him how wonderful he was.

A sycophant is a person who flatters way, way too much, overdoing the praise. You would probably call this type of person a kiss-up.

You may know a sycophant, someone who is so gushing she "makes you sick." Think of a sycophant as a sick-o-phant because you're sick of all her insincere praise.

toady (rhymes with, *road* he): a sycophant; a fawning, obsequious hanger-on.

> The new employee was so desperate to be accepted by the others that she became a toady, hanging around the top salesmen and flattering them every chance she got.

A toady is a yes-man or a kiss-up; someone like a groupie who praises too much. Picture a toad: a slimy, icky thing that's always hanging around you.

upbraid (*up* braid): criticize or rebuke sharply.

> *The morning I flunked my driver's test, I was afraid to tell my mother because I knew she would immediately upbraid me for not having studied harder.*

Don't define upbraiding as simply "braiding up." When you braid something, you put it together. Think of upbraid as un-braiding or ripping apart; what your mom would do if you goofed off, didn't study, and flunked your test.

Bonus trivia: Here's a word you won't see too often, but it's a fun word to know: fustigate. To *fustigate* is to beat someone with a stick. I often use fustigate in a humorously threatening manner: "If you don't stop eating all my Cheesy Puffs, I shall fustigate you!" (Can't you just see one of the *South Park* kids using this word?)

vilify (rhymes with, *will* he try): use abusive language about.

> *I heard my mother vilify me and my driving abilities to my father when he came home that night.*

–Ify is a suffix meaning "to make." You probably know that a *villain* is a bad guy, someone vile (the villains in movies always wear black). You can think of vilify as to make into a villain, a bad guy.

Bonus: What do you suppose you do when you *revile* someone? You insult, criticize and abuse him. In other words, you treat him as if he's vile or like a villain.

vituperate (rhymes with, my *group* her eight): to find fault with, to vilify, revile, abuse.

> *My personal trainer vituperated me for not exercising more, telling me, "Your figure is so bad, it looks as if the contents settled during shipment!"*

Everyone's a Critic: Practice Exercises

Here comes your favorite part of the chapter, your chance to show off what you've gained. When you've finished, check your answers with the "Answers to the Exercises" section at the end of this chapter.

Would you like a hint?

Do you ever just want to give a little hint, without coming right out and giving away the answer? Here are some words you can use to sound *erudite* (scholarly) while doing so.

- *implicit* (rhymes with, him *this* it): When you give an implicit comment, you suggest or hint, but don't plainly express what you're talking about. The word is related to imply. The opposite of implicit is *explicit,* which means clearly stated, plain, outspoken. You explicitly tell your beau you don't want another set of windshield wipers for your car this Valentine's Day.

- *inkling* (rhymes with, twinkling): An inkling is an indirect suggestion; a slight indication; a hint. A child hopes to get an inkling of what he'll be getting for Christmas by shaking the boxes under the tree.

- *innuendo* (rhymes with, win you *friend* dough): An innuendo is an indirect remark, especially one derogatory. For example, a gossip newspaper, the kind sold in the supermarket checkout lines, often has innuendoes that a famous couple is breaking up because one party cheated on the other.

- *insinuate* (in *sin* you ate): You insinuate when you work something into a conversation indirectly and artfully; when you suggest or hint indirectly. A good teacher knows how to insinuate during a lecture that the students had better learn this material especially well, because it has a good chance of showing up on the final exam.

- *intimation* (rhymes with, win *Tim* nation): An intimation is a hint; an indirect suggestion. When you have a scavenger hunt, you don't draw a complete map of how to find the treasures; instead, you provide clues and intimations.

- *subtle* (*sut* tull): Subtle means delicately suggestive, not grossly obvious. You start out by giving your parents a subtle hint about what you want for your 16th birthday and hope they get a clue before you have to stop being subtle and start leaving Porsche and Ferrari ads on their desks.

- *tacit* (rhymes with, *lass* it): Tacit means not expressed or declared openly, but implied or understood. If your boss gives tacit approval to your project, he hasn't specifically told you it's okay, but he hasn't rejected it either, leading you to believe that you can go forward.

Exercise one

Directions: Select the appropriate word to complete the sentence.

1. My friend is such a great baker that we all (extol/denounce) his cookies.

2. I was afraid that my best friend would (laud/upbraid) me for losing her Robin Hood book after I had borrowed it from her.

3. After seeing all the gorgeous women on campus, Steve broke into a (panegyric/vilification), saying he couldn't wait to begin college!

4. With a huge grin on his face, Sgt. Zia accepted the commendation and the (accolades, chastisement) of the crowd.

5. Although Donna tried hard to (eulogize/belittle) the substitute teacher, she could find very little good to say about him.

6. Expecting (kudos/censure) for the excellent job he did reorganizing the office, Fred was dismayed to get only a brief nod.

7. The criminal received a (paean/rebuke) from the judge who said that his crime was so heinous it deserved the most severe punishment possible.

8. It is common for sportscasters to (acclaim/castigate) hockey players who take cheap shots and create a power play for the other team because they have to sit in the penalty box.

9. The psychiatry student was discouraged by the (fawning/disparagement) she got on her paper after she had spent long hours doing the best job she could.

10. When I heard the instructor at clown college (laud/malign) me, I knew I was not going to get any plaudits for my performance that afternoon.

Exercise two

Directions: Choose the antonym (opposite) of each word.

1. acclaim: (accolade, censure)
2. castigation: (rebuke, encomium)
3. plaudits: (vilification, panegyric)
4. upbraid: (eulogize, denigrate)
5. extol: (castigate, fawn)
6. malign: (denounce, extol)
7. panegyric: (belittlement, paean)
8. laud: (acclaim, malign)
9. belittle: (eulogize, revile)
10. kudos: (censure, paean)

What's for lunch?

If your buddy in med school informs you you're suffering from borborygmus, should you panic? Nope. Just grab a sandwich. *Borborygmus* is simply tummy growling — the sound you hear when you're hungry. If you're hearing borborygmus right now, you'll especially enjoy the following food-related words.

- *comestible* (rhymes with, home *best* nibble): Comestible is simply a fancy name for food. A chi-chi (affected, showy) restaurant may call itself Classy Comestibles.

- *epicure* (rhymes with, *pep* pick cure): Are you an epicure? An epicure is a person who enjoys and has a discriminating taste for fine foods and drinks. Today's term might be foodie, as in food groupie — someone who goes to the latest restaurants and keeps track of celebrity chefs as if they were rock stars.

  Bonus trivia: Epicure comes from the name of a Greek philosopher, Epicurus, 341–279 B.C., who held that the goal of a man should be a life characterized by the enjoyment of moderate pleasure.

- *esculent* (rhymes with, *yes* you'll lent): Something esculent is fit to be used for food; edible. You may look at a weed in the field and wonder whether it is esculent. My cooking, sad to relate, is definitely not esculent.

- *fodder* (rhymes with, *nod*der): Usually, fodder is coarse food, the kind used to feed cattle and horses, such as straw, hay, and so on. Fodder can also be used metaphorically, in a non-food sense. For example, when your mailbox is full of junk advertising, you may label that promotional fodder.

- *glutton* (rhymes with, *but*ton): A glutton is a person who eats too much. Interesting point: The term is derived from the same word as *gullet,* which is your esophagus — the tube that sends the food down from the mouth to the stomach. Put too much food in your gullet, and you're a glutton.

- *gourmand* (rhymes with, your *pond*): Gourmand actually has two meanings. The preferred meaning is one who pigs out, someone who eats to excess. A secondary meaning is a gourmet; one who is an epicure and is an excellent judge of fine food and drinks. However, if someone calls you a gourmand, he's more likely to be insulting than complimenting you.

- *gustatory* (rhymes with, *bust* a story): Gustatory means having to do with the sense of taste. Eating a bowl of your favorite ice cream is a gustatory delight.

- *savory* (*save* or he): Something savory is appetizing, pleasing to the taste or smell. In some countries, such as Britain and Canada, a savory is an appetizer.

- *sustenance* (rhymes with, *bus* ten dense): Sustenance is nourishment, food. The word is also used metaphorically for anything that sustains you. Hearing good music is sustenance to a music lover.

- *viands* (rhymes with, *try* ands): Viands are foods, especially choice dishes. At a formal party, the viands may include caviar and *fois gras.*

- *victuals* (rhymes with, *skit*tles): Although the word is now used more in a slang or dialectical sense, victuals means food. A sitcom character affecting a hillbilly turn of phrase may ask, "Maw, are the victuals ready yet?"

Exercise three

Directions: Select the best answer to each question.

1. Unhappy with the ---- he received from the critics, the actor resolved to stick with action films in the future and not attempt to do any more light comedy.

    (A) plaudits

    (B) censure

    (C) acclaim

    (D) kudos

    (E) paeans

2. The attorney was mildly surprised when he heard the judge had ---- him, because he had always thought he had the judge's respect and admiration.

    (A) eulogized

    (B) extolled

    (C) acclaimed

    (D) disparaged

    (E) lauded

3. Refugees from foreign countries at war are eager to come to a country noted for its safety and peace, and they offer ---- to the stability of the nation.

    (A) a vilification

    (B) a rebuke

    (C) a denunciation

    (D) an encomium

    (E) a denigration

4. Intrigued by the ---- he heard the enthusiastic students giving the latest rock group's performance, the recording executive resolved to hear their music for himself and went to one of the group's concerts.

    (A) paean

    (B) censure

    (C) vituperation

    (D) vilification

    (E) rebuke

5. The nuclear scientist was unwilling to - - - - the virtues of her career, saying that although the hours were long and the work difficult, the rewards made all the effort more than worthwhile.

   (A) extol

   (B) laud

   (C) malign

   (D) acclaim

   (E) eulogize

6. Calling his colleague a(n) - - - -, the worker claimed that excessively complimenting the boss and doing the boss's errands were not the best ways to earn respect and ultimately promotion within the corporation.

   (A) kudos

   (B) paean

   (C) encomium

   (D) eulogy

   (E) toady

7. When the editor of the paper wrote an article highly critical of the police force, he was - - - - by the publisher who stated that it was the paper's policy to support law enforcement whenever possible.

   (A) fawned over

   (B) offered kudos

   (C) termed a sycophant

   (D) upbraided

   (E) given plaudits

8. When the practical joke went too far, the prankster was - - - - by his friends who said that the jokester needed to learn when to stop.

   (A) given an encomium

   (B) rebuked

   (C) extolled

   (D) labeled a toady

   (E) acclaimed

9. Myrrh, which has been used as a medicine for more than two centuries, used to be - - - - for its painkilling abilities; today myrrh is most commonly used in mouthwash and toothpaste.

   (A) demeaned

   (B) denigrated

   (C) belittled

   (D) lauded

   (E) defamed

10. Refusing to be a(n) - - - -, the sales clerk told the customer the truth, that the outfit was not flattering and, in fact, made her look quite unattractive.

   (A) accolade

   (B) plaudit

   (C) vituperation

   (D) sycophant

   (E) reviler

My hero: Words about bravery (and cowardice)

When the talk turns to bungee jumping, exploring the Amazon, or wrestling alligators, are you the first to sign up or the first to run away and hide under the bedcovers? These words can describe you no matter which action you take.

✔ **audacious** (rhymes with, clawed *a* shuss): Someone audacious is bold, daring, or fearless. You have probably used another form of this word, **audacity,** as in, "You have the audacity to tell me to my face that I'm so skinny my uniform has only one pin stripe? How dare you!" While audacity can mean boldness, it more commonly is used to mean shamelessness, brazenness, or chutzpah.

✔ **cow** (rhymes with, *now*): Did you read this word and wonder what a browsing bovine had to do with brave/afraid words? Cow has a secondary meaning. To cow is to intimidate, to make afraid or submissive. Don't let all these words cow you; they're not as frightening as they look.

✔ **craven** (rhymes with, *rav*en): Someone craven is very cowardly, abjectly afraid. The word is strong. If it were in, for example, an analogy, such as CRAVEN: AFRAID::, you would make the sentence, "Craven is very afraid."

✔ **dastard** (rhymes with, *bas*tard): A dastard (careful to note the d) is a cowardly evildoer. A dastard isn't simply a coward, mind you, but a wicked, evil coward. You don't call the friend who refuses to jump off the high dive a dastard. The dastard is the friend who would never do anything to your face but who sneaks into the locker room as you're showering (after jumping off the high dive) and hides your swimsuit, cut off shorts, T-shirt, and towel.

(continued)

(continued)

✔ **daunt** (rhymes with, *haunt*): To daunt is to make afraid; to intimidate; to dishearten. You should know two other forms of this word that both mean unafraid: **dauntless** and **undaunted.**

✔ **doughty** (rhymes with, *doubt* he): Doughty means brave.

Don't confuse this word with doughy. Pillsbury has a giggling doughy boy, not a doughty boy (although in my opinion, it takes someone pretty brave to jump into a hot oven!).

✔ **foolhardy** (rhymes with, *school* party): Foolhardy people are hardy (brave) and bold, but in a foolish way. For example, if you rush into a burning building to save a baby, that's hardy or brave. If you rush into a burning building to save a scrapbook of baby pictures, that's foolishly brave or foolhardy.

✔ **intrepid** (rhymes with, in *step* hid): Intrepid means bold, fearless, very brave.

Your roots can help you define this word (see Chapter 2). The prefix *in–* usually means not; the root *trep* means fear. If you're intrepid, you are not fearful.

✔ **mettle** (rhymes with, *kettle*): Someone with mettle has courage, but more than that: She also has spirit and a high quality of character. You've probably heard the expression, "test your mettle." The SAT, GRE and other exams test your mettle. They see what you're made of, testing your courage and character.

✔ **poltroon** (rhymes with, whole *goon*): A poltroon is not just a coward but a thorough coward. If you're a poltroon, you are afraid of everything. Interesting tidbit: The word poltroon comes from the same root as *poult,* as in poultry, meaning — you guessed it — a chicken.

✔ **pusillanimous** (pew sill *an* im us): Pusillanimous means timid, cowardly, fainthearted. This word has an interesting derivation. It combines two roots, one meaning child or little boy one meaning mind. When you are pusillanimous, you have the mind of a child, in the sense of being afraid of many things.

✔ **timorous** (rhymes with, *him* or us): Timorous is the pompous, ten-dollar word for timid or afraid.

Bonus trivia: Have a friend named Tim or Timothy? Sorry, you can't call him timorous and think his name came from the same root. Timothy actually came from a root meaning "honor to God."

✔ **trepidation** (rhymes with, *step* hid nation): Trepidation is fear, especially fearful uncertainty. When you have a sore tooth, you feel trepidation going to the dentist, unsure of whether the pain is nothing special, or whether the tooth is rotten to the core. The root *trep* means fear, but the word originally came from the same root as tremble. When you have trepidation, you tremble with anxiety.

Bonus dentist joke: Why do dentists have a reputation for being sad? Because they're always looking down in the mouth.

✔ **valiant** (rhymes with, *gal* he sent): Being older than the dawn of time, I recall a Sunday cartoon strip called *Prince Valiant.* The prince went around rescuing princesses, slaying dragons, and generally proving his valor and bravery. Valiant means brave.

Answers to the Exercises

Put down that red pencil; you won't need to make any corrections . . . or will you? Check the following answers to see just how many questions you answered correctly.

Exercise one

1. **extol.** To extol is to praise. Try to remember the tip that you ex*tol* Toll House cookies (you like chocolate chip cookies).

2. **upbraid.** When your friend "unbraids" you or "rips you apart," she is upbraiding or criticizing you.

   Bonus joke: Why did Robin Hood have to remodel Sherwood Forest? Answer: It had a Little John!

3. **panegyric.** A panegyric is a song of praise. If Steve was drooling over the gorgeous women, he was praising the college.

4. **accolades.** Accolades are praises, kudos, or congratulations. If Sgt. Zia was grinning and got a commendation (an award for doing something well), he was receiving accolades.

5. **eulogize.** To eulogize is to praise. You eulogize a good teacher; you belittle a bad one.

6. **kudos.** Kudos are praises, congratulations, or an "attaboy!" for a job well done. If Fred did an excellent job reorganizing the office, he expected praise.

7. **rebuke.** A rebuke is a criticism.

   Bonus word: The judge called the crime heinous, which means outrageously evil or wicked; abominable. Many of my jokes have been called not just horrible, but heinous.

   Bonus joke: Judge to locksmith who had been caught in the commission of a crime: "What were you doing when the police arrived?" Locksmith: "I was making a bolt for the door."

8. **castigate.** To castigate is to criticize harshly. A sportscaster would not praise but would criticize a player who incurred a penalty.

9. **disparagement.** Disparagement is criticism, ridicule.

   Bonus joke: Did you hear about the psychiatrist who had two boxes on her desk? They were marked Outgoing and Inhibited.

10. **malign.** If the student got no plaudits or praises, the instructor maligned, or criticized her.

    Bonus joke: Why is it good to be an unemployed jester? Because you're nobody's fool!

Exercise two

1. **censure.** Acclaim is praise; censure is criticism.

2. **encomium.** Castigation is public criticism; encomium is formal praise.

3. **vilification.** Plaudits are praises; vilification is abusive language.

4. **eulogize.** To upbraid is to criticize sharply; to eulogize is to give high praise.

5. **castigate.** To extol is to praise highly; to castigate is to criticize sharply.

6. **extol.** To malign is to speak evil of; to extol is to praise.

7. **belittlement.** A panegyric is high praise; belittlement is speaking slightingly of.

8. **malign.** To laud is to praise; to malign is to speak evil of.

9. **eulogize.** To belittle is to criticize, to put down. To eulogize is to praise, to say good things about.

10. **censure.** Censure is strong disapproval. Kudos are praise.

Exercise three

1. **B.** Censure is criticism or *disapprobation* (disapproval). The actor is unhappy with criticism. He is, on the other hand, happy with plaudits, acclaim, kudos, and paeans, which are all praise.

2. **D.** To disparage is to insult or speak badly of. If the attorney thought the judge respected and admired him, he would be surprised at hearing that the judge insulted him. To eulogize, extol, acclaim, and laud are all to praise.

    Bonus joke: Of course, no one can have a question about lawyers without including a lawyer joke: Why don't sharks eat lawyers? Professional courtesy!

3. **D.** Encomium is praise. Refugees who go to another country for peace offer praise to that country. They would not offer a vilification, rebuke, denunciation (the noun form of denounce; when one denounces, one gives denunciation), or denigration, all words meaning criticism or insult.

4. **A.** If the students were enthusiastic about the group, they liked the music, and, therefore, offered a paean, or song of praise, about it. They didn't offer censure, vituperation, vilification, or rebuke, all of which are words of insult or criticism.

5. **C.** This question was a little tricky, but you could have used the process of elimination to get it correct. The scientist was unwilling to criticize or speak badly of, or malign, her career, saying that even though she worked hard, the rewards were worth the effort. By predicting you need a negative word in the blank, you can eliminate all the other choices. Extol, laud, acclaim, and eulogize all mean to praise.

   Bonus joke: What is the most common illness suffered by nuclear scientists? Atomic ache.

6. **E.** A toady is a yes-man, a kiss-up, or someone who praises and flatters way too much. You want a negative word to fit in the blank; all the choices except toady are positive.

7. **D.** To upbraid is to rebuke, to criticize harshly. If the paper wanted to support law enforcement but the editorial was critical of the police, the publisher was not happy and criticized the writer. To fawn over or to be a sycophant is to flatter excessively. Kudos and plaudits are praises, just the opposite of what the reporter was given.

8. **B.** Predict that you need a negative word to fill in the blank. To rebuke is to criticize. Given encomium means given praises. Extolled means praised. Acclaimed means praised. Choice D is also negative, but doesn't fit the meaning of the sentence. A toady is a yes-man, a kiss-up, or someone who flatters to excess.

   And speaking of pranks and practical jokes, my own favorite prankster was the writer Robert Benchley, who often sent telegrams to his friends. I followed his lead and sent one from Venice, Italy, saying, "Streets full of water. Advise."

9. **D.** To laud is to praise. Something that kills your pain, that makes you feel better, is certainly going to be praised. The other words are all negative. To demean, denigrate, belittle, and defame all mean to put down, to speak badly of.

10. **D.** A sycophant is a toady, a yes-man, a kiss-up, someone who flatters to excess. If the clerk refused to flatter someone by saying she looked good, she was not a sycophant. An accolade is praise, as is a plaudit. (Both words are more commonly found in the plural: accolades, plaudits.) Vituperation is harsh criticism; a reviler is one who reviles, or speaks negatively about.

    Hearing someone called unattractive reminds me of my of my favorite putdowns I once heard at a comedy workshop: "You're so ugly you'd go to a Haunted House and come out with an application!"

Chapter 8

It Was the Best of Times, It Was the Worst of Times: Words of Joy and Sorrow

• •

Words in This Chapter

▶ badinage

▶ beatific

▶ bemoan

▶ carp

▶ choleric

▶ despondent

▶ dirge

▶ disconsolate

▶ disgruntled

▶ doleful

▶ droll

▶ felicitous

▶ funereal

▶ incensed

▶ jocular

▶ lachrymose

▶ lamentation

▶ lugubrious

▶ peevish

▶ peckish

▶ querulous

▶ risible

▶ sanguine

▶ surly

▶ woebegone

• •

*O*ne afternoon, your significant other calls and tells you in a completely neutral voice, "Come over quickly; I'm in a very lachrymose mood." Do you run to the doughnut shop to get goodies to cheer up a sad sweetie . . . or do you look forward to an afternoon of jokes and laughter? Is someone *lachrymose* tearful or joyful? When you've finished this chapter, you'll know that a lachrymose lassie (or lad) is using her or his lachrymal glands — tear ducts — and that it's time to grab the glazed on your way over.

Happy as a Clam with New Vocabulary Words

The words in this chapter describe someone who is happy or sad. Some terms are words you use when you're on top of the world, in a great mood, laughing at everything, and thinking that things just don't get much better than this. Other words are on the gloomy side, describing the days you wish you could fast forward through and get over with.

badinage (rhymes with, *sad* in midge): humorous banter or ridicule.

> *The catcher and batter engaged in such witty badinage that the umpire couldn't stop laughing long enough to call the game.*

Bonus trivia: You may know that Shakespeare is called the Bard (a ***bard*** is a poet). When scholars use Shakespearean quotes humorously, mangling the quotes for fun, the process is called ***bardinage,*** a take-off on the word "badinage." Use this word on your English teacher to impress him with how smart you are.

beatific (be uh *tiff* ick): serenely happy, blissful.

> *Seeing the beatific smile on our friend's face, we realized she had finally solved the puzzle.*

Bonus joke: Why was the toy store customer happy when she completed the jigsaw puzzle in only six weeks? Answer: The box said "Three to Six Years!"

bemoan (he *groan*): weep, lament, express sorrow for.

> *I bemoaned the fact that my temporary financial embarrassment caused me to be unable to go on the class trip visiting colleges over Spring Break.*

The prefix be– means completely, but in most instances, you can just ignore the prefix. For example, to ***becloud*** the issues is to cloud the issues (ignore the be–). To ***belittle*** someone is to make him feel little (ignore the be–). To ***bewail*** is to wail (ignore the be–). Therefore, what do you do when you ***bemoan*** something? Right, you moan about it (ignore the be–).

carp (rhymes with, *harp*): find fault with, take exception to.

> *The guest carped about everything in the hotel, from the food in the dining hall to the color of the towels at the pool.*

You may have heard of a fish called the carp. To remember this word, think of a "fish-faced old grump," complaining (or carping) about everything.

As easy as a walk in the park

Ever hear the cliché, "take a stroll down memory lane?" When you've mastered these words that have to do with walking, any punster can do just that.

✔ *amble* (rhymes with, *gamble*): to walk in a leisurely manner.

✔ *ambulatory* (rhymes with, *scam* you'll a story): able to walk, moving from one pace to another.

✔ *gambol* (*gam* bowl): to jump and skip about in play, to frolic. (Don't confuse this with gamble. People in Las Vegas gamble; lambs in the meadows gambol.)

✔ *perambulate* (rhymes with, her *scam* you'll late): to walk about, stroll. (Note that ambulatory and perambulate both have the root *ambula,* meaning to move.)

✔ *ramble* (rhymes with, *gamble*): to roam about, to stroll idly without any particular goal.

✔ *swagger* (rhymes with, *stagger*): to walk with a bold, arrogant stride.

✔ *trudge* (rhymes with, *budge*): to walk wearily or laboriously.

---

choleric (rhymes with, go *there* ick): hot-tempered, angry, wrathful.

> *Everyone tried to avoid taking the choleric professor's class, knowing that he was always exploding over the most minor problems.*

Bonus trivia: Cholera is an intestinal disease that can cause vomiting and diarrhea. No wonder someone choleric is irritable!

In medieval times, yellow bile (also called ***choler***) was considered the source of anger and irritability. Bile, which helps in digestion, is a greenish fluid secreted by the liver and stored in the gallbladder. (Bet you never thought you'd see so much biology in a vocabulary book, did you?)

despondent (rhymes with, yes *pond* dent): dejected, losing hope, losing heart.

> *After her tenth blind date turned out badly, Monica was despondent, saying she wasn't going to accept another date unless she could find a more evolved person.*

dirge (rhymes with, *purge*): a song of mourning, sung at a funeral (a dirge can also be the wake itself).

> *"Can we pick up the pace on this song," the drummer asked, "before it starts to remind people of a dirge?"*

disconsolate (rhymes with, this *con* soul yet): unhappy, forlorn, unable to be comforted.

> *The little child was disconsolate, unable to be comforted when she found out her dog had to be put to sleep.*

You may be more familiar with the positive form of this word: console. You *console*, or comfort, someone who is unhappy.

disgruntled (dis *grunt* tulled): discontented, in a bad mood or bad humor.

> *After having to spend the day listening to his friends talk about the great vacation he chose not to take, Mark was disgruntled and eager to change the subject.*

I think of a disgruntled person as someone who is sitting there, grunting rudely at you because he's in such a bad mood. "Want to go to the mall, honey?" "Grunt, grunt." "Want to go to the library and study?" "Grunt, grunt."

doleful (rhymes with, *soul*ful): sorrowful, mournful, discontent.

> *The doleful look on Lee's face showed all too clearly his unhappiness at the fact that he had to eat a healthy bowl of pineapple slices for desert instead of the ice cream he had been anticipating.*

Yes, the example above did intentionally play off of Dole pineapple, the brand of fruit. Hey, anything to help you remember, right? You may also see this word in another form: dolorous. Given that the suffix *–ous* means "full of," *dolorous* and doleful are the same word.

droll (rhymes with, *troll*): amusing, especially in an odd or surprising way.

> *Steven Wright, my favorite comic, often makes droll comments like, "I'm not afraid of heights — I'm afraid of widths!"*

felicitous (rhymes with, so *this* it us): very happy.

> *The wedding was such a felicitous occasion that even the previously feuding divorced parents put aside their differences and were happy for the day.*

Bonus trivia: Ever see *Felix the Cat* cartoons in your misspent youth (or see Felix the Cat clocks in the store)? Ever wonder why the grinning feline was called Felix? He was one happy cat.

funereal (few *near* he ull): gloomy, dismal, appropriate to a funeral.

> *The funereal expression on the model's face showed she wasn't happy having to wear clothes that the magazine critic said "must have some pharmaceutical explanation."*

incensed (in *sens*ed): angry, enraged, exasperated.

> *Juan was incensed when his girlfriend corrected the spelling in his love letters, accusing her of being a grammar Nazi.*

What do you do with a stick of incense? You burn it. Someone who is incensed is "burning mad."

jocular (rhymes with, *clock* you'll er): speaking or acting in jest or merriment, jokingly.

> *The eye doctor pointed at his wall of eyeglasses and jocularly said, "If you don't see what you want, you're in the right place!"*

You may have heard the expression, "Going for the jugular," meaning going in for the kill (slitting the jugular vein). A comedian who is closing the routine with his very best joke may be said to be "going for the jocular!"

lachrymose (rhymes with, *back* him gross): tearful, sad, mournful.

> *The lachrymose expression on Jessica's face told her friends that Jessica had just been dumped by her boyfriend.*

Know where your lachrymal ducts are? They are your tear ducts. When you cry, you're lachrymose.

lamentation (lam men *tay* shun): bewailing, mourning, regret.

> *The student's lamentations could be heard throughout the dorm, as he whined about the careless mistakes he made on his test, resulting in a low score that cost him the position of valedictorian.*

Bonus trivia: What's a valedictorian? You probably said, "It's the person with the top GPA." Well, yes and no. In the United States, usually the person with the best GPA (grade point average) is the valedictorian of his or her class, but that's not what the word means. *Valedictory* means "said or done at parting, pertaining to goodbye." A *valedictorian* is the person who gives the goodbye speech for the class. The honor may go to the top student, but anyone who says goodbye is a valedictorian. Therefore, whenever your friends talk about school, you can casually say you are going to be the valedictorian — then wave goodbye and make your prediction come true!

lugubrious (loo *gyoo* bree us): mournful, doleful, dismal.

> *The lugubrious expression on the basset hound's face made him look sad, even when his tail was wagging so hard he knocked over three lamps and two toddlers!*

You use the word lugubrious in a comic, almost ridiculous way. You don't call someone who is having the blues one day lugubrious; you call a clown who goes over the top pantomiming huge tears and a broken heart lugubrious.

peevish (rhymes with, *heave* fish): irritable, fretful, spiteful.

> *When he found out he couldn't get the day off from school to go to the game, Jarold was peevish, and pouted all day, refusing to participate in class.*

Peevish has a "childish" connotation. Someone peevish is angry and acting like a pouting baby. You may have heard the slang form of this word, peeved. When you're *peeved* about something, you are childishly annoyed.

peckish (rhymes with, *deck* fish): irritable, touchy, often from hunger.

> *Knowing that her child became peckish when he hadn't eaten for a while, the mother made a point of stopping the car every few hours and letting her son grab a snack.*

Peckish can mean just plain grouchy, but it usually has the idea of being grouchy from lack of food. This is a fun, classy word to use to get off the hook when you have just snapped at someone: "Sorry, my blood sugar is low, and I'm a mite peckish." (Personally, I think "peckish" could be a name in a law firm: "Peckish, Grumbler, and Grouch, Attorneys at Law.")

querulous (*k'were* you luss): full of complaints.

> *Because Rudy was not a naturally querulous person, we were surprised when he complained all day long that his new shoes were too tight, his pants didn't fit right, and his shirt wasn't in fashion anymore.*

Bonus trivia: Speaking of shoes, here's a fact you can work into the conversation to sidetrack your parents the next time they are querulous because you've spent too much money buying yet more footwear: There was no difference between right and left shoes until the mid-1800s.

risible (rhymes with, *visible*): laughable, humorous.

> *Your suggestion that I go to the party with Monty the Mouth-Breather is risible; when I said I wanted to date an IQ donor, I didn't mean someone who gave away all his brain cells!*

sanguine (*sang* win): cheerful, optimistic.

> *I was not sanguine about the chances of my friend's relationship getting serious when I realized her boyfriend listed his profession as "philogynist" on his resume.*

This word is interesting. Students often confuse it with *sanguinary,* which means bloodthirsty (an assassin is sanguinary). Both words have the same root, *sanguis,* meaning blood. Sanguine people were originally ruddy, or red-faced; red-faced people were considered good-tempered, jolly, optimistic, cheerful.

Bonus word: Did you figure out from the example sentence above what a philogynist is? *Phil* means love, *gyn* means woman, and *–ist* means "a person who." Therefore, a ***philogynist*** is a person who loves women. (It's a sad commentary on our society that the word ***misogynist,*** a person who hates women, is more widely used and understood than philogynist.)

surly (rhymes with, early): bad-tempered, unfriendly.

> *The surly polar bear worried the park rangers, who reiterated their warnings that the tourists should not feed any of the animals, especially the bears.*

Right on the recommendation

Here are some good words to use in a letter of recommendation to impress the readers.

✔ *diligent* (rhymes with, *pill* he gent): A diligent person is persevering and careful in work; painstaking.

✔ *dogged* (rhymes with, *frog* Ed): Being dogged, which is stubborn, not giving in easily, would be a good thing for a person tacking a difficult and time-consuming task.

✔ *exemplary* (ex *semp* lury): Exemplary means serving as a model or example; worth imitating.

✔ *industrious* (in *duss* tree us): Someone industrious is steady and hard-working.

✔ *meticulous* (rhymes with, ri*dic*ulous): Meticulous people are detail-oriented, very careful, even finicky.

✔ *probity* (rhymes with, *grow* bitty): A person with probity has integrity and is upright in her dealings.

✔ *proficient* (rhymes with, know *fish* scent): A proficient person is highly skilled; competent.

✔ *punctilious* (punk *till* he us): A punctilious person would be excellent in a job requiring protocol, as she is scrupulous about every detail of behavior.

✔ *scrupulous* (*screw* pyew luss): Someone scrupulous is extremely careful to do things right.

✔ *veracity* (rhymes with, her *gas* city): Veracity is truthfulness.

✔ *virtuoso* (rhymes with, *fur* chew oh so): A person displaying great skill is a virtuoso. After mastering the words in this book, you're a vocabulary virtuoso!

Bonus trivia: Don't ask me who discovered the fact, but according to biologists, all polar bears are left-handed.

woebegone (*whoa* be gone): overwhelmed with grief, distress and sorrow.

> *When he realized that he had won the lottery but that the dog had eaten the winning ticket, Lance was woebegone.*

Woebegone is an interesting word. It means the opposite of what logic would seem to indicate. Wouldn't you think that woe-be-gone would mean happy, because the woe (sadness) is gone? Not so. Woebegone is not just sad, but very, very sad. If you miss this word on a test, I shall be woebegone, thinking I have failed you.

Sadder but Wiser: Practice Exercises

When you've finished having fun going through exercises in this section, check your answers against those in the "Answers to the Exercises" section at the end of this chapter — and hope the result won't leave you disgruntled.

Exercise one

Directions: Select the appropriate word to complete the sentence.

1. In a (jocular/woebegone) mood, one cannibal turned to the other and teased, "Does this clown taste funny to you?"

2. Latifa (bemoaned/rejoiced over) the fact that her husband never asked directions, and that they were often lost for hours.

3. The (woebegone/incensed) expression on the face of the farmer was common; he wasn't any sadder than usual.

4. Hearing the (hymn/dirge), we looked to see whether a funeral was in progress at the mortuary, worried we would be interrupting.

5. My cousin often comes up with (peevish/droll) questions that make me giggle, with questions I can't answer, like, "Why do noses run and feet smell?"

6. We enjoyed the (wrath/badinage) between the two leading characters in the sitcom, laughing over their topping each other's jokes and one-liners.

7. The heavyweight girl was (disgruntled/peckish) when she heard the comic say he didn't want her to think he was "having fun at your expanse, young lady!"

Words not to use on a letter of recommendation

This chapter also has a sidebar on words to use on a recommendation. Here is the flip side of that concept, words *not* to use.

✔ *flippant* (rhymes with, *hip* ant): Flippant people are disrespectful, saucy, or impertinent. They sass and talk back to the boss.

✔ *intransigent* (in *trans* sig gent): An intransigent person refuses to compromise. An intransigent person insists on always getting her way. (I have a sign on my computer that shows how intransigent I am. It reads: "Be reasonable. Do everything my way.")

✔ *plagiarism* (rhymes with, *sage* her ism): To plagiarize is to steal someone else's ideas, to take another person's work and pass it off as your own.

✔ *procrastinator* (pro *crass* tin eight her): A procrastinator is one who habitually postpones or puts off things. A procrastinator would not be good at meeting deadlines.

✔ *rash* (rhymes with, *dash*): If you are rash, you are too hasty, to the point of being reckless.

8. The (lugubrious/beatific) look on the teacher's face made us believe that we had all flunked the midterm, a fact that was confirmed as she passed back our tests.

9. After hiking for hours with no food, we were all (despondent/peckish) and snapping at each other, eager to get to the nearest McDonald's as soon as possible.

10. The music in the elevator wasn't just slow, it was positively (risible/funereal), making us all depressed.

Exercise two

Directions: Choose the synonym (word with the same meaning) of each word.

1. lugubrious: (disconsolate/sanguine)

2. risible: (humorous/disgusting)

3. felicitous: (happy/ furious)

4. peevish: (disgruntled/funereal)

5. choleric: (mellow/hot-tempered)

6. beatific: (wrathful/calm)

7. lamentation: (praise/grief)

8. incensed: (furious/joyous)

9. disconsolate: (elated/sorrowful)

10. doleful: (sad/happy)

Exercise three

Directions: Select the best answer to each question.

1. Steve was - - - - over having been fired from his job for misrepresenting his background and qualifications, but understood that the firm was unable to continue his employment, given his lack of credibility.

   (A) sanguine

   (B) disconsolate

   (C) jocular

   (D) droll

   (E) peckish

2. The astronomy professor, normally a very mild-mannered man, became - - - - and yelled at everyone when his students broke an expensive telescope for which he was responsible.

   (A) incensed

   (B) despondent

   (C) querulous

   (D) lachrymose

   (E) peckish

3. Well-known for her dogmatic insistence on imprisoning those who were guilty of even minor infractions of the law, Judge Stras quickly became - - - - when she was forced to release prisoners because the jails were already filled.

   (A) carping

   (B) jocular

   (C) surly

   (D) beatific

   (E) felicitous

4. The angry teenager, by flouting the rules at every opportunity, showed his disdain for them, ---- that the majority of the rules were simply aimed at keeping teenagers in trouble.

    (A) lamenting

    (B) quibbling

    (C) lampooning

    (D) carping

    (E) risible

5. The badinage of the announcers so incensed the basketball player that he climbed into the broadcasting booth and ---- the speakers.

    (A) lauded

    (B) congratulated

    (C) questioned

    (D) attacked

    (E) fired

6. Unlike a dog that actively seeks human companionship, a cat often seems unhappy — even ---- — when forced to suffer the indignity of being picked up and petted.

    (A) woebegone

    (B) sanguine

    (C) droll

    (D) jocular

    (E) beatific

7. In colonial days, little effort was made to embellish the ---- that were played at funerals, but it is this very simplicity that makes those songs timeless and still used in services today.

    (A) games

    (B) dirges

    (C) badinage

    (D) lampoons

    (E) games

We're not who you think we are

You've heard the expression, "We see what we want to see, we hear what we want to hear," right? The same is true on exams with vocabulary. For example, if you saw the word proscribe, would you read it as prescribe? Here are some of the most commonly misread twosomes of words.

✔ **aggregate** (*agg* gree gate) / **aggravate** (*agg* grah vate): An aggregate is a group or mass of things. The expression "in the aggregate" means taken all together, as in "In the aggregate, teenagers are harder working and more serious than television portrays them to be." Note the root *greg,* meaning group or herd. To aggravate is to make worse, to make more troublesome. You aggravate a rash when you scratch it.

✔ **causal** (*cause* ull) / **casual** (*cazh* you ull): These words are incredibly easy to confuse. Causal means relating to cause and effect, as in, "There's a causal connection between smoking and lung cancer."

✔ **dearth** (rhymes with, *birth*) / **death** (rhymes with, *Beth*): A dearth is a scarcity or lack. You have a dearth of time to party when teachers are assigning an abundance of homework.

✔ **disparate** (*diss* per it) / **desperate** (*dess* per it): Disparate means different, not alike. The root *par* means equal (as in parity, two bullets down) and *dis* means not. There is a disparity between how many words you knew when you began reading this book, and how many you know now.

✔ **froward** (*fro* word) / **forward** (*four* word): Many students tell me they think froward is a typo! Froward is a real word, meaning stubbornly willful, contrary, not easily controlled. Think of a two-year-old shouting, "no! no!" all the time as a froward child.

✔ **parity** (*pair* itty) / **parody** (*pair* oh dee): Parity is equality. You know this word in its more common form, par. If you are at par on the golf course, you are equal to the course. A parody is a humorous imitation.

✔ **proscribe** (pro *scribe*) / **prescribe** (pre scribe): These words are actually opposites. To proscribe is to forbid the practice or use of. When you are ill, the doctor prescribes bed rest and proscribes partying.

Do you use aggravate to mean annoy, telling your little brother he constantly aggravates you? Many grammar Nazis, myself included, consider that informal usage incorrect in proper English. You can aggravate an illness by running around chasing your little brother when you should be in bed resting; your brother doesn't aggravate you when he slips that rubber frog into your bed to scare you half to death. (The grammar checker on many computers tries to substitute "irritate" for "aggravate" when the word is used in the "to annoy" sense.)

Bonus joke (you need to read this joke aloud to get it): A stagecoach was transporting two nuns across the West in 1846 when robbers came up and made the coach stop so they could steal everything. While the older nun sat calmly, the younger nun was terrified and asked the older nun what she should do. Said the older nun, "Show them your cross." The younger nun jumped out, wagged a finger at the robbers and said, "I'm really aggravated now!"

8. Although the first to admit that the charlatan had duped him with his fake remedies, Dr. Drake was still - - - - because his arthritis had, in fact, become less painful.

   (A) sanguine

   (B) choleric

   (C) peevish

   (D) beatific

   (E) doleful

9. Unaccustomed to receiving any compliments from the normally - - - - supervisor, the worker was understandably wary.

   (A) querulous

   (B) lugubrious

   (C) doleful

   (D) lachrymose

   (E) felicitous

10. Emily was - - - - about her chances at beating her opponent in the race, claiming the other girl was so slow she'd come in third in a race with a pregnant woman.

    (A) disgruntled

    (B) peckish

    (C) peevish

    (D) sanguine

    (E) lugubrious

Answers to the Exercises

This section gives you the answers and explanations for the exercises you've completed so brilliantly. I'm hoping your results don't leave you disconsolate, lugubrious, or lachrymose!

Exercise one

1. **jocular.** Jocular means joking, merry. The word is pronounced "jock-u-lar," not "joke-u-lar," but you can remember it by thinking of jokes.

2. **bemoaned.** To bemoan is to express sorrow for, to bewail or lament over.

Bonus joke: Why did *Apollo 13* have such trouble getting to the moon? The astronauts refused to ask the guys in *Apollo 12* for directions.

3. **woebegone.** Woebegone means sad, mournful. For some reason, farmers always seem to be portrayed in pictures as sad and mournful (think of Grant Wood's famous painting, "American Gothic," of the farmer and his daughter/niece). Most of the farmers I know, however, have great senses of humor. My favorite insult was from a farmer who tapped my brain and said, "No grain in that silo."

4. **dirge.** A dirge is a sad, mournful song, often played at a funeral. I once stood up at a community forum and suggested that the parking meters be programmed to play dirges when the time on them had expired! (Only a few brave souls in the audience admitted to getting my joke . . . expired . . . died . . . get it?)

5. **droll.** Droll means amusing, especially in an odd or surprising way. Puns and sarcasm can be droll. Slapstick comedy, on the other hand, is not droll because it is obvious.

6. **badinage.** Badinage is humorous banter or ridicule. Think of trash talk, when two people are constantly teasing each other. Brothers and sisters at the dinner table usually indulge in good-hearted badinage.

7. **disgruntled.** Disgruntled means in a bad humor, discontent. If the woman were unhappy with her weight and being teased about it by the comic, she would be in a bad mood or disgruntled.

8. **lugubrious.** Lugubrious means mournful, sad. A teacher whose class flunks the midterm is sad. The students themselves were probably lugubrious as well.

9. **peckish.** You are peckish when you are irritable from lack of food. I picture a bunch of cranky chickens pecking at anything that comes near them, hoping to get something edible.

10. **funereal.** As you can probably figure out, funereal is rather like a funeral, gloomy, dismal, mournful. You have a funereal expression on your face when you find out that the card you hoped was from your sweetheart was, in fact, an appointment reminder from your dentist.

Bonus joke: When is the best time to go to see the dentist? Answer: When it's two-thirty (tooth-hurty).

Exercise two

1. **disconsolate.** Disconsolate and lugubrious both mean sad, mournful.

2. **humorous.** Something risible is humorous or funny.

3. **happy.** Felicitous means full of happiness.

4. **disgruntled.** A peevish person is disgruntled, irritable and acting in a pouty, childish manner.

5. **hot-tempered.** Someone choleric is hot-tempered, quick to get angry.

6. **calm.** Beatific is calm, serene, happy and mellow.

7. **grief.** Lamentation is grief, mourning. There is a book of the Bible called Lamentations, in which the writer expresses grief over the state of events.

8. **furious.** If you are incensed, you are furious, burning mad.

9. **sorrowful.** A disconsolate person is sorrowful, unhappy, unable to be consoled.

10. **sad.** You are doleful when you are very sad.

Exercise three

1. **B.** Predict that the blank must have a negative word. Steve would not have been happy over being fired. Disconsolate means unhappy, forlorn, or unable to be consoled.

   Bonus: Did you get the word "credibility?" *Cred* is a root meaning trust or belief. Someone *credible* is trustable, trustworthy. You more commonly know this word as incredible. Your story that you were abducted by aliens is incredible; if you go around telling it, your credibility will suffer.

2. **A.** Incensed means angry, enraged. Because the professor yelled at the students, he was angry rather than sad (despondent, lachrymose), complaining (querulous), or irritable (peckish).

3. **C.** If the judge really wanted to throw everyone in jail, she would not be happy at having to let the bad guys go free. She would, therefore, be surly, or bad-tempered.

4. **D.** The teenager complained, or carped, about the rules. Choice A was tempting, but to lament is to be mournful over. The teenager was flouting (showing his disrespect for or breaking) the rules, so he wasn't sad about them, but rather grumpy.

   Choice C has an interesting bonus word. Ever hear of National Lampoon, like *National Lampoon's Christmas Vacation,* or *National Lampoon's Ben Wilder,* the movies? To lampoon is to ridicule, to make fun of. The movies made fun of the people involved in the adventures.

5. **D.** For a change of pace, the vocabulary words weren't in the answer choices, but in the question itself. Badinage is humorous banter or ridicule, often at someone's expense. A person who is incensed is furious, "burning" mad. Therefore, a player who has been ridiculed and is furious would climb into the booth to attack the broadcasters, not to praise (laud), congratulate, or question them. And it is unlikely a player would have the ability to fire the broadcasters.

6. **A.** To be woebegone is to be overwhelmed with grief. Choices B, C, D, and E are all positive words, while the question wants a negative word.

7. **B.** The key to this question is the fact that these "songs" are timeless. A dirge is a sad, mournful song, often played at funerals. (Personally, I've often thought that "Dirge" would be a great name for a clown with a painted on frown.)

8. **D.** The key is the word "although," which alerts you to the fact that although the good doctor was conned, he was still happy. Beatific means happy, serenely joyful.

    Bonus: If you understood the words *charlatan* (a fake, a fraud, a quack) and *duped* (tricked, conned), give yourself a pat on the back.

9. **A.** Querulous means full of complaints. A supervisor who normally complains then suddenly compliments is enough to make any worker wary (cautious). Although a sad supervisor may not normally give out compliments, lugubrious and doleful and lachrymose all mean sad. You can't have three right answers; therefore, all three are wrong. Felicitous means happy, joyful. A joyful supervisor is more likely to give compliments than not to give them.

10. **D.** A sanguine person is cheerful and optimistic. Emily was positive she could beat her opponent in the race.

Let's party, dude!

You ready to have some fun? If you're not too into the festivities to remember your vocabulary, here are some great words to use when the good times are rollin'!

✔ **Bacchanalia** (back an *ale* yuh): drunken party. (Bacchus was the god of wine.)

✔ **convivial** (rhymes with, one *give* he uhl): having to do with a feast or festive activity.

✔ **hedonism** (*he* done is um): pursuit of pleasure as a way of life.

✔ **revelry** (*rev* uhl ree): noisy merry-making, boisterous festivity.

✔ **Saturnalia** (sat urn *ale* yuh): period of unrestrained revelry.

✔ **soiree** (rhymes with, par *day*): party or gathering in the evening.

Chapter 9

When Your IQ Is a Fraction: Words about Intelligence

Words in This Chapter

- acumen
- acute
- astute
- befuddle
- coruscation
- discerning
- dolt
- erudite
- fatuous
- folly
- inane
- incisive
- ingenious
- judicious
- nescient
- obtuse
- omniscient
- pedant
- perspicacious
- polymath
- prodigy
- pundit
- resourceful
- sagacious
- vacuous

Smart? There's no doubt in my mind what a genius you are; after all, you bought this book, didn't you? However, while the purchase demonstrates your shopping *savvy* (know-how, shrewdness), it doesn't necessarily indicate your status as a sesquipedalian. *Sesqui* means one and a half; for example, a *sesquicentennial* is a one-and-a-half century or 150-year event. *Ped* means foot; for example, a pedestrian goes on foot. A *sesquipedalian* uses foot-and-a-half-long words, or in other words, knows a lot of big vocabulary. While I can't promise you'll encounter words quite that long (pause for a sigh of relief!) in this chapter, you do find words that indicate your intelligence . . . and the lack thereof in others who don't know this fun — and challenging — vocabulary.

Words of Wisdom: New Vocabulary

You know, of course, that I have nothing but the utmost admiration for you and your intelligence. However, just on the remote chance that there are a few words you haven't mastered yet, please take a look at the vocabulary given in this section.

acumen (rhymes with, *back* you men): shrewdness, keenness, and quickness in understanding and dealing with a situation.

> *Noted for his political acumen, Kent was hired as a consultant to help various candidates win elected office.*

Bonus joke: Politicians make strange bedfellows . . . but they soon get used to the bunk.

(If you didn't get the joke, you're probably not familiar with a second meaning of bunk. Besides being a type of bed, bunk is short for *bunkum,* meaning insincere talk or empty talk that's merely for effect — like some political speeches.)

acute (rhymes with, a *suit*): keen or quick of mind, shrewd.

> *The acute lawyer was able to understand the points of even the most complicated cases, and thus was in demand by all the firms.*

An acute angle is sharp, less than 90 degrees — think of it as quick to come to the point. Think of an acute mind quickly grasping the point.

astute (rhymes with, us *toot*): having or showing a clever or shrewd mind; cunning.

> *The astute detective was able to break the alibi of the criminal by proving that the pictures he supposedly took in the afternoon showed shadows that would occur only in the morning.*

Have you ever taken a so-called idiot test? You have to be very astute to catch the tricks in those. For example, one question is, "A plane crashes on the exact border of the United States and Canada. The survivors are buried in which country?" The answer of course is, "Survivors aren't buried!"

befuddle (rhymes with, wee *pud*dle): to confuse.

> *The Beatles, just to befuddle everyone, dedicated their movie* Help! *to Elias Howe, the inventor of the sewing machine.*

The prefix *be–* means completely. To befuddle is to fuddle completely (isn't that helpful?). To remember this word, think of Elmer Fudd, Bugs Bunny's nemesis. He's always getting so confused and befuddled by Bugs that he ends up blasting himself instead of the wascally wabbit.

What's a nemesis? In Greek mythology, Nemesis was the goddess of vengeance or revenge. Today, you say something is a *nemesis* if it is the inevitable cause of someone's downfall or defeat. When I was in high school, I considered chemistry my nemesis.

coruscation (rhymes with, chorus *say* shun): a sudden brilliant display of wit.

> *Mandy shocked everyone with her coruscation during history class, because usually she sat quietly, not volunteering answers, and rarely knowing the answers when called upon.*

Literally, coruscation is sparkling or giving off a gleam of light. When a cartoon character gets the light bulb over her head to show she has a brilliant idea, that's coruscation.

discerning (rhymes with, this *turn*ing): having or showing good judgment or understanding.

> *The busy star's personal assistant had to be discerning and determine which media representatives would be allowed to see the star and which would be given a polite excuse.*

Bonus joke: Sometimes assistants, receptionists, and "gatekeepers" (people who determine who gets to see The Big Man and who doesn't) can get a little officious. The last time someone asked me very snootily, "Do you have an appointment?" I responded, "Yes, and if this takes too long, I'll be late for it."

dolt (rhymes with, *bolt*): a stupid, slow-witted person, a blockhead.

> *During presidential elections, each side attempts to make the other side's candidate look like a dolt, unable to understand the intricacies of power brokering and decision making.*

Bonus joke: Speaking of politicians, know who's the vice-president of pumpkins? Al Gourd!

erudite (rhymes with, *there* you bite): learned, scholarly.

> *Although Sergio was the most erudite instructor at the school, the author of many papers published in educational journals, and a top researcher in his field of history, he was fond of puerile jokes, such as, "Why were the Dark Ages called that? Because there were a lot of knights then."*

Erudite doesn't mean innately or inherently brilliant, but well-read and having knowledge gained from literature. In other words, you're not born erudite, you become erudite.

fatuous (rhymes with, *that* you us): silly, foolish, complacently stupid, or inane.

It was clear from the fatuous expression on Jim's face that he was totally infatuated with Georgia, unwilling to be out of her presence for even a few minutes.

Even though the suffix *–ous* means full of, fatuous does not mean "full of fat," or very fat. Fatuous comes from the same Latin root as infatuated. When you are infatuated with someone, you act foolishly around her, think you're in love, get all tongue-tied, and say silly things when she tries to talk with you.

folly (rhymes with, *trolly*): a lack of understanding or sense, foolishness.

> *Secretary of State Seward's 1867 purchase of Alaska from Russia for $7,200,000 was called Seward's Folly because people believed the land was worthless.*

Folly comes from the same word as fool. A fool is known for his folly.

inane (rhymes with, in-*sane*): lacking sense, foolish, silly.

> *Ryan started a T-shirt company called, Say Whaaa?, selling T-shirts with such inane sayings as, "Garrulous people leave me in a state of earitation!"*

An inane comment is just plain dumb. The word has a second meaning: empty or vacant. An inane person is empty of common sense.

To get the joke on the T-shirt, you need to know that garrulous means excessively talkative, never shutting up. (And, of course, "earitation" is a play on irritation.)

incisive (rhymes with, we *sighs* give): sharp, keen, or acute.

> *When asked to describe her blind date, Amanda incisively said, "He's a non-practicing adult."*

You know that an incision is a cut, like an incision a surgeon makes to get access to your heart. When you make an incisive comment, it cuts through the baloney and gets sharply to the heart of the matter.

ingenious (rhymes with, in *gene* ee us): clever, resourceful.

> *The ingenious travel agent was able to save her client several hundred dollars by booking fares to smaller airports.*

If you're ingenious, you're not so much book smart as street smart. You find a way to solve problems by being resourceful.

judicious (rhymes with, you'd *dish* us): wise and careful, showing sound judgment.

> *The young girl judiciously decided to call her parents to come give her a ride home after she heard her car making loud noises, not wanting to risk getting stuck on the freeway during rush hour.*

As you guessed, this word comes from the same root as judge — that a wise person who makes the decision.

Did you notice the correct spelling of the word judgment? There's no middle "e." The way to remember this is to say to yourself, "There's no judge in judgment." People misspell judgment all the time, especially on tests.

nescient (rhymes with, *mesh* cent): ignorant, lacking knowledge.

> *When the nescient shop teacher substituted for the Calculus teacher, his students ignored him, realizing quickly that they knew more about Calculus than he did.*

Bonus joke: What kind of tools should a shop teacher use in math class? Multipliers.

Don't confuse nescient with **omniscient,** meaning all-knowing. The words are opposites.

obtuse (rhymes with, blob *loose*): slow to understand, dull.

> *Mr. Watson was too obtuse to understand the doctor's humor when the gastroenterologist said, "Well, it's alimentary, my dear Watson!"*

Earlier in this list, you're told that an acute person, like an acute angle, is sharp and to the point. An obtuse person, like an obtuse angle, is dull and not so sharp.

omniscient (ahm *nish* ent): knowing all things.

> *The father liked to tell his daughter that he was omniscient, and give her trivia such as, "The most common disease in the world is tooth decay."*

Omni means all; *scien* means knowledge. Little children think their parents are omniscient and are shocked to find that some matters are beyond even Mom and Dad's knowledge.

pedant (rhymes with, *said* dent): a schoolteacher, especially one who puts unnecessary stress on minor or trivial points of learning.

> *When the English teacher gave Jenna's paper an F because of one dangling modifier, Jenna shrugged it off, saying that you can never fully please a pedant.*

You may see a synonym: pedagogue. A *pedagogue* is a teacher, specifically a dogmatic, pedantic teacher. *Pedagogy* is the art or science of teaching.

perspicacious (purse pick *kay* shuss): having keen judgment or understanding, acutely perceptive.

> *We're looking for a perspicacious stockbroker, one who doesn't merely follow the trends but can predict what they mean and what the future will bring.*

Don't confuse perspicacious, meaning having good understanding, with *perspicuous,* meaning easily understood or lucid. A person is perspicacious; an argument is perspicuous. Perspicacious comes from the same root as perspective. When you see things in perspective — that is, when you have a good view of the matter — you are perspicacious.

polymath (rhymes with, *trolly* path): a person of great and diversified learning.

> *During a cruise across the Atlantic, we had a polymath at our table who was able to keep us entertained with trivia, such as the fact that a volcano in Costa Rica is the only place in the world from which you can see both the Atlantic and Pacific oceans at the same time.*

The root *poly* means many; *math* comes from a root meaning learning. A person who has learned many things is a polymath.

prodigy (rhymes with, *rod* smidge he): a child of highly unusual talent or genius.

> *Mozart was a prodigy, composing symphonies at age five.*

Bonus joke: What is Mozart doing now? Decomposing.

Don't confuse prodigy, a genius, with *prodigious,* meaning enormous or huge. A prodigy has a prodigious talent. In the same way, don't confuse prodigy, a genius, with *prodigal,* meaning recklessly wasteful. A parent may lament that her prodigy was prodigal with his talent, wasting it on video games rather than using it in school.

pundit (rhymes with, *one* zit): a person who has or professes to have great learning or authority.

The zoo hired a pundit to give speeches to schoolchildren, enthralling them with such little- known trivia as the fact that a giraffe can go without water longer than a camel can.

Pundit can be used two different ways. It can mean a person who actually does know what she's talking bout . . . or someone who only thinks she knows what she's talking about. You often hear the term used in government circles: "The political pundits believe that the next election will be very close."

resourceful (re *source* full): able to deal creatively and effectively with problems and difficulties.

The lead character on the television show was highly resourceful, using whatever was at hand such as shoelaces and ashtrays to get out of difficult situations.

A resourceful person is not so much brilliant as capable. You can share an IQ with someone else (in other word, not have too many brains of your own!) and still be highly resourceful.

sagacious (suh *gay* shuss): showing keen perception and sound judgment.

The sagacious writer impressed everyone with his ability to understand and discuss human frailness and idiosyncrasies.

A more common form of sagacious is sage. A **sage** is a very wise person, especially an elderly man noted for his wisdom, experience, and judgment. One of the qualifying answers/questions when I was on *Jeopardy!* years ago was "He was known as the Sage of Baltimore." The question: Who was H. L. Mencken (a famous political commentator)?

A sage is also an herb. You may have heard on an Oldies station a Simon and Garfunkel song that has the line, "Parsley, sage, rosemary, and thyme." Those are all herbs used in cooking.

Bonus: Did you catch the word idiosyncrasies in the example? An idiosyncrasy is a personal mannerism or peculiarity. For example, your idiosyncrasy may be twirling your hair or tapping your fingers.

vacuous (rhymes with, *sack* you us): stupid, showing lack of intelligence.

When asked how Vikings communicated, the student had a vacuous expression on her face betraying her ignorance. Then suddenly, she smiled and hazarded a guess: "With Norse Code?"

The write stuff

Has learning all this vocabulary made you decide you'd like to do a little writing, make a few ink spots of your own? Here are some related words to get you started.

✔ **bowdlerize** (rhymes with, *loud* her eyes): to remove passages considered offensive; to expurgate. This word comes from Thomas Bowdler, 1754–1825, who published an *expurgated* (cleaned up) version of Shakespeare for the family, including young children.

✔ **doggerel** (*dog* er ull): trivial, awkward, often comically bad verse. If you are being self-deprecating, putting yourself and your work down, you respond to a compliment on your poem by saying, "Oh this? It's just some doggerel I scribbled quickly."

✔ **ellipsis** (rhymes with, he *lips* kiss): the omission of a word or words necessary for complete grammatical construction but understood in the context. For example, you may say, "The zookeeper gives lions more meat than tigers." The "he gives" is understood before "tigers."

✔ **expurgate** (rhymes with, *hex* berg gate): to remove obscene or objectionable passages. A book may be expurgated and rewritten before being released to children.

You see the word "purge" in this term. To expurgate material is to *purge* (take out, eliminate) the dirty parts.

✔ **graffiti** (rhymes with, laugh *he* tea): inscriptions, slogans, and so on scratched or drawn on a wall or other public surface.

Bonus trivia: The singular of graffiti is graffito. What's unusual about that? It's rare for a singular form to end in a vowel rather than a consonant. Think about it: Phenomena's singular is phenomenon. Criteria's singular is criterion. Even data has a singular, datum.

✔ **graphologist** (rhymes with, laugh *all* oh gist): a handwriting expert; one who studies handwriting. If "you stink!" is written on the principal's office door, she may bring in a graphologist to determine who penned the put-down.

✔ **illegible** (ill *ledge* ibble): difficult or impossible to read. An illegible prescription (doctors are infamous for their poor handwriting) may mean you leave the pharmacy with not the Prozac you wanted (an antidepressnt) but Premarin (a female hormone)!

✔ **orthography** (rhymes with, north *hog* graph he): spelling in accord with common usage; the study of spelling. Small children often have highly original systems of orthography, different from those of adults.

Bonus joke: Why was the ink spot crying? His mother was in the pen, and he didn't know how long the sentence would be!

A vacuous person has a vacuum where her brain should be; she is empty-headed. The word is often used in the cliché, "a vacuous expression." When you're totally clueless and your face shows the fact, you have a vacuous expression.

Proving You're Smart as a Whip: Practice Exercises

What's the verdict? Did you already know some of the words, or did you have to master quite a few new ones? Try the exercises in this section to make sure everything is firmly fixed into your brain. The answers are in the "Answers to the Exercises" section at the end of this chapter.

Exercise one

Directions: Choose the synonym (word with the same meaning) for each word.

1. resourceful: (ingenious/fatuous)
2. polymath: (dolt/pundit)
3. judicious: (discerning/inane)
4. acumen: (folly/perspicacity)
5. incisive: (befuddled/acute)
6. vacuous: (acute/inane)
7. sagacious: (erudite/nescient)
8. prodigy: (polymath/dolt)
9. befuddled: (ingenious/obtuse)
10. folly: (pedantry/vacuity)

Exercise two

Directions: Choose the most appropriate word to complete the sentence.

1. The psychiatrist treating the shoplifter told him that while his excuses for his behavior were quite - - - - and may fool the police and even the judge, the truth of the matter was that he didn't have kleptomania or any other mental illness, just excessive greed.

    (A) ingenious

    (B) doltish

    (C) nescient

    (D) befuddled

    (E) fatuous

It all "ADs" up

ADmit it: You ADmire people with more than ADequate vocabularies. ADd the following words to your own vocabulary to gain the ADulation of others.

✔ *adage* (rhymes with, *bad* smidge): an old saying that has been popularly accepted as truth. An adage is something like a proverb, almost a cliché, like, "A stitch in time saves nine" or "A watched pot never boils."

I've seen people confuse adage, a saying, with *adagio,* a command meaning to go slowly. A musician may be told, "adagio," meaning to slow down her playing. An adagio is also the slow part of a ballet, the part requiring special skill and balance.

✔ *adamant* (*ad* uh mint): unrelenting, unyielding. You are adamant in your statement to the police officer that the parking meter had the bag over it *before* you parked in the space.

Bonus trivia: In ancient times, adamantis was considered the hardest metal, something supposedly unbreakable. If you are adamant in your statements, no one can "break" them.

✔ *addendum* (rhymes with, then *den* dumb): something added; an appendix or supplement. An addendum is just a fancy name for an addition. You have an addendum to a book, for example, when the publisher realizes too late that she left out a portion and has to print a special supplement.

✔ *addle* (rhymes with, *pad*dle): muddle or confuse. The word these days is usually used as part of a longer word, such as *addle-brained* or *addlepated,* both meaning confused.

✔ *adroit* (rhymes with, uh *boy't*): skillful or expert. You will become an adroit test-taker when you master all these impressive vocabulary words.

✔ *adulation* (rhymes with, *sad* you nation): intense admiration; excessive flattery. A rock star receives adulation from groupies.

✔ *adulterate* (a*dult* her eight): to make inferior by adding a less valuable substance. For example, if you're selling silver coins but you've shaved off some of the silver and put in copper or brass instead, you've adulterated the coins.

✔ *adumbrate* (rhymes with, a *dumb* date): to foreshadow in a vague way; to sketch in an outline of; to give a sketchy idea of.

The words umbrella and adumbrate have the same root, *umbra,* meaning shade.

2. The father, keeping a - - - - eye on his college son's finances, quickly discovered a problem with an unbalanced checkbook and met with the bank officer to remedy the situation.

(A) polymath

(B) discerning

(C) vacuous

(D) obtuse

(E) pedantic

3. Noted for his ---- in dealing with numbers, Ahmad was voted treasurer of the fraternity.

   (A) nescience

   (B) coruscation

   (C) acumen

   (D) inanity

   (E) incisiveness

4. We were amazed at the ---- of the accountant, who seemed not to know any of the latest changes in the tax code and was oblivious about the problems that had been in the news lately.

   (A) resourcefulness

   (B) perspicacity

   (C) omniscience

   (D) sagacity

   (E) nescience

5. His friends urged the ---- man to try out for the quiz show, saying that because he was such a polymath, he was a natural for anything testing trivia.

   (A) fatuous

   (B) doltish

   (C) inane

   (D) acute

   (E) erudite

6. To prove her typing skills were better than those of the other job applicants, the ---- student cleverly devised several pangrams and challenged the others to a timed typing test.

   (A) coruscating

   (B) resourceful

   (C) fatuous

   (D) omniscient

   (E) judicious

7. The graduate school professor quickly realized his ---- in attempting to teach Ph.D.-level material to students who had just recently graduated college, and lowered his teaching to what he considered an abecedarian level.

   (A) folly

   (B) ingenuity

   (C) prodigy

   (D) vacuity

   (E) sagacity

8. Although she enjoyed learning to play new musical instruments, Mrs. Lai laughingly admitted she was no ----, given that she picked up her first instrument when she was over 40.

   (A) pundit

   (B) dolt

   (C) prodigy

   (D) polymath

   (E) sage

9. The television commentator was hired because of his ---- wit, which allowed him to see past the puffery and self-aggrandizement of the candidates and evaluate the issues clearly.

   (A) resourceful

   (B) pedantic

   (C) obtuse

   (D) inane

   (E) incisive

10. The young man operating the carousel was quite ----, using anything available, such as a penknife or even a pair of scissors, to fix the ride whenever it broke down.

    (A) fatuous

    (B) judicious

    (C) resourceful

    (D) befuddled

    (E) nescient

The law

Want to strike terror into your parents' hearts? Tell them you got involved with the law today and watch them *blanch* (turn pale). Make 'em sweat a bit before you let on that you were talking about the law in terms of legal vocabulary, not a constable with a truncheon hauling you off to juvenile court.

✔ *arbitration* (are bit *tray* shun): the settlement of a dispute by a person selected to hear both sides and come to a decision. You may have heard of binding arbitration in sports. When a ballplayer wants 10 million dollars and the team wants to pay him 5 million, instead of going to court and spending money on the lawyers, both sides agree to binding arbitration. That means what the *arbiter,* the decision-maker, says is binding, or must be done.

✔ *bequeath* (rhymes with, be*neath*): to leave by Last Will and Testament; to hand down to another. Your parents (after they've forgiven you for scaring them half to death) may bequeath you their house, car, and other property in their wills. The noun form of bequeath is *bequest.* What is left to you is the bequest.

✔ *fiat* (rhymes with, *me* hot): an order issued by legal authority. The Latin term *fiat* literally means "let it be done." You may hear of a judicial fiat, which is an order given by a judge.

✔ *intestate* (rhymes with, in*vest* eight): without a will. A testament is a will, as in Last Will and Testament. The word is similar to testify. When you testify, you give testimony or make a statement. When you die intestate, you die without a will (*in-* means not or without). An intestate person's property usually goes to the next of kin or to the state.

I've seen people confuse intestate with interstate, as in an interstate highway. Watch out for that r in the middle of the road, so to speak!

✔ *jurisprudence* (jur is *prew* dence): the science or philosophy of law. My business card reads, "Suzee Vlk, J.D." That doesn't mean Juvenile Delinquent (contrary to popular opinion), but Juris Doctorate, a doctorate of law.

✔ *mediate* (rhymes with, *bed* it eight): to bring about a conciliation or settlement. When two neighbors have a dispute, they may choose to go to a neutral third party and have her mediate the argument, rather than going to court. The root *medi* means middle. The mediator gets in the middle of the argument, listening to both sides.

✔ *perjury* (rhymes with, *fur* jury): the willful telling of a lie while under oath. When a witness in a trial intentionally lies about something, she is committing perjury and can go to prison for doing so.

Bonus joke (best if read aloud): Why is it dangerous for a lawyer to walk onto a construction site when plumbers are working? Because the plumbers may connect the drain line to the wrong suer.

Exercise three

Directions: Select the appropriate word to complete the sentence.

1. The interviewer was so favorably impressed by the applicant's (folly/coruscation) that she offered the job to him right there and then.

2. The (sagacious/nescient) philosophy teacher was happy to share his knowledge with his students, but encouraged them to think for themselves as well, saying that, "the world has many echoes, but few voices."

3. The (pedant/pundit) couldn't understand why her boyfriend became upset when she corrected the grammar in his loveletters, saying he should be pleased that she cared enough to make the changes.

4. The (judicious/obtuse) shopper was not clever enough to realize that the so-called beaver fur coat for which he had paid a lot of money was actually synthetic fabric because the sale of real fur was prohibited in his state.

5. Looking completely (astute/befuddled), the young girl didn't understand the pun she saw on the sign at an Italian restaurant offering "pizza and quiet."

6. The well-read and (erudite/inane) science major was able to tell us the most interesting facts, such as how you can use crickets to tell temperature.

7. The (astute/pedantic) criminal was able to predict what direction the police officers would travel and go in the opposite direction, thus eluding capture.

8. Marvin's friends have nicknamed him Mr. (nescient/omniscient) because he is such a know-it-all.

9. The camper, lost and stranded in the wilderness for three days, was (fatuous/resourceful) enough to find materials to build a small tepee-like shelter and a fire to melt snow for drinking water.

10. The math (dolt/pedant) taught an evening Calculus class and ended every session with a reminder to his students that they "shouldn't drink and de-rive!"

Answers to the Exercises

The material in this section is meant to reinforce what you already know: You're one smart student and becoming more erudite by the minute!

Exercise one

1. **ingenious.** Someone resourceful is able to deal creatively and effectively with problems. Someone ingenious is clever and resourceful.

2. **pundit.** A polymath, just like a pundit, is a person of great learning.

3. **discerning.** Judicious means wise and careful, showing sound judgment. Discerning means having good judgment or understanding.

4. **perspicacity.** Acumen is shrewdness, keenness, and quickness in understanding and dealing with a situation. Perspicacity — the noun form of perspicacious — is acute perception, keen understanding.

5. **acute.** An incisive comment is keen, sharp, acute. An acute comment is shrewd, keen.

6. **obtuse.** A vacuous person is stupid, lacking intelligence (think of a vacuous person as "vacant in the mind"). An obtuse person is slow to understand, dull.

7. **erudite.** Sagacious means showing keen perception and sound judgment. Erudite means learned, scholarly. Note that while these two words are not exact synonyms, they are closer to being synonymous than are sagacious and nescient. Nescient means ignorant, lacking knowledge.

8. **polymath.** A prodigy is a child of highly unusual talent or genius. A dolt is a slow-witted person.

9. **obtuse.** Someone befuddled is confused completely. Someone obtuse is slow to understand.

10. **vacuity.** Folly is a lack of understanding or sense. Vacuity, which is just the noun form of vacuous (keep in mind that the suffix *–ity* makes a word a noun) is stupidity or a lack of intelligence.

Exercise two

1. **A.** An ingenious excuse is one that's clever and resourceful.

   Bonus humor: Actually, it's not all that bad having kleptomania. You can always take something for it!

2. **B.** Discerning means showing good understanding. A discerning father discerns, or recognizes and understands, a problem before it gets out of hand. I only wish my own father had kept an eye on me during my school days. I kept telling him my finances were fluid, when what I really meant was that they were going down the drain!

3. **C.** Acumen is quickness in understanding and dealing with a situation. The term "financial acumen" is often heard describing people who are good with numbers and economics.

4. **E.** Nescience is ignorance or lack of knowledge. An accountant who doesn't know the tax code is definitely ignorant. My own accountant knows everything and tells me he has a photographic memory. I told him I had one, too, but that mine was always out of film!

5. **E.** Someone erudite is learned, scholarly. Did you note the second vocab word in the sentence, polymath? A polymath is a person of great and diversified learning, just exactly what quiz shows want.

6. **B.** A resourceful person is able to deal creatively and effectively with problems and difficulties.

   Bonus trivia: What's a *pangram?* It's a sentence that contains every letter ("pan" means all) of the alphabet. The most commonly known pangram is "The quick brown fox jumps over the lazy dog." When I was taking typing, I had a particularly interesting teacher who taught us pangrams like, "Pack my box with five dozen liquor jugs."

7. **A.** Folly is a lack of understanding or sense, foolishness. It's folly to teach material that's over the heads of students.

   Bonus: What's *abecedarian*? It's pronounced A-B-C-darian and it means "simple as ABC" or, in other words, elementary. It can also mean pertaining to the alphabet, as in "The first graders enjoyed their abecedarian lessons, shouting out the letters as the teacher pointed to them," but I personally find the word more fun to use in the simpleton sense. "I'm sorry, was I using too many big words for you? I'll attempt to utilize a more abecedarian vocabulary in the future."

8. **C.** A prodigy is a child of highly unusual talent or genius.

   Bonus joke: What musical instrument did the Ancient Britons play? Anglo-Saxaphones!

9. **E.** Incisive means sharp, keen, acute. An incisive wit cuts like an incision through everything to get to the truth of the matter.

   What's *self-aggrandizement?* It's the act of making yourself more powerful or wealthy, especially in a ruthless way. You see the word "grand" in the middle of self-aggrandizement; you make yourself grander when you practice self-aggrandizement.

10. **C.** Someone resourceful is able to deal creatively and effectively with difficulties. A person who can use whatever is at hand to fix a broken-down ride is resourceful.

Exercise three

1. **coruscation.** Coruscation is a sudden brilliant display of wit. If the candidate were to suddenly say something so brilliant that it wowed the interviewer, it's likely he would be offered the job on the spot.

2. **sagacious.** Someone sagacious is showing keen perception and sound judgment.

3. **pedant.** A pedant is a schoolteacher, or someone who puts unnecessary stress on minor or trial points of learning. I, by the way, did what the question above stated, corrected my boyfriend's sweet nothings and haven't heard the end of it since!

4. **obtuse.** Someone obtuse is slow to understand, dull.

   Bonus trivia: What is a *plew?* It's a beaver pelt or skin. The next time you see someone in a fur coat, ask sweetly, "Oh my, is that real plew?"

5. **befuddled.** To be befuddled is to be confused. People often look befuddled around me, because I am prone to puns, as you can see throughout this book.

6. **erudite.** Someone erudite is learned, scholarly.

   Bonus trivia: Want to find cricket temperature in degrees Fahrenheit? Count the number of chirps the cricket makes in a 14-second interval. Add 40 to the result, and there's your temperature (roughly). Why does this work? Crickets are cold-blooded, meaning their metabolisms are determined by the temperature. They move faster and chirp faster as the temperature gets warmer.

7. **astute.** An astute criminal is cunning, having a clever or shrewd mind.

   Did you catch the extra vocabulary word in the question: eluding? To *elude* is to avoid or escape by cunning or quickness. The root *lude* comes from the Latin *ludere,* meaning to play. You see *lude* in such words as *prelude* (literally, to play beforehand, but in more common sense, an introduction, something before the principal event) and *interlude* (literally, between the play, but in a more common sense, anything that fills time between two events). And yes, even though the word is rare, you may hear of such a thing as a *postlude.* It's a musical selection that concludes a performance, such as the organ music that plays as you're exiting a church after the service.

8. **omniscient.** *Scien* is a root meaning knowledge; *omni–* is a prefix meaning "all." Someone omniscient knows everything.

9. **resourceful.** Someone resourceful makes good use of the available resources and is able to deal creatively and effectively with problems and difficulties.

   Bonus joke (which you have to say aloud to understand): A patient tells his doctor of his recurring dream that he's a wigwam on weeknights and a tepee on weekends. The doctor says, "Oh, your problem is easy to spot: You're two tents!"

10. **pedant.** A pedant is a schoolteacher, especially one who puts unnecessary stress on minor or trivial points of learning.

Stop that right now!

When I was in college, the girls in my sorority decided we didn't want anything as *pedestrian* (commonplace) as a stop sign in front of our house. Instead, we made our own signs with some of the following words on them. They worked: Everyone stopped to try to figure out what the heck was going on!

✔ *abeyance* (uh *bay* unce): temporary suspension.

✔ *cessation* (rhymes with, mess *sta*tion): stopping, ceasing.

✔ *desist* (rhymes with, see *wrist*): to stop, abstain, cease from.

✔ *deter* (rhymes with, see *fur*): to stop or discourage a person from doing something.

✔ *refrain* (rhymes with, see *train*): to hold back, stop from doing.

✔ *surcease* (rhymes with, fur *crease*): an end or cessation.

Chapter 10

Couch Potatoes Need Love, Too: Words of Energy and Laziness

• •

Words in This Chapter

- animated
- celerity
- dawdle
- dilatory
- dynamic
- ebullient
- effervescent
- enervated
- expedite
- indolent
- laggard
- languid

- lassitude
- lethargic
- listless
- peripatetic
- precipitate
- procrastinate
- sluggish
- somnolent
- soporific
- torpor
- vim
- vivacious

• •

There are two types of people in this world: Those who can't pass a couch without wanting to take a nap on it, and those who can't pass a couch without wanting to bench press it. This chapter introduces you to words you can use to describe both types.

Examining New Vocabulary Words That Are Full of Energy

Use all that mental energy you've been saving up over the years to attack and master the words in this chapter. The couch will still be there waiting for you when you're done.

animated (rhymes with, *ban* him wait Ed): lively, vigorous, spirited.

> *The two debaters got into such an animated argument that the arbiter had to declare a ten-minute recess to let them settle down.*

Think of animation at the movies. When the artists draw Pocahontas or Buzz Lightyear and make the characters "come to life," they are animating the drawings.

Bonus: There's a second good vocab word in the example sentence: arbiter. An **arbiter** is an umpire or an **arbitrator** (a longer form of the same word): someone chosen to judge a dispute. You may have heard of a sports figure's accepting "binding arbitration," which occurs when a third party is allowed to make a decision as to the athlete's eligibility or paycheck.

celerity (rhymes with, so *there* kitty): speed, swiftness.

> *When my friend told me he had tickets for the Brittany Spears concert and would I go, I accepted with such celerity that he didn't have a chance to end the sentence with, "— ask Tiffany to go with me."*

The root *celer* means speed. In a car, you can accelerate (add speed) or decelerate (take away speed).

dawdle (rhymes with, *paw* dull): waste time by being slow or idle.

> *Noting how her son liked to dawdle on weekends, the mother joked that she timed his chores by the calendar, not the clock.*

dilatory (rhymes with, *thrill* a story): causing delay; slow or late in doing things.

> *Because my boss was dilatory in making the bank deposit, every check I wrote on my account bounced.*

You probably know this word in a more common form, dilly-dally. To **dilly-dally** is to waste time, to loiter, to dawdle.

Don't confuse dilatory with dilate. When your pupils are **dilated** during an eye exam, they become larger, not slower.

dynamic (rhymes with, try *ham* ick): energetic, vigorous.

> *Wearing the Halloween costumes of the Dynamic Duo, Batman and Robin attempted to live up to their names by cannonballing off the roof of the house into the swimming pool, causing an explosion of water that drenched everyone at the party.*

Bonus trivia: Speaking of explosions and dynamic people, the man who invented dynamite, Alfred Nobel, was a Swedish industrialist and philanthropist who created the Nobel Prize.

Bonus word: What's a philanthropist? *Phil* means love; *anthro* means humankind. A ***philanthropist*** loves his or her fellow humans and is generous and giving toward them.

ebullient (ih *bull* yent): overflowing with enthusiasm, high-spirited.

> *The ebullient young car salesman, when asked how he stayed so enthusiastic after losing a big sale at the used vehicle lot, said, "We Yuppies never weep; we Saab!"*

effervescent (rhymes with, deaf fur *yes* sent): lively, vivacious, high-spirited.

> *The effervescent girl became the head cheerleader even though she was a total klutz because her bubbly personality inspired the team and the other cheerleaders.*

Television features commercials for the denture cleaner Efferdent. When you watch the commercial, you see a tablet drop into water and create bubbles. Someone effervescent is bubbly.

enervated (rhymes with, *when* her dated): weakened, devitalized.

> *The teacher stated that he was so enervated from a long day in the classroom that when he stopped to think, he forgot to start again!*

Even though enervated energized, don't confuse the two; they are opposites. Literally, enervated means "out of nerves," as when your nerves are shot.

expedite (rhymes with, *hex* speed height): to speed up, hasten, facilitate.

> *In an attempt to expedite the physical, the patient had printed out a long list of his symptoms, including a sore throat and sneezing fits.*

Bonus joke: What direction does a sneeze go? A(t)-choo!

Don't confuse expedite, to speed up, with extradite. To ***extradite*** is to turn over a criminal or a person accused of a crime to the place where the crime occurred. For example, if a man robs a Las Vegas casino and runs away to Honolulu, the state of Hawaii may extradite the criminal back to Nevada.

indolent (rhymes with, *win* dough lent): lazy, idle.

> *The bloodhound was so indolent, lounging on the front porch, that Justin jokingly claimed the dog was seven months behind on his scratching.*

You may have heard of Dole pineapples. I remember in-Dole-nt by thinking that the Dole pineapples are in me as I lounge around, lazy and mellow, in Hawaii, being a beach bum.

laggard (rhymes with, *hag*gard): a slow person, one who falls behind.

> *The three-year-old complained that he wasn't a laggard in school; it's just that it took him so long to spell Jeremiah Wojciechowska that all the other kids had finished their tests by the time he signed his name!*

You probably use this word all the time in a more familiar form, lag, as in, "He was lagging behind in his studies and needed to stay after school for some extra help from his teacher."

Bonus joke: Speaking of teachers, what's the best thing about geography instructors? They always know their place!

languid (rhymes with, *bang* wid): drooping, weak, sluggish.

> *The overwhelming heat left everyone languid, especially the Inuit student who had just transferred to San Diego from Anchorage, Alaska where he had been used to temperatures below zero.*

Bonus joke: Speaking of Alaska, do you know why the people there wash their clothes in Tide? It's too cold to wash them out'tide!

lassitude (rhymes with, *gas* it, Dude): weariness, languor, listlessness.

> *Suffering from lassitude, the exhausted parents, shopping for their tenth birthday party gift of the summer, simply wrapped up some batteries and wrote on the card, "Toy not included."*

lethargic (rhymes with, Beth *barge* it): drowsy, dull, sluggish.

> *Sitting around after Thanksgiving, stomachs full and conversation desultory, everyone was feeling lethargic and couldn't be bothered even to fight over who would get to lie on the couch.*

Bonus trivia: The word lethargy is closely related to Lethe, the Greek river of forgetfulness. According to mythology, anyone who drank the river water would have a loss of memory. Wouldn't this be a great excuse for a bad test score: "Sorry, Dad, I did study, but I had some Lethe water by mistake, thinking it was Gatorade, and well, everything went out of my mind."

Second vocab word: desultory. *Desultory* means passing from one thing to another in an aimless, disconnected manner. When you chat about this and that, not sticking to one topic for very long, your conversation is desultory.

listless (*list* less): weary, spiritless, languid.

> *When their 16-year-old daughter was so listless she didn't want to go to the mall with her friends and preferred to stay home in bed, Mr. and Mrs. Tsang were so concerned they made an appointment with their doctor.*

A good way to remember listless is to think of having gone through a loooooong shopping list. By the time your list is done, you are list-less, and listless (weary).

peripatetic (pair uh pah *tet* ick): walking or moving about, itinerant.

> *The professional dog walker called his business Peripatetic Pups, and was known to walk as many as ten rambunctious puppies at a time.*

The root *peri* means around, as in the perimeter of a circle. Someone peripatetic is walking around (and if he has ten rambunctious, or boisterous, wild, unruly puppies, he's probably not so much walking in circles as being dragged around in circles!).

Bonus: The definition says that peripatetic means itinerant. What word do you know that's close to itinerant? Itinerary. An *itinerary* is your "walking around plan," your route or detailed outline for a journey.

precipitate (pre *sip* it tate): acting, happening, or done very hastily or rashly.

> *Marla realized she had been precipitate in accepting a date with a man she thought was a millionaire when she saw that his suit was not Sergio Armani but Salvation Armani!*

You may know that a *precipice* is a steep cliff. Someone who is precipitate is "rushing headlong over a cliff," leaping before looking and acting before thinking.

procrastinate (pro *crass* tin eight): put off, postpone.

> *Mrs. Guzman attempted to procrastinate as long as she could, dreading the moment when she and her husband — whose toupee looked as if a sheep had crash landed on his head — had to make an entrance into her high school reunion.*

I have never been around teenagers who didn't know the word procrastinate. When you think about it, this knowledge is logical, because the word procrastinate — preceded by "don't" — is probably the word kids hear most often from their parents.

sluggish (rhymes with, buggish): lacking energy, slow-moving.

> *The ridiculously slow basketball player was so sluggish that his sarcastic teammates nicknamed him "Escargot."*

Did you get the preceding reference? ***Escargot*** (ess car *go*) is the French word for snail, especially an edible variety. When you go to a nice French restaurant, you may order escargot for an appetizer.

In some old novels you may encounter the charming word "slugabed." A ***slugabed*** is someone who stays in bed longer than she should.

somnolent (rhymes with, *Mom* no lent): sleepy, drowsy.

> *The math professor's students were habitually so somnolent in the 7:00 a.m. class that he placed pillows on the seats, delighting the sleepy students until they realized that beneath each pillow was a pop quiz.*

I really had a professor do this one time. We nicknamed him the "Tooth Un-Fair-y" and stayed awake in his class from that point on.

soporific (rhymes with, cop or *if* ick): causing sleep.

> *Professor Zimmerman was complimented by what he considered his hip nickname, "Dr. Zzzzzz," not realizing the students gave it to him because he was the most soporific teacher on campus.*

Two roots, *sop* and *som,* mean sleep. Soporific is the most common word using *sop,* but many use *som,* including ***somniferous*** (putting to sleep), ***insomnia*** (inability to sleep; *in-* means not), and in the drugstores, Sominex (a pill that helps you go to sleep).

torpor (*tore* pour): sluggishness, inactivity.

> *The varsity players, knowing they were a better team than their opponents, were in such a state of torpor that they couldn't get the job done, causing the coach to send in the second string who could hustle much better.*

Bonus joke: When's the best time for a coach to send in the subs? When the court is flooded!

vim (rhymes with, him): energy, vigor.

> *When Tawny's father, getting ready to go for a long run, said he was starting his day with vim and vigor, Tawny thought he was referring to a new sports drink and energy bar.*

Bonus: If you ever watch some of the old Doris Day and Rock Hudson movies in repeats, you may catch one that displays a fictional product called Vim, which is supposed to give you energy.

vivacious (rhymes with, try *play* bus): lively, energetic.

> *Accustomed to a far more vivacious class, the phys ed teacher berated her students in terms they could understand, telling them they were playing as slowly as 22K modems.*

Feeling sleepy?

In this chapter, you find out that soporific means causing sleep and somnolent means sleepy, drowsy. How many of these other sleep-related words can you define?

✔ *narcolepsy* (*nark* oh lep see): The root *narco* also means sleep, although it is less common than *sop* and *som*. A narcotic, for example, puts you to sleep before an operation. Narcolepsy is medical condition marked by a frequent and uncontrollable desire for sleep. If you just can't keep your eyes open during government class, tell the teacher it's not because you were up until 3:00 a.m. at the party, but because you suffer from narcolepsy.

✔ *pandiculation* (pan dick you *lay* shun): This is one of my all-time favorite words. It's just for fun, not one you're likely to see on an exam, but certainly one you can get a lot of use out of in real life. Pandiculation is the act of stretching and yawning. If your mother is going on and on and on about something, you probably indulge yourself in a little pandiculation to express your boredom.

✔ *somnambulism* (som nam byou *lay* shun): *Som* means sleep, and *ambu* means walk or move. Somnambulism is sleepwalking. Knowing this word lets you come up with a great excuse: "No, I didn't mean to eat the last jelly doughnuts you were hoarding in the back of the fridge; you can't hold me responsible for something I did while somnambulating."

✔ *somniloquist* (som *nill* oh quist): You know that *som* means sleep, and *loq* means speech or talk. The suffix *–ist* means a person. Therefore, a somniloquist is a person who talks in his or her sleep. Be sure that if you are a somniloquist, you use the big, impressive words you've mastered in this chapter.

Vi is a root meaning life; *–ous* means full of. Someone vivacious is full of life, moving as if she were a 144K modem, not a 22K one.

As you probably deduced from the context of the sentence, to **berate** is to scold or rebuke severely. I remember this word by thinking that I would berate ("B-rate") someone who rated only a B when she could in fact easily earn an A.

$E=mc^2$: Practice Exercises About Energy

If you're still full of vim and vigor and not too enervated, take a few minutes to complete the exercises in this section. Check your work in the "Answers to the Exercises" section at the end of this chapter.

Exercise one

Directions: Select the appropriate word to complete the sentence.

1. Claire was known to (procrastinate/expedite) so much that she often could be found writing her essay on the bus on the way to school the day the paper was due.

2. The (lethargic/animated) personal trainer told her client that she should be outside training on a day so gorgeous it seemed faxed from heaven.

3. The company decided to name its new computer (celerity/enervated) to remind the public of the incredible speed of the machine.

4. The installer promised to (dawdle /expedite) put the linoleum in our new kitchen when he heard we were having a housewarming party in just two weeks.

5. Wesley was so (lethargic/animated) that he never worked out, claiming he got winded just winding up a conversation.

6. The mattress company claimed it had the perfect job for an (effervescent/indolent) worker, napping on the beds to show how comfortable they were.

7. Refuting the claim that he was a laggard, Yogi stated that he worked twice as hard as anyone else at work and was the most (animated/languid) employee in the entire Forest Service.

8. After receiving the operation that gave her a new hip joint, Mrs. Andropov was full of (lassitude/vim), eager to go out dancing.

9. The (vivacious/ somnolent) math teacher livened up his lectures by telling math jokes to his students.

10. Noted for his (torpor/ebullience), the school mascot customarily spent the entire football game doing cartwheels on the sidelines, running up into the stands to sit in cute girls' laps, and in general revving up the students' enthusiasm.

It's a common mistake

The next time you want to raise a supercilious eyebrow, give a disdainful glance, or in some way express that what was just said or done is too common for the elite likes of you, use a little classier word, like one of the following.

✔ *banal* (rhymes with, men *pal*): Banal means commonplace, dull, stale. A boring person is noted for saying nothing original but everything banal.

✔ *bourgeois* (boo *zwah*): Someone bourgeois is of the middle class; conventional. The exciting jet setters you read about in the magazines are not bourgeois; your neighbors and friends are bourgeois.

✔ *cliché* (rhymes with, we *play*): A cliché is an expression or idea that has become overused. Every generation has its cliché, from "That's groovy, man!" of the '60s to "Radical, dude!" of the '80s.

✔ *hackneyed* (rhymes with, *back* need): Something hackneyed is overused. The saying, "Have a happy day!" is hackneyed.

✔ *mundane* (rhymes with, fun *gain*): Given that mundo means "world" in Spanish, you may know that mundane means "of this world," in the sense of commonplace and ordinary. Brushing your teeth is a mundane activity.

✔ *pedestrian* (rhymes with, red *yes* tree un): Yes, a pedestrian is someone who walks, but the word has a second meaning. Pedestrian means ordinary and dull, lacking interest or imagination. A pedestrian paper shows no insight or perception and would probably be given a grade of C. I think of a pedestrian job as one you "just walked through," didn't put much effort into.

✔ *platitude* (rhymes with, *attitude*): A platitude is a commonplace or trite remark, but one uttered as if it were fresh and original. For example, if you and your buddies are bored, bored, bored and one of you says, "Summertime has a lot of leisure hours to fill," as if none of you had figured that out yet, that's a platitude.

✔ *prosaic* (rhymes with, mo*sa*ic): Prosaic means commonplace, dull, and ordinary. Prose, which is everyday writing, is more prosaic than poetry.

✔ *trite* (rhymes with, *bite*): Something trite is stale, overused, and no longer fresh and original. Something innovative at one stage, like wearing a baseball cap turned backwards, becomes trite when everyone starts doing the same.

✔ *vulgar* (rhymes with, *gull* grrrr): Ah, you thought this word meant crude and indecent, didn't you? Get your mind outta that gutter! While vulgar does have that meaning, it's the fourth one listed in my dictionary. The primary meaning of vulgar is "common and popular," belonging to or characteristic of the common people. English is the vulgar language of America.

Exercise two

Directions: Choose the best word to complete the sentence.

1. Although many people believe alcohol is a stimulant, it is actually a depressant that leaves drinkers more - - - - than they were before imbibing.

   (A) peripatetic

   (B) somnolent

   (C) dilatory

   (D) precipitate

   (E) ebullient

2. The castaway who had been floating for days became - - - - when he spotted a plane, screaming "May Day! May Day!" as loudly as he could, and waving his arms to get attention.

   (A) soporific

   (B) listless

   (C) indolent

   (D) sluggish

   (E) animated

3. The trademarks of the architect's - - - - style were sharp lines and 90-degree angles that made the houses look as if they were poised on the edge of the bluff, ready to leap into the ocean.

   (A) torpid

   (B) enervated

   (C) lassitudinous

   (D) animated

   (E) somnolent

4. Because the clouded leopard is in danger of extinction due to the deforestation of its habitat, the zoo director accepted with - - - - the offer of a breeding pair, hoping to start a breeding program as soon as possible.

   (A) indolence

   (B) vim

   (C) listlessness

   (D) lassitude

   (E) celerity

5. Mrs. O'Leary shed her usual - - - - and began screaming and yelling, jump-ing up and down, when she discovered that she had in fact won the lottery.

   (A) vim

   (B) dynamism

   (C) ebullience

   (D) torpor

   (E) animation

6. The - - - - pansy was drooping on its stem. It needed water and fertilizer if it were going to survive another day.

   (A) precipitate

   (B) procrastinating

   (C) vivacious

   (D) languid

   (E) dawdling

7. Because the worker was paid by the hour, not the job, it wasn't uncom-mon for her to - - - - and take more time than was absolutely necessary.

   (A) dawdle

   (B) enervate

   (C) expedite

   (D) precipitate

   (E) effervesce

8. The economist labeled the sluggish market "a time of - - - -," as very little activity was occurring.

   (A) dynamism

   (B) celerity

   (C) effervescence

   (D) animation

   (E) lassitude

Words you may overhear in a gym

You may think that all you hear in a gym are grunts and groans, but if you listen carefully, you may hear the following vocabulary used to describe the people who are there working out.

- ✔ *brawny* (rhymes with, *dawn* see): strong and muscular.

- ✔ *burly* (rhymes with, *curly*): big and strong, heavy and muscular.

- ✔ *lissome* (rhymes with, *this* some): limber, moving gracefully and easily.

- ✔ *lithe* (*lie*-th): flexible, limber, bending easily.

- ✔ *narcissism* (*nar* siss is um): excessive interest in one's appearance.

- ✔ *strapping* (rhymes with, *clap*ping): tall and well-built; robust.

- ✔ *supple* rhymes with *coup*le): limber, able to bend and move easily.

9. Cynthia learned quickly that the mere fact she was working in a government position didn't mean she couldn't be fired for - - - - and resolved to work more energetically and enthusiastically at her next job.

    (A) indolence

    (B) ebullience

    (C) vim

    (D) vivacity

    (E) celerity

10. The tepid bath acted as a - - - -, relaxing Pavel almost to sleep.

    (A) peripatetic

    (B) soporific

    (C) laggard

    (D) precipitate

    (E) vim

Exercise three

Directions: Choose the antonym (word with the opposite meaning) for each word.

1. laggard: dawdler/ expediter

2. listless: (indolent/animated)

3. precipitate: (sluggish/dynamic)

4. torpor: (lassitude/vim)

5. dawdling: (celerity/lethargy)

6. lethargic: (enervated/vivacious)

7. dilatory: (expeditious/somnolent)

8. dynamic: (languid/animated)

9. precipitate: (effervescent/sluggish)

10. enervated: (ebullient/torpid)

Answers to the Exercises

Did you turn to this portion with celerity, rushing eagerly to see how many you answered correctly? I hope your reward is a perfect score.

Exercise one

1. **procrastinate.** If Claire is still working on her paper on the bus, she postponed (or put off doing) the work until the last minute.

2. **animated.** A personal trainer who wants to go outside and start exercising is lively, vivacious, and spirited.

3. **celerity.** Celerity is speed, which actually would be a pretty good name for a computer.

4. **expedite.** To expedite is to speed up, to hasten.

   Bonus joke: What do you call a little Frenchman who lets you walk all over him? Linoleum Bonaparte!

5. **lethargic.** Someone lethargic is drowsy, dull, sluggish.

6. **indolent.** A lazy, indolent person would be ideally suited for a job that required her to lie around all day.

7. **animated.** Someone animated is lively, vigorous, spirited.

8. **vim.** Vim is energy and vigor.

   The root *vi* means life; someone full of vim is full of life, lively.

9. **vivacious.** Someone vivacious is lively and energetic (*vi* means life).

   And speaking of math jokes, here's one you can use on your friends: Know how many seconds there are in a year? Twelve: January 2nd, February 2nd . . . .

10. **ebullience.** Ebullience is enthusiasm and high spirits, just what a school mascot should have. Torpor is sluggishness and inactivity. Believe it or not, there is a school whose mascot is the Banana Slug (University of California at Santa Cruz). I'm thinking that mascot may not have to be in top shape to perform his job!

Exercise two

1. **B.** Someone somnolent is sleepy, drowsy. The sentence is calling for a word that means the opposite of stimulated. Imbibing is drinking. If you speak Spanish, you know that beber means to drink. Another related term, *bibulous,* is a fun word meaning "fond of alcoholic beverages." Can't you just see some frat group calling itself the Bibulous Boys?

   Bonus trivia: You've heard of a magnum of champagne, right? Can you name the different size bottles in order? Here's the list for your next party:

   • Magnum 1600 ml

   • Jeroboam 3200 ml

   • Rehoboam 4800 ml

   • Methuselah 6400 ml

   • Salmanazar 9600 ml

   • Bathazal 12,800 ml

   • Nebuchadnezzar 16,000 ml (more than four gallons!)

2. **E.** An animated person is lively and spirited, which is just what you would be if you thought you had a chance of being rescued.

   Bonus trivia: The expression "May Day" actually came from the French *m'aidez,* meaning "help me."

3. **D.** Animated means lively, vigorous, and spirited. A house that looks ready to leap off a bluff is certainly spirited!

4. **E.** Celerity is speed (the root *celer* means speed). A director would jump on such an offer, accepting it quickly. Choice B was something of a trap. Yes, vim means energy and vigor, but the sentence would more logically imply speed rather than energy.

5. **D.** Torpor is sluggishness, inactivity. If jumping up and down is different than what Mrs. O'Leary usually did, she usually was torpid.

6. **D.** Languid means weak, drooping. Flowers that are on their last legs — last stems? — are languid. You can remember this word by relating it to a more familiar word, languish. The weak flowers may languish for one more day before dying.

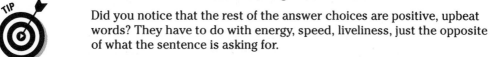

Bonus trivia: Pansies are named after the French word for thought, *pensée,* because of the way the blossom resembles a quiet, still face, deep in contemplation.

7. **A.** To dawdle is to waste time by being slow or idle. Many people dawdle over coffee in the morning before leaving to face the day. Of course, if you were going to have a fun day at, say, Disneyland, you would try to expedite (speed up) breakfast and get going quickly.

8. **E.** Lassitude means weariness, languor, listlessness.

Did you notice that the rest of the answer choices are positive, upbeat words? They have to do with energy, speed, liveliness, just the opposite of what the sentence is asking for.

9. **A.** Indolence is laziness, idleness. The kind of worker who has to resolve to become more energetic lest she be fired must be lazy to begin with.

Bonus joke: What do you call a worker for the government in a big Spanish city? A Seville servant!

10. **B.** A soporific is something that causes sleep, like a glass of milk, a warm (tepid) bath, or a boring teacher.

The root *sop* means sleep.

Bonus joke: Did you know that the planet Saturn actually has such low mass that it could float in a bathtub? Yeah, but it would leave a ring.

Exercise three

1. **expediter.** To expedite is to speed up.

If you pronounce the word in an exaggerated manner as "ex-speeeeeeeed-up," you'll remember the meaning. When you're trying to get a passport at the last minute before a vacation, you hope that the clerk is an expediter. A laggard is a slow person, one who falls behind.

2. **animated.** Someone animated is lively and energetic; someone listless is weary, spiritless.

3. **precipitate.** You are precipitate if you rush headlong or act too swiftly. Someone sluggish is slow-moving.

4. **torpor.** Torpor is sluggishness, inactivity. If the weather outside is so bad you can't open the door without being covered with snow and are content to stay in by the fire, you may suffer from torpor, or couch-potato syndrome. Vim is liveliness.

5. **celerity.** Celerity is swiftness (the root *celer* means speed). If you dawdle, you move slowly. I've often thought that Dawdling would be a good name for a sleepy, slow little town by Mt. Rushmore: Dawdling, South Dakota.

6. **vivacious.** Someone lethargic is drowsy, sluggish. You are lethargic on a hot Sunday afternoon when all your work is done and you see absolutely no reason to budge from your chair for the next few hours. Someone vivacious is energetic and lively, the type of spoil-sport who would probably come and yank you out of that chair to go to the gym.

7. **expediting.** Expediting means speeding up. Dilatory is causing delay, being late. You want the cable TV guy to expedite setting up your TV before the big game. You scream in frustration when he is dilatory, talking on his cell phone every five minutes instead of paying attention to the job.

8. **languid.** Dynamic means energetic and vigorous; think of a dog in the morning before her walk on the beach. Languid means drooping, weak, sluggish. Picture that same dog two hours later after a full morning running through the surf, chasing seagulls.

    Bonus joke: Why do seagulls fly by the sea? If they flew by the bay, they'd be bay gulls (bagels)!

9. **dawdle.** To *precipitate* is to act hastily. You meet someone this weekend and rush off to Las Vegas to get married next weekend. To dawdle is to waste time by being slow or idle. If you meet someone in high school, but don't get married until after your friends have grandchildren, you have dawdled.

10. **ebullient.** Enervated means weakened or devitalized. A marathon runner is enervated when he crosses the finish line (or as a runner friend of mine says, "Right now, I'm too tired to run a bath"). Ebullient means overflowing with enthusiasm, high-spirited. A moderate amount of exercise can actually revitalize a person and leave her ebullient.

Words you hate to see

Did you laugh when you read the heading of this sidebar and say to yourself, "Words I hate to see? All words on the SAT are the words I hate to see!" After you master the words in this book, you won't want to say that any more, although knowing the words in this sidebar means that you could.

✔ *abhor* (rhymes with, dab *shore*): to hate; to shrink from in disgust.

✔ *abomination* (a *bomb* in nation): anything hateful and disgusting.

✔ *animosity* (an nim *mas* itty): strong feeling of hatred or dislike.

✔ *detest* (rhymes with, see *test*): to hate; abhor.

✔ *execrable* (*ex* scribble): detestable, abominable.

✔ *odious* (*oh* dee us): arousing or deserving hatred; disgusting. (Don't confuse odious with odorous, meaning having a pronounced odor or smell.)

✔ *rancor* (*ran* core): continuing and bitter hate; deep spite or malice.

Chapter 11

I'm Not Always Right, But I'm Never Wrong: Words about Stubbornness

*W*hat do the following things have in common: bulldogs, mules, and toddlers who are going through the terrible twos? They are all stubborn critters. Anyone can say a mule is stubborn, but after you've gone through this chapter, you'll be able to use a much classier vocab to get the same message across.

Agreeing to Disagree: New Vocabulary Words

The words in this section have to do with people who stubbornly refuse to do what you want (how dare they!) or who intelligently agree to go along with your wishes.

acquiescent (rhymes with, *back* we yes sent): agreeing or consenting without protest.

> *The acquiescent college student agreed to finish the summer reading list, saying she felt that books were batteries for the brain.*

The prefix *ac–* means to, toward. **Quiescent** means to become still or quiet (you can see the "quiet" in that word). To **acquiesce** is to go toward quietly and without protest.

compliant (rhymes with, Mom *try* ant): yielding, submissive. The verb form is to **comply.**

> *Candice told her fiancée that she wanted to comply with the wishes of her soon to be mother-in-law and wear the same dress that Ruth had worn 30 years before, but that the gown unfortunately made her look so much like Bridezilla that something else had to be found.*

A compliant person complies, or goes along, with someone else. She is not stubborn, but readily gives in.

docile (rhymes with, *floss* while): submissive, easy to manage.

> *The horse was so docile that even a small child could ride her, making her perfect for giving rides to beginners at the dude ranch.*

Docile is from the same Latin root — *docere,* meaning to teach — as decent. A decent person has been taught well, been shown approved social standards.

dogged (rhymes with, *frog* Ed): persistent, stubborn.

> *Clancy doggedly pursued the woman of his dreams, following her for years even though she told him repeatedly that she kept him around only because it was illegal to dump toxic waste.*

Ever see a dog with a bone? You try to take his bone away, and Rover is going to hang on doggedly. You can lift the bone up and take Rover with it, still hanging on persistently and stubbornly.

dogmatic (rhymes with, frog *mat* pick): stating opinions in a positive or arrogant manner.

> *Although the debater was knowledgeable on the topic, his arrogant, pompous, and dogmatic manner of speaking, refusing to acknowledge, or accept any conflicting points of view annoyed his listeners.*

A *dogma* is a doctrine, tenet, or belief. You have probably heard people speak of religious dogmas, such as the Ten Commandments.

fractious (rhymes with, *back* shuss): hard to manage, unruly, rebellious.

> *The sweet-looking little old ladies from the Senior Center became a fractious bunch after a few drinks on their outing, running around and refusing to get back on the bus.*

Frac is a root meaning break. When you have people breaking free, breaking the rules, or breaking out, they are fractious.

Speaking of little old ladies, my own rule-breaking mother is fond of saying, "I'm 80 years old and don't need glasses. I drink right outta the bottle!"

froward (rhymes with, *throw* word): stubbornly willful, not easily controlled.

> *The froward child refused to step onto the plane unless he could go into the cockpit and meet the pilot, saying he wanted to see whether the pilot had a beanie hat with a propeller, like his favorite cartoon character.*

Bonus joke: Speaking of flying, do you know what type of luggage a vulture takes on a plane? Carrion only!

hidebound (rhymes with, *side* hound): obstinately conservative and narrow-minded.

> *When accused of being narrow-minded and hidebound, my father responded he'd rather be close-minded than so open-minded his brains fell out.*

When your brain is bound up, tied up and unable to open itself to new ideas, you're hidebound.

intractable (in *track* table): hard to manage, stubborn.

> *The lawyer realized that his client was intractable and would not take the advice offered but would insist on having the case tried his own way, much to the detriment of his case.*

If intractable means not easy to manage, what do you suppose *tractable* means? Right, easy to manage. The word comes from the root *tractare,* meaning to drag or haul. You use a tractor to haul brush on the farm; you use a tractor beam to haul a spaceship back to the docking station for repairs.

irresolute (ear rez so *loot*): indecisive, wavering, vacillating.

> *The house shopper was irresolute and couldn't make up her mind whether to buy a modern house or wait until she found the same kind of house she'd grown up in and looked back on with nostalgia.*

My grammar teacher used to tell me that nostalgia was like a grammar lesson: present tense, past perfect!

malleable (rhymes with, *gal* he able): capable of being changed or trained.

> *Gold is considered one of the most precious metals because it is so malleable that it can easily be bent or hammered into many different shapes.*

Think of using a mallet to beat something until it changes to what you want. Malleable actually does come from the same root as mallet, meaning hammer. Your coach keeps hammering the fundamentals into your brain, hoping you're malleable enough to change your bad habits and learn things the way he thinks is best.

obdurate (rhymes with, *blob* fur ate): stubborn, not giving in readily.

> *The president was obdurate when it came to his tax initiative, insisting that no taxes would be raised during his administration.*

Obdurate comes from the same root as durable. Someone obdurate is hardened and strong, durable, and stubborn.

obstinate (rhymes with, *blobs* tin ate): stubborn, dogged, mulish, not yielding to reason or plea.

> *Frustrated by his friend's obstinate attitude and refusal to compromise, Nicholas began braying at his buddy, saying he was as stubborn as a mule.*

Okay, you probably know that calling someone mulish means he's like a mule, stubborn. But what is muliebrity? It has nothing to do with mules. *Muliebrity* is womanhood, the characteristics of a woman. If you are *mulierose,* you are fond of women. What a great word to use: "How are you, Doug?" "Quite mulierose, thank you."

pertinacious (rhymes with, fur tin *hay* shuss): holding firmly and stubbornly to a purpose.

> *My friend repeatedly criticized me for eating meat, pertinaciously attempting to convince me to become a vegetarian.*

Bonus trivia: What famous vegetarians can you name? How about Leonardo da Vinci, Pythagora (he of the famous formula that plagued you during geometry class), Mahatma Gandhi, and Adolph Hitler.

pliable (rhymes with, *fry* able): easily influenced or persuaded.

> *The pliable passenger was easily persuaded to change seats with his buddy, saying that it didn't matter where on the plane he sat, because he was bound to get fanny fatigue anywhere.*

Think of someone pliable as willing to com*ply*.

recalcitrant (re *cal* sit trant): stubbornly defiant; refusing to obey authority.

> *The recalcitrant horse continually bucked off his passengers and attempted to kick every human who got close.*

Recalcitrant is from a Latin word meaning "to kick back." A stubborn horse kicks back when it refuses to obey commands.

refractory (rhymes with, she *back* story): hard to manage, stubborn.

> *The hair gel company decided to call its product an anti-refractory, because it tamed even the most unruly and unmanageable hair.*

Bonus joke: Did you hear about the anti-baldness drug? It was called a pate accompli! (Don't get the joke? Pate is a humorous term for the top of the head. The joke is a take-off on the expression *fait accompli,* meaning something accomplished or done.)

resolved (re *zol*ved): determined, fixed in purpose.

> *The student was resolved to get an A in gemology, studying her notes and going on field trips to examine various types of precious stones.*

Bonus joke: What do you call a counterfeit diamond? A shamrock.

servile (rhymes with, *curve* vile): like a slave, yielding, submissive.

> *The captive of the pirates pretended to be servile and go along with the whims of the buccaneers, but she was simply biding her time until she got an opportunity to escape.*

Bonus trivia: You know that a buccaneer is a pirate, but do you know the origin of the word buccaneer? It comes the word *boucans,* which were the wooden frames on which the men cured their meat.

submissive (sub *miss* ive): yielding; unresisting; docile. The verb form is to **submit.**

> *The young girl stood submissively as the animal expert coiled a snake around her neck, telling her that the animal was safe and wouldn't hurt her.*

Bonus joke: Why can't some snakes multiply? Because they're adders.

tenacious (rhymes with, when *play* shuss): persistent, stubborn.

> *The nutritionist was tenacious in telling her client that he had to lose weight, reminding him daily that he was growing out of his 501s and soon would have to look for 747s.*

If the nutritionist makes that same lame joke every single day, she's persistent in attempting to get her client to do what she wants.

Don't confuse tenacious (and its noun form, **tenacity**) with tentative. Someone tentative is hesitant, timid, uncertain, just the opposite of someone tenacious.

unruly (un *rule* he): hard to control or restrain.

> *The substitute teacher found the class so unruly that he was unable to do any actual teaching because he was so busy trying to enforce discipline.*

Note the "rule" root in this word. Someone who is "un" rules — or against or without the rules — is unruly.

I once had a substitute teacher who would get so frustrated, overwhelmed, and at the end of his rope that he would look at us and say, "You all make me wish I had a lower IQ so I could enjoy your company!"

vacillate (rhymes with, *gas* till eight): to waiver in mind, show indecision.

> *Dana couldn't decide what type of flowers to plant in her garden, vacillating between roses and tulips.*

Bonus trivia: Most people associate tulips with the Dutch. However, the flower came to Europe from Turkey in the mid-1500s, and the word tulip is derived from the word for turban, referring to the appearance of the closed blossoms.

We can't all be Michael Jordan:
Clumsy words to describe everyone else

Do the people at the neighborhood gym shake when you approach . . . because they're laughing so hard? Some people are gifted with grace and athletic abilities — but they're out spending those superstar salaries. Perhaps you're better described by the words that follow:

✔ *bungle* (rhymes with, *jungle*): to do or make things clumsily. You bungle a golf shot when you hook or slice it, sending it into a sand trap or a water hazard.

✔ *elephantine* (*elephant* tine): huge, heavy, slow, clumsy, or like an elephant. Although I think elephants are getting a bad rap here because many of them are quite graceful, if you move in a lumbering sense, you're considered clumsy and elephantine. Remember that the suffix *–ine* means similar to or like.

✔ *footless* (*foot* less): not efficient, clumsy, or inept. Never heard this word before, you say? The dictionary says "considered informal," meaning it's almost slang. It is a great word, however, sounding like the kind of trashy insult you'd yell at someone who just missed the winning goal in soccer.

✔ *foozle* (rhymes with, *whose'll*): to make or do something awkwardly, to bungle. You foozled your attempt to dance with the cutest girl in school when you tripped over the end of the tablecloth on the way to go ask her to boogey and managed to pull the punchbowl on top of yourself.

✔ *gauche* (*go* shhhh): lacking grace, especially social grace; awkward; tactless. If you're clumsy with words more than with actions, you are gauche. A gauche comment leaves you with your foot in your mouth, which is a pretty agile move, come to think of it!

✔ *gawky* (rhymes with, squawky): awkward, often from being disproportionately tall. A teenage boy who seems to trip over his own feet because his legs are so long they're always getting in the way is gawky.

✔ *inept* (rhymes with, win *slept*): clumsy or bungling, inefficient. I am inept at tennis, usually managing to run into my partner in every doubles match. The root *ept* comes from *apt,* meaning appropriate or suited to its purpose. If you are inept; that is, you are not apt, you can't do what you want to do, such as returning serve without colliding with your partner.

✔ *maladroit* (rhymes with, pal uh *boy't*): awkward, clumsy, bungling. Most of us make a maladroit effort to hop in a potato sack race at a picnic, falling on our faces. Note that the prefix *mal–* means bad. The opposite of maladroit is *adroit,* meaning skillful. Adroit literally means "to the right," as in right-handed. Most people are more skillful with their right hands than their left hands.

✔ *ungainly* (un *gain* lee): awkward, clumsy. A little puppy makes an ungainly attempt to jump on the couch, collapsing in a heap at your feet.

✔ *untoward* (un *toward*): awkward, clumsy. The dictionary says that this word is obsolete, but you may still see it in some old novels. An untoward young girl tries to curtsey and flops on her face.

wishy-washy (*wish* he *wash* he): indecisive, vacillating.

> *Giselle was a wishy-washy shopper, picking up and putting down item after item, driving the sales clerks crazy with her inability to make up her mind.*

My boyfriend tells me I never have trouble deciding what to buy: I purchase anything that's on sale. He accused me once of trying to buy the elevator because it was marked down!

yielding (rhymes with, *field* ding): giving up under pressure, surrendering, submitting.

> *After hearing her children beg for Rice Krispies for ten minutes, the mother, who was yielding in nature, agreed to serve that cereal instead of eggs for breakfast.*

Bonus joke: Did you hear about the illegitimate Rice Krispie? It had no Pop!

Yielding to These Practice Exercises

Yielding and compliant soul that you are, you'll have no trouble agreeing with me when I ask you to do the following exercises. The answers are given at the end of this chapter in the "Answers to the Exercises" section.

Exercise one

Directions: Choose the best word to complete the sentence.

1. Mikaela was noted for being - - - - before making a decision, changing her mind frequently and having difficulty making and sticking to choices.

   (A) yielding

   (B) vacillating

   (C) dogmatic

   (D) fractious

   (E) hidebound

2. The dance coach said that she preferred to acquire very young students because they were more - - - - than the older ones and could be trained the way she wanted them to be from the start.

   (A) recalcitrant

   (B) obstinate

   (C) unruly

   (D) malleable

   (E) intractable

3. Although many others tried to convince the astronaut that the plan for repairing the capsule in space could be done more quickly and efficiently a different way, she was - - - - in sticking to her original version, stubbornly insisting it was the best way to accomplish the job.

   (A) irresolute

   (B) pliable

   (C) acquiescent

   (D) servile

   (E) pertinacious

4. The - - - - student readily agreed to do all the vocal exercises her teacher asked of her, including practicing very difficult tongue-twisters to improve her enunciation.

   (A) froward

   (B) refractory

   (C) obdurate

   (D) fractious

   (E) docile

5. After hearing a speech from her father on how she needed to make up her own mind and not be so - - - -, following the crowd in everything she said or did, Tamara resolved to become more independent.

   (A) obstinate

   (B) fractious

   (C) servile

   (D) dogged

   (E) tenacious

Stealing with style

When your sister confronts you just after you've eaten the last bite of that jelly doughnut she was saving for herself, you can either self-righteously say you didn't steal it (and hope there's no jelly on your face to give away your lie), or you can attempt to confuse the issue by using one of the classier words given in this sidebar. With any luck, your sibling will be so bewildered by — or in awe of — your vocabulary that you can, well, steal away.

✔ **bilk** (rhymes with, *milk*): to cheat or defraud. The urban cowpoke took his ten-gallon hat back to the hat store, claiming he was bilked because the hat held only about six pints.

✔ **defalcate** (rhymes with, the *tall* Kate): to steal or misuse funds; to embezzle. A worker may defalcate with the office payroll, using it to buy lottery tickets he hopes to use to win big and replace the money.

✔ **filch** (*fil*ch): to steal something small or petty. You don't filch a Michaelangelo statue worth a million dollars; you filch a Michelangelo Teenage Ninja Turtle stuffed animal worth a buck.

✔ **kleptomaniac** (rhymes with, *slept* toe maniac): a person with an abnormal, persistent impulse to steal, not prompted by need. A person who is starving and steals a loaf of bread isn't a kleptomaniac; a person who is wealthy but takes a lotta' dough from the bakery because she can't help herself is a kleptomaniac.

✔ **peculate** (rhymes with, *spec*ulate): to steal or misuse funds, to embezzle. This word tends to be used more to refer to dealing with public funds. A government worker peculates the pension plan. Note the root *pecu,* as in **pecuniary,** meaning to do with money, or impecunious, not having money.

✔ **pilfer** (*pill* fur): to steal small sums or petty objects. You pilfer a few quarters from your mom's purse to buy yourself a soda.

✔ **plunder** (rhymes with, *blun*der): to rob by force, especially in warfare. Pirates plunder a ship, taking all the treasure chests.

✔ **purloin** (rhymes with, *sir*loin): to steal. You purloin, pilfer, and pinch (a great name for a law firm, doesn't it?) bubble gum from the neighborhood store when you are a child, only to get marched back by your mother and forced to confess your transgressions.

✔ **rifle** (rhymes with, *trifle*): to ransack and rob a place. You rifle through the drawers in your sister's bedroom, hoping to find her diary, which you can use to blackmail her forever.

✔ **swindle** (rhymes with, *spin*dle): to cheat, to get money or property from another by false pretenses. You swindle a friend out of his paycheck by selling him your old computer games, which he could just as easily download for free from the Web.

✔ **yegg** (rhymes with, *egg*): a criminal, especially a safecracker or burglar. When you're getting introduced to someone and find out, "He's a good egg," be sure you're not really hearing, "He's a good yegg."

6. The - - - - worker, after making up excuses and holding out as long as he could, finally started to do the job the way the supervisor wanted, showing all the enthusiasm of teenagers asking for more homework.

   (A) wishy-washy

   (B) irresolute

   (C) froward

   (D) malleable

   (E) acquiescent

7. The - - - - woman told her fiancée that she would not accept a diamond engagement ring, but insisted on having emeralds to match her eyes.

   (A) unruly

   (B) obdurate

   (C) irresolute

   (D) tenacious

   (E) pliable

8. The couple was - - - - in their insistence that their relationship could be saved, despite the fact that both families and several marriage counselors had recommended that they consider separation.

   (A) dogged

   (B) malleable

   (C) wishy-washy

   (D) docile

   (E) acquiescent

9. The attorney was held in contempt of court for telling the judge he was - - - -, too conservative, and narrow-minded to consider the facts of the case objectively.

   (A) irresolute

   (B) recalcitrant

   (C) vacillating

   (D) hidebound

   (E) pliable

10. The worker - - - - refused to alter his method of assembling widgets, despite proof that his method was slower, was more inefficient, and could cause serious wrist and muscle injury over time.

    (A) obstinately

    (B) submissively

    (C) irresolutely

    (D) pliably

    (E) acquiescently

Exercise two

Directions: Choose the antonym (opposite) of each word.

1. obstinate: (compliant/hidebound)

2. vacillating: (acquiescent/dogged)

3. froward: (wishy-washy/pertinacious)

4. recalcitrant: (yielding/fractious)

5. malleable: (intractable/submissive)

6. irresolute: (obdurate/docile)

7. tenacious: (servile/refractory)

8. fractious: (pliable/unruly)

9. dogmatic: (irresolute/tenacious)

10. intractable: (compliant/recalcitrant)

Exercise three

Directions: Select the appropriate word to complete the sentence.

1. Annoyed that the union representative was so (obdurate/pliable) in his demands and refused to compromise, the management representative cancelled further negotiations.

2. The little girl said that her dog, a (docile/recalcitrant) Corgi, would be easy to train to be a therapy dog.

3. Realizing that Kevin was (resolved/wishy-washy) about his decision to go bungee jumping, his parents gave up trying to talk him out of doing so and simply made sure he got the proper training.

Will work for vocabulary: Words about begging

On my drive to work, I often encounter street people with signs saying, "Will work for food." I've become friendly with several of them, giving them a little cash along with a not-so-little lecture on expanding their vocabularies. I laughed all day long the morning I pulled up to the light and saw one gent holding a sign that read, "Will entreat for entrees!" Here are some classy ways to beg.

✔ *beseech* (rhymes with, she *peach*): to ask for earnestly; to beg for. You beseech your friends not to go to Egypt without you, but to wait until you can cajole and wheedle your parents into giving you the cash to accompany them.

> *Bonus joke:* Where does an Egyptian park his camel? In Camelot!

✔ *cadge* (*cage*): to get by begging or scrounging. A child can cadge some cash from his parents either by begging them for it or by going through the couch cushions and finding it for himself.

✔ *cajole* (rhymes with, the *hole*): to persuade or prevail upon, to coax. When you cajole, you beg in the sweetest, nicest way possible. A girlfriend cajoles her boyfriend into going to the political rally with her when he'd rather stay home and work on his car.

> *Bonus political joke:* What do you call a republican turkey? One with two right wings!

✔ *entreat* (rhymes with, when *beat*): to plead for. Think of a dog entreating you for treats, begging for goodies.

✔ *implore* (rhymes with, him *sore*): to beg earnestly. You implore the teacher to change your B+ to an A– so that your GPA will be high enough to get you into your first-choice college.

✔ *importune* (rhymes with, him sore *goon*): to urge, ask or beg for persistently. Importune has an element of nagging about it. When you ask for something over and over and over, you are importuning.

✔ *mendicant* (rhymes with, *when* Dick can't): a beggar. In history class you may have read about mendicant monks. They are the begging monks, ones who don't work in the fields but travel on foot from place to place with their begging bowls, asking the faithful for food.

✔ *supplicant* (rhymes with, *yup* lick can't): one who begs or asks humbly. Supplicant is often used in a religious sense, as one who goes to the church to pray for intervention.

✔ *wheedle* (rhymes with, *need*le): to coax or persuade by flattery or endearments. You wheedle your parents into taking you to Hawaii for vacation, sweet talking them by telling them how wonderful they are and what a good job of parenting they are doing.

Speaking of Hawaii, it was there that I saw my favorite bumper sticker: "Maui Rain Festival. January 1–December 31."

4. The biologist (doggedly/submissively) pursued the moose, finally spotting him after hours of hiking.

5. The child psychiatrist assured the exhausted parents that the (fractious/pliable) behavior of their child was normal, because most two-year-olds were difficult, if not impossible, to manage.

6. Roger was (unruly/vacillating) in his decision on whether or not to acquire a tattoo, changing his mind every few minutes.

7. The school's music director was (wishy-washy/tenacious) over which musical to choose, alternating among *Music Man, My Fair Lady,* and *Oklahoma.*

8. Given how (acquiescent/fractious) all the athletes were on both sides, it surprised no one when a fracas broke out, sending several people to the emergency room with broken bones.

9. Moshe did an excellent imitation of his (dogmatic/pliable) father, pronouncing his opinions in an arrogant, overly positive manner.

10. Aware that years of living in cold climates and avoiding warmer ones left her boyfriend (submissive/hidebound), the girl didn't bother trying to open his mind to new places to go on summer vacation.

Answers to the Exercises

If you're looking at the answers before attempting the questions, shame on you! Go back right now and do things in the proper order. But if you've already answered the questions, enjoy seeing from the following explanations just how clever you really are.

Exercise one

1. **B.** To vacillate is to waiver in mind, to show indecision. If you change your mind back and forth, back and forth until you drive your friends crazy, you vacillate. (I have a vacillating friend whom I tell constantly, "You drive me out of my mind!" The smart alec went out and bought me a bumper sticker that says, "Out of my mind. Back in five minutes.")

2. **D.** Someone malleable is capable of being changed or trained. (Do you dance? The one time I tried, I was asked whether I'd recently had a rhythmectomy!)

3. **E.** Someone pertinacious is holding firmly and stubbornly to a purpose, as the astronaut here is doing with her repair plan.

   Bonus joke: What's an astronaut's favorite food? Fission chips!

4. **E.** A docile person is submissive, easy to manage, like a child who works hard and does what the vocal coach suggests.

   Bonus trivia: Speaking of vocal exercises, here's one that my speech teacher told me years ago he thought was the most difficult tongue-twister of all: Say "red leather, yellow leather" three times, very fast. Almost no one can get through three repetitions perfectly.

5. **C.** Someone servile is like a slave, yielding, submissive. A servile person follows the crowd. A friend of mine once was giving her own daughter this same "be more independent/think for yourself " lecture and cracked me up by saying, "If you saw a sign saying 'Wet Floor,' you probably would!"

6. **C.** Someone froward is stubbornly willful, not easily controlled, like a worker who holds out as long as possible against doing something.

7. **D.** A tenacious person is stubborn, not giving in. The woman knew that she wanted emeralds, and stubbornly insisted on getting them.

   Bonus trivia: Anyone can say emerald or emerald green. It takes a classy Dummies vocab pundit to say ***smaragdine*** (sma-*rag*-din), which means of emerald. "The movie star has smaragdine eyes that make him stand out on the screen."

8. **A.** Dogged means persistent, stubborn. The couple stubbornly, persistently insisted that their relationship would endure.

9. **D.** A hidebound judge is obstinately conservative, narrow-minded.

   Bonus joke: A musical lawyer I know never lost a case. Whenever he questioned the appropriateness of testimony with a long drawn out, "Objectiooooooooooon," the judge had to admit it was sustained!

10. **A.** If you are confronted with proof that your way is wrong and dangerous, yet you continue to do something that same way, you are obstinate and stubborn.

Exercise two

1. **compliant.** Someone obstinate is stubbornly dogged, not yielding. A compliant person is yielding and submissive.

2. **dogged.** Someone vacillating waivers in mind, is indecisive. A dogged person is persistent and stubborn, like a dog with a bone.

3. **wishy-washy.** If you're froward, you are stubbornly willful, not easily controlled. If you're wishy-washy, you are indecisive and vacillating.

4. **yielding.** A yielding person surrenders, submits, gives up under pressure. A recalcitrant person is stubbornly defiant, refusing to obey authority.

5. **intractable.** If you're malleable, you are capable of being trained. If you're intractable, you're hard to manage and stubborn.

6. **obdurate.** An irresolute person is indecisive, wavering, vacillating. An obdurate person is stubborn, not giving in readily.

7. **servile.** Someone tenacious is persistent and stubborn. Someone servile is like a slave, yielding and submissive.

8. **pliable.** A fractious person is hard to manage, unruly, rebellious. A pliable person is easily influenced or persuaded.

9. **irresolute.** Someone dogmatic states his opinion in a positive or arrogant manner. Someone irresolute is indecisive, wavering.

10. **compliant.** An intractable person is hard to manage, stubborn. A compliant person is submissive, yielding.

Exercise three

1. **obdurate.** An obdurate person is stubborn, not giving in readily or in this case, not compromising. Remember that the root *ob* means block. An obdurate person blocks progress.

2. **docile.** A docile dog is submissive, easy to manage.

   Bonus trivia: A Corgi is one of my favorite breeds of dog. If you've seen one, you know it's very short and low to the ground. The name Corgi is actually Welch. "Corr" means dwarf; "ci" means dog. A Corgi is a dwarf dog!

3. **resolved.** A resolved person is determined and fixed in purpose.

4. **doggedly.** To be dogged is to be persistent and stubborn.

   Bonus trivia: Did you know that moose is an Algonquin (Native American) word meaning "eater of twigs?" Given that a moose can tip the scales at 1,500 pounds, that's a lot of lumber!

5. **fractious.** A fractious child is unruly, rebellious, hard to manage.

6. **vacillating.** To vacillate is to waiver in mind or show indecision, exactly as Roger does when he repeatedly changes his mind.

   Bonus trivia: Tattoo is a word from the Tahitian language. If you were to learn the language, you'd have to memorize only 13 letters, the five vowels (A, E, I, O, U) and only eight consonants (F, H, M, N, P, R, T, and V). Just think: Tahitian tots don't learn their ABCs, but their AFHs!

7. **wishy-washy.** A wishy-washy person is indecisive and vacillating.

   Bonus trivia: Speaking of Oklahoma, here's something even my friends from that state didn't know: Oklahoma means "red people" in Choctaw (Native American) language.

8. **fractious.** A fractious person is unruly, rebellious, hard to manage.

   Did you notice the inside joke in the sentence? The root *frac* means break, as in a fraction is a broken number. A fracas (a noisy fight, loud brawl) *broke* out, resulting in *broken* bones.

9. **dogmatic.** A dogmatic person is sure of himself, convinced his opinions are correct.

10. **hidebound.** A hidebound person is narrow-minded and not open to new ideas. I had a hidebound boyfriend once. He was from Alaska and loved cold weather so much that his definition of summer was three months of bad skiing!

Chapter 12

Classy Chat: Impressive Words for Impressive Scores

. . . .

Words in This Chapter

- aberration
- abjure
- abstemious
- acme
- adjure
- Brobdingnagian
- candor
- coeval
- hackneyed
- halcyon

- inundate
- noisome
- noxious
- peregrinate
- perfunctory
- prolific
- salubrious
- serendipity
- superfluous
- turpitude

. . . .

Sesquipedalianist (long-word user) that I am, I have a bumper stick on my car that reads, "Eschew Obfuscation!" That's a classy (albeit pretentious) way of saying that I like to avoid confusion (to *eschew* is to shun or avoid, and to *obfuscate* is to make things more confusing or bewildering).

Sometimes, though, using longer, classier words can help make a point. In the case of your upcoming entrance exam, knowing longer, classier words can help you score points.

Making an Impression with New Vocabulary

This chapter introduces you to longer, more impressive-sounding words you can use to replace shorter, easier ones in every day. You'll also likely see many of these words on your entrance exam.

aberration (rhymes with, scab her *nation*): a departure or deviation from the norm. (Why say "abnormality" when you can say "aberration"?)

> *While Europeans are often fluent in three or four languages, an American who speaks more than two languages is an aberration.*

Bonus joke: A momma mouse and her two babies were out for a stroll, when suddenly they were confronted by a big cat, licking its chops. The cat eyed them greedily and said, "Meow!" The momma mouse looked right back at the cat and as loudly as she could, yelled, "Bow-wow! Ruff!" The cat scampered away. Momma looked at her babies and said, "See? Didn't I tell you speaking a second language would be useful?"

abjure (rhymes with, scab *sure*): to give up, renounce. (Why say "dump" when you can say "abjure"?)

> *My geometry teacher promised us he would abjure his sick jokes if we all got As on the final.*

Geometry joke: What did Humphrey Bogart say to the Greek mathematician? "Here's looking at Euclid!"

abstemious (rhymes with, crabs *them* he us): moderate, temperate, especially in eating and drinking. (Why say "doing in moderation" when you can say "abstemious"?)

> *Realizing the bikini season was only a few months away, Brittany became even more abstemious than usual, eschewing desserts and drinking only water.*

Abstemious may remind you of the related word, abstain. When you **abstain,** or stay away from alcohol, you are abstemious.

Bonus: There's another good word in the example sentence: eschew. (It is also at the very beginning of the chapter, if you were paying attention.) To **eschew** is to shun, avoid, keep away from. You eschew chewing foods you don't like.

acme (rhymes with, *back* me): the highest point, the peak. (Why say "top" when you can say "acme"?)

> *Wile E. Coyote, in his never-ending quest to annihilate the Roadrunner, used only the finest products, such as Acme slingshots and Acme dynamite.*

Bonus: Did you catch the extra vocab word in that sentence? To **annihilate** is to destroy completely or demolish.

adjure (rhymes with, *bad* sure): to command solemnly, often under oath; to entreat or appeal to. (Why say "order" when you can say "adjure"?)

> *The judge adjured the jury members to consider all the evidence presented to them by lawyers on both sides before making their decision.*

Be careful not to confuse adjure, meaning order, with *adjourn,* meaning to close a session or meeting. When the judge adjourns (closes) the court at 5:00 p.m., she adjures (orders) the jury not to discuss the case with anyone at home.

Bonus joke: Know why lawyers are always buried 12 feet under? Because deep down, they're good guys!

Brobdingnagian (rhymes with, Bob din *nag* he un): giant. This word comes from the novel *Gulliver's Travels:* Brobdingnag was a land inhabited by giants about 60 feet tall. (Why say "big" when you can say "Brobdingnagian"?)

> *The most Brobdingnagian herb in the world is the banana plant, which can grow quite tall in the tropics.*

Bonus trivia: Are you surprised that a banana plant is an herb, because you think of herbs as little teeny things grown in boxes on window sills? An herb is any vascular plant that has water-carrying vessels but doesn't have woody tissue. (Woody tissue is that in which the cells have died but still carry water.) How about that: vocabulary and botany all in one question. Could life get any better?

candor (rhymes with, *grand* or): fairness, honesty, or frankness. (Why "openness" when you can say "candor"?)

> *Marcia didn't appreciate John's candor when he told her that when she bent over in her new floral-patterned dress, she looked just like the sofa in the mall's discount furniture store.*

John either has a death wish or a really sick furniture fetish (a *fetish* is an irrational devotion or attraction to something).

coeval (rhymes with, no *evil*): all of the same age or period; contemporary. (Why say "at the same time" when you can say "coeval"?)

> *When teens talk to their coevals, they can use slang like "butt munchies" that adults wouldn't know means a spectacular fall, as if off a skateboard or snowboard.*

The root *ev* means age or time, as in primeval (of the earliest times or ages) and medieval (of the Middle Ages).

hackneyed (rhymes with, *black* weed): overused or trite. (Why say "too common" when you can say "hackneyed"?)

> *Sometimes the best (okay, worst) jokes are the hackneyed ones told by the five-year-olds, to whom the humor is still fresh, such as "Why did the turtle cross the road? To get to the Shell Station!"*

halcyon (rhymes with, *pals* he on): happy, tranquil, or idyllic. (Why say "calm" when you can say "halcyon"?)

> *In England, in more halcyon days, mistletoe always hung over the door as a sign of peace, and any visitor to the house was greeted with a kiss.*

inundate (*in* uhn date): to flood or deluge; to overwhelm with a great amount of anything. (Why say "overdo it" when you can say "inundate"?)

> *The kindergarten teacher found herself inundated by a flood of knock-knock jokes every Monday after the kids had watched cartoons all weekend.*

Bonus joke: Speaking of knock-knock jokes, here's my favorite one that's good to use to remember the word inundate: Knock knock. Who's there? Dwayne. Dwayne who? Dwayne the bathtub; I'm dwowning!

noisome (rhymes with, *boys* some): having a bad odor, foul-smelling, injurious to the health, harmful. (Why say "stinky" when you can say "noisome"?)

> *The noisome stench coming from the restaurant's kitchen made us decide we would rather eat somewhere else.*

noxious (rhymes with, *box* shuss): injurious, harmful to the health, or unwholesome. (Why say "bad for you" when you can say "noxious"?)

> *A friend of mine, tired of hearing her bad cooking called noxious, said she'd prefer to have her meals referred to as "detestable comestibles."*

Comestible is the ten-dollar word for food. If you speak Spanish, you know that "comer" means to eat, which should help you remember this word. **Detestable** is hateful, execrable, or odious. Every schoolchild who learns detestable remembers it by saying de-*test*-able to mean he or she hates vocabulary tests.

peregrinate (rhymes with, *there* rig grin ate): to travel or walk. (Why say "wander around" when you can say "peregrinate"?)

> *At a picnic, I always manage to work into the conversation my favorite piece of trivia: Heinz ketchup peregrinates out of the bottle at 25 miles per year.*

perfunctory (rhymes with, her *funk* tore he): done merely as form or routine; superficial. (Why say "automatic" or "routine" when you can say "perfunctory"?)

> *The dating service counselor made only a perfunctory attempt to match the applicant, whispering to her secretary, "That poor kid couldn't get a date on a tombstone!"*

prolific (rhymes with, go *jif* ick): fruitful, abounding, producing many/much. (Why say "giving much" when you can say "prolific"?)

> *The prolific novelist wrote at least two books a year, much to the delight of her faithful fans.*

salubrious (rhymes with, gal *lube* free us): healthful, wholesome, (you may know a similar word, ***salutary***). (Why say "good for you" when you can say "salubrious"?)

> *When the English professor accused his forgetful class of reading too many comic books that were not salubrious, one student responded, "Yes, Prof, we're sick; we have the mnemonic plague!"*

You can guffaw at my lame joke (assuming you get the play on "bubonic plague," a disease that was called Black Death in the Middle Ages) only if you know the word ***mnemonic***, which means helping the memory. My favorite mnemonic device is "My Very Educated Mother Served Us Nine Pickles." That helps me to remember the planets in order of their respective distance from the sun: Mercury, Venus, Earth, Mars, Saturn, Uranus, Neptune, and Pluto.

serendipity (rhymes with, care in *dip* pity): luck or good fortune, especially in finding something accidentally. (Why say "luck" when you can say "serendipity"?)

> *Ms. Kozak named her junk shop Serendipity, explaining to her customers that she hoped they would be lucky enough to find exactly what they wanted as they sorted through her boxes and bins.*

Bonus trivia: Did you know that Serendip was the old name of Sri Lanka (an island off the tip of India)? The fairy tale, the "Three Princes of Serendip," was all about how three lucky young men had one good piece of fortune after another.

superfluous (sue *per* flew us): surplus, excessive. (Why say "too much" when you can say "superfluous"?)

> *The anatomy professor joked that a prosthetic appendix would be superfluous.*

Do you note the root *super,* meaning above or extra? The suffix *–ous* means full of, such that superfluous is "full of extra."

Hint: Ever see the hair remover for legs, Nair? On the bottle, it says, "for superfluous body hair," meaning that it's for hair you think is unnecessary or too much.

turpitude (rhymes with, *burp* it rude): vileness, depravity. (Why say "evil" when you can say "turpitude"?)

> *One time, when a parent thought I was teaching her son "number sex" instead of "number sets," I was accused of moral turpitude.*

That's a true story, by the way. Someday I am going to write a book called *Confessions of a Test Prep Tutor,* full of stories of the zany (crazy) things that have happened to me. (You'll find some of them in the short stories in this book, too.)

Talkin' trash

When your sports coach tells you he wants to hear some chatter on the field, he usually doesn't mean he is hoping you'll compliment the opposing team. Instead, he wants you to do the things mentioned here.

✔ *belittle* (be *little*): To belittle — logically enough — is to make seem little or less important, to speak slightingly of. You belittle your opponent's accomplishments in a school election to make yours look better by comparison.

✔ *besmirch* (rhymes with, she *perch*): To besmirch is to bring dishonor to, to sully. You besmirch your opponent's reputation by saying you caught him trying on the Cafeteria Lady's hairnet.

✔ *calumny* (rhymes with, *gal* yum knee): A calumny is a false and malicious statement meant to hurt someone's reputation. You calumniate an opponent when you say that he cheated on his exams.

✔ *derogatory* (rhymes with, her *jog* a story): A derogatory comment is disparaging, belittling, lessening someone's good name. The new derogatory nickname for your opponent is Hairnet Harry.

✔ *malign* (rhymes with, uh *line*): To malign is to speak evil of, to defame. Your opponent says he's had enough of your maligning him and drops out of the race.

✔ *traduce* (rhymes with, duh *goose*): To traduce is to say untrue or malicious things about; to slander. It can also mean to betray. You traduce your opponent when, contrary to the agreement you both had to run a positive campaign, you start spreading lies about his past.

✔ *vilify* (rhymes with, *will* uh pie): To vilify is to use abusive or slandering language about. You know that the suffix *–ify* means to make; to vilify is "to make vile," to make seem wicked, base, inferior.

Keeping Up Appearances: Practice Exercises

You may find yourself vilifying, belittling, and maligning me (to use words from the "Talkin' trash" sidebar) as you go through the following exercises. Check your answers against the "Answers to the Exercises" section at the end of the chapter.

Exercise one

Directions: Choose the antonym (opposite) of each word.

1. abjure: embrace/reject
2. salubrious: healthy/noxious
3. perfunctory: dutiful/meticulous
4. halcyon: turbulent/peaceful
5. peregrinate: amble/stagnate
6. hackneyed: clichéd/original
7. Brobdingnagian: little/big
8. abstemious: overindulging/refraining
9. superfluous: insufficient/excessive
10. candor: deception/honesty

Exercise two

Directions: Select the appropriate word to complete the sentence.

1. I promised my father that I would remain (abstemious/salubrious) until my 21st birthday, not drinking any alcohol, even beer.
2. The (prolific/perfunctory) author has written more than 30 books, averaging three a year for the past decade.
3. It was sheer (serendipity/coeval) that the penny I found in the gutter turned out to be very rare, worth hundreds of dollars.
4. The teacher would always (inundate/adjure) the students with homework during vacations, making him very unpopular with the teenagers, who just wanted to relax during their time off school.

"Honey, no one can tell it's cubic zirconium:"
Words about fakes and frauds

False teeth. Fake nails. Faux fur. The word is full of items that aren't the genuine article. It's up to you to recognize the vocabulary that lets you know something isn't exactly what it seems. The words below are a start.

✔ **bogus** (rhymes with, *go* Gus): Bogus means not genuine. Many years ago, before we actually had a two-dollar bill, the saying, "As bogus as a two-dollar bill" was common. Now bogus is often used in teen slang, as in, "That final exam was bogus; it didn't test anything we've learned over the year."

✔ **brummagem** (rhymes with, *come* a gem): Something brummagem is a cheap and gaudy substitute for the real thing, such as brummagem jewelry that's made up of rhinestones instead of diamonds. This word is a classy way to make a catty comment about another woman's jewelry: "Oh look, Lori's wearing her brummagem baubles again." (Brummagem is a corruption of Birmingham, a city in England once noted for selling cheap, fake jewelry.)

✔ **ersatz** (rhymes with, *her* flats): Coming from the German word meaning to replace, something ersatz is a synthetic (okay, fake) version of a product meant to replace something else. For example, "designer" colognes that sell at the swap meet for $1

each and supposedly smell just like the expensive colognes in the stores are ersatz.

✔ **pinchbeck** (*pinch* beck): Something pinchbeck is sham, a cheap imitation. This word, too, is often used to describe fake jewelry. I think a great name for a store that sells costume jewels would be Pinchbeck and Brummagem.

✔ **pseudo** (rhymes with, *you* know): Pseudo means counterfeit, pretended, or sham. The word can be an adjective, a noun (a person who pretends to be an intellectual) but is most often used as a prefix: pseudonym (fake name), pseudoscience (false science, such as predicting hurricanes by counting the number of rocks in a chicken's gizzard), and so on.

✔ **sham** (rhymes with, *ham*): A sham is a counterfeit, a fake.

Bonus joke (courtesy of a five-year-old): What do you find at the bottom of Shamu the Killer Whale's tank? Sham-poo!

✔ **spurious** (rhymes with, *fury* us): Spurious means false or counterfeit. A way I've always remembered this word is to think that if a man gives me a spurious diamond, I'm a furious woman. Forget the cubic zirconium; gimme the real stuff!

---

5. The actor had a (turpitude/acme) clause in his contract, saying that if he committed a crime or did anything immoral, he would be fired immediately.

6. The (noisome/hackneyed) reek that came from the sewers made all of us gag, except for the puppy who was eager to jump into the drain and roll around.

7. He claimed that the careless mistake was a mere (aberration/turpitude), and that he always double-checked his work very carefully.

8. The police psychic wrote a tell-all book, claiming that the (acme/Brobdingnagian) of her career was finding the small child who had been lost in the forest for three days.

9. The local newspaper editor was fond of clichés and (hackneyed/noxious) sayings, claiming they lent the paper a certain homey charm.

10. The comic (peregrinated/abjured) through the crowd, going slowly enough to lean over and tell everyone a folksy joke or make a cornball comment.

Exercise three

Directions: Choose the best word to complete the sentence.

1. The painter was noted for his - - - - landscapes, portraying calm and peaceful countryside scenes.

   (A) acme

   (B) perfunctory

   (C) coeval

   (D) hackneyed

   (E) halcyon

2. The novelist wrote an amusing "what if" story, portraying events that may have occurred had George Washington, Napoleon, and Bill Clinton been - - - - and met at a summit conference.

   (A) coeval

   (B) noisome

   (C) abstemious

   (D) noxious

   (E) superfluous

3. When asked what he felt about the scandal, the politician gave a - - - - "No comment" and refused to respond further.

   (A) prolific

   (B) perfunctory

   (C) noisome

   (D) Brobdingnagian

   (E) superfluous

4. When released at its own home, a homing pigeon usually will not - - - - but will remain content in its own domicile.

   (A) peregrinate

   (B) inundate

   (C) adjure

   (D) abjure

   (E) candor

5. We considered the lengthy explanation of the molecular structure - - - - to our design class, as all we really needed to know was whether the material would drape fluidly in long gowns.

   (A) serendipity

   (B) acme

   (C) superfluous

   (D) turpitude

   (E) noisome

6. The police chief intentionally chose the most - - - - officers he had to accompany the plenipotentiary, hoping to create an impressive and intimidating escort.

   (A) perfunctory

   (B) halcyon

   (C) hackneyed

   (D) Brobdingnagian

   (E) abstemious

7. A background check in case of - - - - and immorality is highly recommended for anyone who is going to be a teacher or work with young people.

   (A) inundation

   (B) serendipity

   (C) peregrination

   (D) acme

   (E) turpitude

Pompous words to impress pompous people

A friend of mine who runs a used bookstore tells a great story of the time a customer came in wanting to know where "the intelligent books" were. It turns out she wasn't looking for books on intelligence or the brain, but for big, fat, impressive-looking books she could put on her coffee table and make her guests think she was smart. These words are the counterparts of those books, "intelligent" words to impress people.

✔ *callipygian* (calluh *pige*-ee un): Callipygian means having shapely buttocks. Yes, this is a real word. A famous statue of a young woman, recently out of her bath, turning around to check out her tushie, is called The Callipygian Venus.

✔ *feckless* (rhymes with, *reck*less): A feckless person is weak and ineffective, careless and irresponsible. Feckless would make an excellent name for a character in a novel, one who is a total loser.

✔ *horripilation* (rhymes with, sore uh pill *ay* shun): When do you suffer from horripilation? When you're at a horror movie, of course. Horripilation is the state of having your hair standing on end. When you're so scared that the hair on your arms tingles and stands up, that's horripilation.

✔ *minatory* (*min* uh tory): A minatory glance is a classy way of giving a "Don't-even-think-about-it!" look. Minatory means threatening or menacing. The bad guy in the movies always gets a close up of the minatory look on his face as he closes in on the good guy.

✔ *opprobrium* (oh *pro* bree um): Done something you're ashamed of? Be prepared to receive opprobrium from your parents and friends. Opprobrium is the disgrace attached to conduct that's viewed as grossly shameful.

✔ *quotidian* (rhymes with, pro *bid* he un): Quotidian means daily, either in the sense of recurring every day or something everyday and common. Taking a vitamin is a quotidian habit.

✔ *sesquipedalian* (rhymes with, yes we said *hale* he un): Given that *sesqui* means one and a half (as in a sesquicentennial is "one and a half hundred" years, or 150 years) and *ped* means foot, sesquipedalian literally means measuring a foot and a half. However, the word usually refers to using foot-and-a-half-long, or very long, words. I pride myself on being sesquipedalian!

8. Nearly overcome by the ---- fumes, the firefighters quickly donned their breathing apparatus.

    (A) superfluous

    (B) coeval

    (C) hackneyed

    (D) noxious

    (E) salubrious

9. After having many troubles with the used car he purchased, Mario - - - - from ever buying anything but a new car in the future.

   (A) peregrinated

   (B) abjured

   (C) inundated

   (D) peregrinated

   (E) adjured

10. Teenagers are a - - - - source of new words, creating dozens, even hundreds, of slang expressions that find their way into mainstream dictionaries within a few years.

    (A) hackneyed

    (B) salubrious

    (C) perfunctory

    (D) inundate

    (E) prolific

Answers to the Exercises

Of course, you were able to get so many correct answers to these questions that it would be unfair of anyone to offer you opprobrium (see the "Pompous words to impress pompous people" sidebar for the definition of this word!).

Exercise one

1. **embrace.** To abjure is to renounce, to give up (the prefix *ab–* means away from). To embrace is to accept, to take as your own; to welcome with open arms (*em* means inside).

2. **noxious.** Something salubrious is healthful, wholesome, or good for you (*sal–* means health; *–ous* means full of). Something noxious is poisonous or harmful.

3. **meticulous.** Something perfunctory is done without much enthusiasm or is done as a matter of routine. Something meticulous is done with much care and attention to detail. A free grocery-store heath checkup given as a store promotion is perfunctory; an exam given by a surgeon prior to operating is meticulous.

Bonus joke: What did the surgeon say to the class clown? "That's enough out of you!"

4. **turbulent.** Something halcyon is tranquil or peaceful, as in a halcyon afternoon spent swinging in a hammock. A turbulent time is full of commotion or wild disorder, as in the craziness and chaos that erupts when your three dogs chasing a cat all jump on top of you and turn the hammock over, trapping the lot of you in a cocoon of claws and paws.

5. **stagnate.** To stagnate is not to move; to peregrinate is to move. To amble is to move or walk leisurely. When you ramble through the mall just window shopping, you're ambling.

6. **original.** Something hackneyed is made dull and trite from overuse. Many sitcoms on TV have hackneyed lines that you can predict long before the actor utters them. A cliché is a hackneyed expression. (It's cliché to say cliché. If you want to sound more original and intelligent, try the synonym "platitude." A *platitude* is a cliché with attitude, a cliché uttered as if it were the freshest and most original thing ever said.)

7. **little.** Something Brobdingnagian is huge. I've always thought that a character named Brobdingnagian Bucks would be a good rich man on a sitcom or a soap opera.

8. **overindulging.** When you're abstemious, you abstain or do without. To overindulge is to pig out, to go overboard. As my father always told me when I got a gleam in my eye as I approached the buffet table, overindulging leads to over-bulging.

Are you sick of big words?

I'm sure you know an instructor who can't stand to use a small, simple word when a *pompous* (self-important), *pretentious* (making claim to some importance, ostentatious) one can be used instead. Here are some fancy terms you can use when conversing with that *pedagogue* (a pedantic, dogmatic teacher).

✔ *febrile* (*fee* brull): feverish (don't confuse this word with feeble).

✔ *hypochondriac* (high poe *con* dree ack): person abnormally anxious over health, especially an imagined illness.

✔ *languish* (rhymes with, *anguish*): to fail in health; become weak.

✔ *malaise* (rhymes with, pal *gaze*): physical discomfort early in an illness.

✔ *nocuous* (*knock* you us): harmful, poisonous, or noxious.

✔ *noisome* (rhymes with, *boys* some): injurious to health; harmful (this word also means foul-smelling).

✔ *valetudinarian* (valley tude in *air* ee un): person in poor health (don't confuse this word with valedictorian).

9. **insufficient.** A superfluous amount is excessive, too much. A redundancy has a superfluity in it, as in, "The Department of Redundancy Department" popularized by William Safire. An insufficiency (*in–* means not) is not enough or a lack of.

10. **deception.** Candor is openness, honesty, frankness.

You may know this word in a more common word, candid. A *candid* snapshot isn't posed; it catches the "honest" or real you. A deception is a fraud, something intended to deceive.

Exercise two

1. **abstemious.** Someone abstemious (*ab–* means away from) abstains or stays away from something, especially from drinking. Salubrious means healthful or wholesome. While a person may remain healthy from not drinking beer, he himself isn't salubrious, or causing health.

2. **prolific.** A prolific writer writes a lot, has a profusion of production. Perfunctory means dutiful, done without much interest. If the writer doesn't care about her subject, she may do a perfunctory job, but if she produces two books a year, she is definitely prolific.

Ever hear the term "nuclear proliferation," maybe in history class? It was used a lot during the Cold War when both the erstwhile (former) Soviet Union and the United States kept stockpiling more and more and more nuclear weapons.

3. **serendipity.** Serendipity is accidental good luck. I had a girlfriend who got pregnant despite (nearly) every precaution possible. Had the child been a girl, my friend would have named her Serendipity, as she was an unexpected piece of good fortune. Luckily for the child, he was a son (who was named Rufus, meaning red or red-haired . . . you be the judge which name was more, uh, special). Coeval means contemporary, of the same age or time.

4. **inundate.** To inundate is to overwhelm, to flood. To adjure is to entreat, to ask solemnly. When the students feel inundated with homework, they may adjure the teacher to give them a break and abjure (do away with or renounce) some of the assignments.

5. **turpitude.** Turpitude is moral depravity, wickedness, vileness. (Wouldn't Turpitude be a great name for a bad guy in a video game?) A turpitude clause is pretty common, by the way, and is used to get rid of teachers who have tenure and sometimes can't be dumped any other way. Acme means the summit, the peak, the best, or the top. Getting fired for turpitude would be the nadir (lowest point) of a teacher's career, not the acme.

6. **noisome.** Something noisome is foul-smelling. Sewers are noisome most of the time. Hackneyed means overused, banal, or clichéd.

    Bonus trivia: Ever been to Paris? Did you know you can take the "Sewer Tour" there? It's true: You can hike through the sewers of Paris, a fascinating tour that I took years ago and have been recommending ever since. You want to be sure, however, to wear clothing you can discard later because the noisome fumes are definitely difficult to get out of your clothing.

7. **aberration.** An aberration is something abnormal, a deviation from the standard. Turpitude is moral wickedness, baseness.

    Remember this word by thinking of an Aberration Vacation, one in which you do something totally bizarre. I've been to Antarctica to slide down the snow and to Borneo to hike through the caves. Both those are not your normal tourist jaunts.

8. **acme.** The acme is the peak, the summit; the word is used metaphorically to mean the highest or best point. The best point of the psychic's life was being able to find the small child. (When I was in college, we hung a sign on the door of the psychiatry lab: "Telepaths wanted. You know where to apply.") Brobdingnagian means huge. The psychic hoped for Brobdingnagian sales for her book by bragging about her successes.

9. **hackneyed.** A hackneyed saying is a cliché, something overused, something trite. After hearing the hackneyed saying, "Keeping up with the Joneses" once too often, a friend of mine said, "To heck with keeping up with the Joneses. I want to drag them down to my level!"

10. **peregrinated.** To peregrinate is to travel, to walk, to move. My all-time favorite comic was Pat Buttram (if you get to watch TV reruns, you may know him as Mr. Haney, a loveable scoundrel from the *Green Acres* show). He had a birthday bit in which he'd say to the celebrant, "Ah don't want to say yer getting old, but ah hear the insurance company sent you a half a calendar!"

Exercise three

1. **E.** Halcyon means tranquil, calm. When you see a landscape with placid bovines (calm cows) munching in front of a Norman Rockwell–type barn, that's a halcyon scene.

2. **A.** Coeval means of the same age or time. The author wanted to write a story of what would have happened had the three men lived simultaneously and worked together.

    Don't think of this word as co-evil. There's nothing evil about coeval.

3. **B.** Something perfunctory is done as a matter of routine, without much care or effort. "No comment" is a perfunctory utterance, an automatic response.

4. **A.** To peregrinate is to move, to travel. If a homing pigeon is already home, it would have no need to travel. A domicile is a residence, a dwelling.

5. **C.** Something superfluous is excessive, extra, or unnecessary. Talking about the molecular content of the material was information overload.

   Bonus trivia: Nylon, the material, was invented by DuPont, which had headquarters in two cities: New York (NY) and London (LON). The combining of the names of the two cities led to NYLON.

6. **D.** Something Brobdingnagian is huge, giant. An escort of very tall, Brobdingnagian police would be impressive.

   Did you catch the extra vocabulary word in the sentence? A *plenipotentiary* is a person, such as a diplomat, given full authority to represent a government. For example, when an ambassador from the United States goes to another country to negotiate a treaty, she or he is a plenipotentiary.

7. **E.** Turpitude is baseness, depravity. Someone with turpitude has bad morals and probably should not be working with youngsters.

   A police officer friend of mine loves this word. He's always using cop slang and calling the bad guy "the perp with turp," meaning the perpetrator (of the crime) with turpitude (evilness).

8. **D.** Noxious means foul-smelling, unhealthful. Ever walk into a new store and have trouble breathing because of the smell of all the plastics and paints? You're inhaling noxious fumes.

9. **B.** To abjure is to renounce, to give up. When Mario decided to buy only new cars, he abjured used vehicles.

   If you chose E, you got two similar words mixed up. To adjure is to entreat or command. To abjure (*ab–* means away from) is to renounce.

10. **E.** Prolific means productive, producing much. Teenagers produce many new slang terms, terms that change as soon as the adults begin using them.

    Bonus trivia: Ever look at a slang dictionary, especially one from long ago? It's fascinating to read what terms we consider common, almost clichéd today, that were slang just a generation or two ago. Even more interesting, to me at least, are the terms that didn't survive: When's the last time you heard anything called "groovy"?

Part III
Story Time: Finding Meaning in Context

The 5th Wave   By Rich Tennant

"Your buddy says the two of you were peripheral to the incident in question. You just said you were superficial to the incident. Now which is it, peripheral or superficial?!"

In this part . . .

Okay, you have a choice when trying to improve your SAT vocabulary: You can open up a dictionary and start memorizing words in order, or you can read ten funny and interesting (I hope) stories that help you remember not just new words and their definitions, but how to use those words correctly.

Which do you feel like doing? If you're a Walking Webster's who chooses to do a little alphabetical reading ("I think I'll finish all the R words today"), you wouldn't have bought this book. If you're more into laughing as you master new words, have a good time going through these stories and adding to your vocabulary the fun and easy way.

Chapter 13

Donna and Larry's Big Adventure

. . . .

Words in This Chapter

▶ alacrity

▶ consternation

▶ dither

▶ hapless

▶ jaded

▶ lampoon

▶ parasite

▶ parry

▶ ravishing

▶ sotto voce

▶ tome

▶ wanderlust

. . . .

Do you like to travel? Have you ever been on a trip where so many things went wrong that all you could do was laugh? The same thing happens to the characters in this chapter's tale.

Telling a Tale

"It was ludicrous and absurd," Larry said, telling his guests about his recent vacation. "We just had to laugh. Who else would be so <u>hapless</u> and unfortunate as to get stuck in a broken-down taxi on the way from the airport to the hotel?"

Donna interjected, "And that's after getting snowed in and missing one flight out of Chicago and having a second flight cancelled for security reasons. We barely caught the third flight."

"We could have made an earlier flight on another airline if you hadn't <u>dithered</u> so much," muttered Larry <u>sotto voce</u>. "I've never known anyone who can get so confused over what to stuff in a suitcase."

"I heard that," said Donna, good-naturedly. "You're just so <u>jaded</u> after all the traveling you've done that going to India is no big deal to you. I, on the other hand, was so excited that I may have overpacked —".

"May have!" bellowed Larry. "There's no 'may' about it." He turned to his audience with an expression of <u>consternation</u>. "She carried a solid-leather three-ring notebook! What's wrong with good old spiral notebooks for trip notes? I did my whole travelogue in one of those."

"Have you read that <u>tome</u> of his?" teased Donna. "It's not so much what he traveled through as what traveled through him!" She turned to Larry. "Page after page is about the food you ate and the bathrooms you had to enter with <u>alacrity</u>. You should have asked Butterbottom's bathroom tissue to sponsor your trip!"

Larry laughed amiably. "Go ahead and <u>lampoon</u> me all you want, but I'll bet you had a good time going through the notebook."

Donna nodded. "You're right, I did. I loved reminiscing about all the fun we had. Remember when that <u>parasite</u> of a guide kept telling me how beautiful and brilliant I was?"

"What do you mean, was? You're still the most <u>ravishing</u> gal around." Larry made a lecherous face at Donna.

"Forget it, buster," admonished Donna. "I know you're trying flattery, hoping to cajole and sweet-talk me into giving up our vacation to the Bahamas in favor of going to your cabin in the Wisconsin north woods. What kind of a vacation would that be? Instead of shoveling down delectable caviar and wearing rubber flip-flops by the swimming pool, I'd be shoveling snow and wearing rubber boots by the cesspool!"

Larry edged closer to his paramour. "But we could snuggle by the fire and kindle the romance again. You don't need drinks with umbrellas served by dumb fellas when you can have hot brandy with a flannel-shirted dandy. Hey, listen to me, I'm a poet!"

Donna put her hands up in front of her face, as if to <u>parry</u> a blow. "Okay, okay, you win. When you start rhyming, I know it's time to stop quibbling and curb my <u>wanderlust</u>. Go ahead and start brushing up your fire-making skills, you overgrown Boy Scout. North woods, here we come!"

Larry gave Donna a bear hug, then pursed his lips and shook his head. "I can't believe you'd give in so easily. I guess I didn't need to go to the travel agency this morning and get these two tickets —".

Donna grabbed the folder out of Larry's hand, opened it, and let out a scream. "I get to be a Bahama Mamma after all! Wonderful! Now, where did I put that bikini of mine?"

As Donna left the room, Larry turned to his guests and gave a big grin and a thumbs up. "Looks like we *both* win!"

Beyond Words: Defining the New Vocabulary

As you read through the story, did you understand the words as they were used in context? This section gives you the definitions, to help you fine-tune your knowledge.

alacrity (rhymes with, a *black* city): eager willingness or readiness. You accept with alacrity an offer to have someone do your homework for you, freeing you to go to the party.

consternation (cons stir *na*tion): great fear or shock that leaves one feeling helpless or bewildered. When you get the news that the teacher has lost all the exams and you have to take them over again (when you have already forgotten everything you crammed in your brain the night before the test), you may look at her with consternation.

Some students have told me that they think this word means "with sternness" because of the "con." Consternation and stern are not related; don't confuse the two on the exam.

dither (rhymes with, *with* her): to be indecisive, vacillate, or waver. If Donna was dithering, she was nervously going back and forth, changing her mind about what to pack, wasting a lot of time in a confused condition.

hapless (rhymes with, *cap* less): unfortunate, unlucky. The root *hap* means luck; a hapless person is luckless. You sometimes hear the expression "the hapless victim of a crime," meaning the unlucky person who got ripped off.

jaded (rhymes with, *faded*): tired, worn out, wearied, or satiated as from overindulgence. A jaded person has been there, done that. If your friend from Kansas visits you in San Diego, she may get all excited over seeing the ocean, but you're so jaded you say, "It's big, it's blue, it's there. Ho hum."

lampoon (rhymes with, cram *soon*): to ridicule or attack. You lampoon your buddy when you make fun of him, posting a picture of his head on Pamela Lee's body on the Internet, complete with a love poem extolling (praising) his "unique beauty."

parasite (rhymes with, *hair* a sight): a person who flatters in exchange for free meals or other items. A parasite is a kiss-up, someone who always tells you how wonderful you are in hopes that you'll give him something. A tour guide who works for tips would kiss-up big time.

You probably know the word parasite from biology class. In biology, a parasite is a plant or animal that lives on or in an organism, usually without benefit to the host.

parry (rhymes with, *hairy*): to ward off or deflect. A fencer parries a blow with a sword. A good witness in court may be clever enough to parry some questions that she doesn't want to answer. The evasive reply itself is called the parry.

ravishing (rhymes with, *lavish* sing): causing great joy or delight; entrancing. Larry was telling Donna that she made him one happy man.

sotto voce (so toe *voh* chay): in an undertone, so as not to be overheard. When you mutter something under your breath, you say it sotto voce, which is Latin for under the voice.

tome (rhymes with, *home*): a book, especially a large, scholarly, or ponderous one. A paperback you stick into your bag to go to the beach isn't a tome. A huge physics book that practically throws your back out every time you lift it is a tome.

wanderlust (*wander* lust): an impulse, longing, or urge to wander or travel. During Spring Break, you may have a wanderlust that sends you to Daytona Beach, Florida or to San Diego, California, to go surfing.

Exercising Your New Vocabulary

Directions: Match the word with its definition.

1. lampoon		a. a large, scholarly book	
2. jaded		b. entrancing; causing joy or delight	
3. ravishing		c. in an undertone	
4. wanderlust		d. to ward off or deflect	
5. sotto voce		e. tired, satiated	
6. tome		f. one who seeks favor by flattering	
7. dither		g. to ridicule or attack	
8. hapless		h. great fear or shock	
9. consternation		i. unfortunate, unlucky	
10. parry		j. to be indecisive; waver	
11. alacrity		k. eager willingness or readiness	
12. parasite		l. an urge to travel	

Answers to the Exercise

1. g	4. l	7. j	10. d
2. e	5. c	8. i	11. k
3. b	6. a	9. h	12. f

Chapter 14

All President and Accounted For

• •

Words in This Chapter

▶ affable

▶ corroborating

▶ dissertation

▶ erstwhile

▶ hiatus

▶ irony

▶ lobbyist

▶ pragmatic

▶ proffer

▶ promulgate

▶ protocol

▶ punctiliously

• •

*H*ave you ever daydreamed about what you and your friends at school will be like in ten or twenty years? You probably know someone you're sure will be a professional athlete or someone else who is going to discover a cure for cancer. The story in this chapter is about a student I know who will probably grow up to be president.

Not the Same Old Story

President Craig Kessler surreptitiously stole a glance at the beautiful <u>lobbyist</u> who was walking into the Oval Office, then looked down and pretended to be working on some papers at his desk, following <u>protocol</u> by waiting for the aide to introduce the lady.

"Mr. President, may I present Dr. Wisniewski," the aide said.

Craig stood up <u>punctiliously</u>. "No need for introductions, Julie; I've known Joy since high school." He <u>proffered</u> his hand and motioned toward the chairs. "Sit down and let's catch up. Well, well, who would have thought all those years ago that you'd become a famous surgeon and the president of the American Medical Association, no less, and that I, well, that I'd be here!"

Joy gave a modest laugh. "Famous is too generous of a description of me, Mr. President, but it's nice to know you haven't changed from your old <u>affable</u> self. I'm hoping you're as <u>pragmatic</u> as you were in high school and can see the practical importance of this new health-care bill."

President Kessler leaned back in his chair. "You're still all business, aren't you? So much for small talk. Yes, I was told by my advisors that you want me to <u>promulgate</u> a plan letting all high school seniors take two weeks off as mental health days just before the SAT. Tell me your reasons for this <u>hiatus</u>."

"Mr. President, I present not just a theory but <u>corroborating</u> evidence that students get little to no real schoolwork done in the weeks leading up to the SAT. Even students with outstanding academic records let their work slip at that time. Why not allow the students to take the time off?"

President Kessler said, "Do you see the <u>irony</u> of cutting school to study for a test to get you into school? I have serious concerns about this proposal."

Joy leaned forward, flirting a bit with her <u>erstwhile</u> schoolmate. "Surely the most powerful man in the world can get a little bill like this passed!"

The president grinned, realizing exactly what his friend was trying to do. "It's true, I could get the bill passed, but I'll need more information. Tell you what, if you'll write up a brief report — a *brief* report, Joy, not a <u>dissertation</u>! — I'll read it and make my decision later." With that the president leaned forward to shake Joy's hand, signaling the meeting had terminated.

"Why Mr. President, I know you have better manners than that." Craig looked startled, but Joy continued, "When you are saying goodbye to a lady, you should get up. Get up. Get up!"

"Whaaaa?" Craig lifted his head groggily to find his friend Joy shaking him. "Craig, lift your head off that Calculus book and get up. You fell asleep and are drooling all over the book. It's time to get to class — get up!"

Exchanging (Vocab) Words

If you're not still shaking your head over the ending of the story, take a few minutes to go through the following material to double-check the definitions of the words introduced in the tale.

affable (rhymes with, *laugh* able): friendly, pleasant, and easy to talk to. An affable person is approachable and has many buddies.

Think of affable as af-friend-able, to help you remember the "friendly" aspect of the definition.

corroborating (core *rob* burr rating): confirming, bolstering, supporting. If your mom doesn't believe your story that you were late because the car had a flat tire, you present the gas station bill for fixing the tire as corroborating evidence.

dissertation (dis ser *tay* shun): a formal and lengthy treatise on a subject. A person who is trying to get a Ph.D. writes a dissertation on her topic. Every school has an over-achieving student (like Hermione Granger in *Harry Potter*) who, when assigned a three-page homework paper, turns in a 30-page dissertation.

Did you catch the bonus word, treatise? A *treatise* is a formal article or book on a subject. The long report you've spent all summer researching and writing (hah!) is a treatise.

erstwhile (rhymes with, *first* while): former. You can threaten your current boyfriend by telling him he's about to become your erstwhile sweetie. When your parents ask whether you changed that C in Algebra class to a B, smile and respond, "I managed to achieve my erstwhile score!" If your parents don't know erstwhile, you won't get into trouble for getting the same score as before.

hiatus (rhymes with, why *hate* us): a break or a gap. You take a hiatus from your studies when you amble over to the @'fridge to look for a snack.

irony (rhymes with, *hi* Ronnie): a circumstance that's the opposite of what may be expected. The classic example of irony is if the firehouse burns down.

lobbyist (rhymes with *hobby* ist): a person acting for a special interest who tries to influence decisions. If you're sent to the school board to plead the case for vending machines in your school cafeteria, you are a lobbyist for the cola cause.

This word derives from the practice of meeting with legislators in the lobby, confronting them and trying to get them to hear your plea or decide in your favor.

pragmatic (rhymes with, hag *matt* ick): practical. While everyone would love to become independently wealthy by winning the lottery, most are pragmatic enough to realize the chances of doing so are pretty slim and that they'd better plan on getting jobs.

proffer (*proff* her): offer. When you offer someone your friendship, you proffer it.

promulgate (*prom* mull gate): to publish or make known officially. If your girl-friend is truly furious at you, she may promulgate the fact by writing an article in the school newspaper.

protocol (rhymes with, *photo* call): the code of ceremonial forms and courtesies accepted as proper for dealings between officials. Protocol is basically the proper manners or etiquette in official situations.

punctiliously (punk *till* he us lee): careful about every detail of behavior; exact. You are punctilious if you mind your manners so well you'd make your mother proud.

Testing Your Mettle with an Exercise

Directions: Match the word to the definition.

1. pragmatic
2. promulgate
3. protocol
4. hiatus
5. dissertation
6. erstwhile
7. lobbyist
8. proffered
9. irony
10. corroborating
11. affable
12. punctiliously

a. a break or a gap
b. a formal treatise on a subject
c. exactly, scrupulously
d. friendly
e. publish or make known officially
f. former
g. confirming, bolstering, supporting
h. a person working to influence a decision
i. offered
j. circumstances opposite of what may be expected
k. code of ceremonies
l. practical

Answers to the Exercise

1. l	4. a	7. h	10. g
2. e	5. b	8. i	11. d
3. k	6. f	9. j	12. c

Chapter 15

Attack of the Killer SAT Book

• •

Words in This Chapter

- agitate
- blanch
- copiously
- curtail
- dubious
- exculpate

- frank
- frenzied
- glower
- solicitously
- ultimate

• •

*I*f you ever meet me at a book signing or see me haunting the bookstore at your favorite mall, come up, introduce yourself, tell me a few good jokes . . . and ask to see my SAT scars. What are SAT scars, you ask? You find out in the story in this chapter.

Making a Long Story Short

"That is sooooo lame!" Josh glowered at me, as if it were my fault that the SAT math had so many tricks in it. "I can't believe you actually did that to me!"

"Hey, don't blame me!" I said, trying to exculpate myself. "I don't write the test; I just teach you how to recognize and avoid the traps that are lurking there waiting for you. Come on, settle down, and let's do the next question. You'll love it: It's even nastier!"

When Josh missed the second problem, his choleric temper got the better of him. He picked up his book in both hands and slammed it down on the table repeatedly. After the third slam, the book slipped out of his hands, and flew across the desk — slamming into my forehead! The edge of the book cut my temple, and blood starting gushing out. Head wounds bleed copiously, and it was only a few seconds before I had what seemed like a geyser of blood flowing down my face.

Josh freaked out. "Oh my gawd — are you okay?" He <u>blanched</u> and looked so pale that I thought for a minute he was going to pass out. He ran to the telephone, and I heard him call 911. I went over and grabbed the phone out of his hand.

"Josh, it's just a cut, no big deal. I'll put some ice on it, and the bleeding will stop. There's no need to panic and call 911, for heaven's sake." In the meantime, the 911 operator was saying <u>solicitously</u>, "Ma'am, are you all right? Do you want me to send an ambulance? Are you able to talk? Is someone threatening you?"

This was getting crazy. I had a <u>frenzied</u> teenager running around, and a 911 operator thinking I was being beaten and unable to talk <u>frankly</u> in front of my "assailant." I forced myself to calm down and explained everything to the operator. It took some doing, but I finally convinced her everything was okay, and no ambulance — or police! — needed to come. That done, I turned to Josh.

"Josh, please put some ice cubes in a towel and give them to me. All I have to do is stop this bleeding. I'm fine, so please stop being so <u>agitated</u>. Really, it's just like a paper cut, except it's on my temple."

I could tell by the <u>dubious</u> look Josh gave me that he didn't believe me, but he did as I asked. In just a few minutes, the bleeding had stopped. We started working again, but as soon as I put my head down to read a question, the wound started bleeding again. Josh jumped up and said, "I'm going to call my dad; he'll know what to do!" Josh's dad was a physician. I tried to wrestle the phone out of Josh's hand, but he was a burly kid and managed to hang on to the receiver. When he told his dad what had happened, his father wanted to talk to me.

I explained everything to Dr. Jones, who insisted I go to the emergency room of the hospital to get some stitches and a head X-ray and have it charged to him. I thought that was really insane, total overkill, but the doctor said, "Look, not only do we care about your health, we don't want you suing us later on!"

To <u>curtail</u> a long story, I went to the emergency room. The doctors didn't even bother with stitches; they just put a bandage on my head. I refused to let Josh go with me; I made him go home to calm down. Of course, I accepted his apology . . . but I couldn't resist having some fun with the guy. The next time he came over, a few days later, I had wrapped an entire roll of gauze around my head and looked like someone from a World War II hospital ward! Unfortunately, I couldn't keep a straight face and was laughing from the moment Josh walked in the door. But he had the <u>ultimate</u> word. He looked at me and said, "I don't know which is sicker, you or the SAT!"

Vocab Words that Stick in Your Throat

Did you understand the vocabulary when you read it in the story? Check your knowledge against the definitions given in this section.

agitate (rhymes with, *badge* it ate): to upset or disturb. You're agitated when you find out that your teacher is giving a pop quiz on material you haven't even read, let alone studied.

blanch (rhymes with, *ranch*): turn white. If you cook, you may know that to blanch vegetables is to boil them until they turn white. When you blanch, all the blood leaves your face, and you turn pale (usually with fear or shock).

copiously (rhymes with, *hope* he us lee): abundantly, a lot. You have a copious amount of homework right before the end of the semester.

curtail (rhymes with, *shirt* tail): shorten. Think of curtail as to "cut the tail" off of something or to shorten it. You ask your friend to curtail her story about her date when your dad tells you to get off the phone because dinner is ready.

dubious (rhymes with, *cube* he us): doubtful. The root *dub* means doubt; the suffix *–ous* means full of. You are wise to be dubious when a TV ad says that a certain product will make you lose ten pounds "without any exercise or diet!"

Dubious can also refer to the thing doubted. For example, you may think a painting is "of dubious authenticity," when you're not sure whether it's a forgery.

exculpate (*ex* culp ate): remove guilt or blame from; get off the hook. The prefix *ex–* means out of or away from; the root *culp* means guilt or blame. You exculpate yourself when you prove you didn't do something your mom is trying to blame you for.

frank (rhymes with, *thank*): openly, honestly, candidly. When you want a frank response to a question, you want your buddy to tell you the truth, not just say what he thinks you want to hear.

frenzied (*friends* heed): hyperactive, upset, running around like a chicken with its head cut off. The last day of school, all of the seniors are frenzied, zooming up and down the halls, unable to concentrate on anything.

glower (rhymes with, *shower*): glare, look angrily. You glower at someone who takes the parking spot you're waiting for.

solicitously (sole *is* it us lee): concernedly, showing care and compassion. You are solicitous toward a friend who has just been dumped, asking, "So are you feeling any better now?"

ultimate (rhymes with, *cult* tim ate lee): final, conclusive. The ultimate word on a topic is the last word. The *penultimate* word is the next-to-last word. Can you guess what the *antepenultimate* word is? *Ante* means before; the antepenultimate word is the "before the second to last word," meaning the third to last word.

Exercising Your Options

Directions: Match the definition to the word.

1. blanched	a. openly, honestly
2. frenzied	b. upset, disturbed
3. solicitously	c. final
4. curtail	d. shorten
5. exculpate	e. glared
6. agitated	g. hyperactive
7. copiously	g. hyperactive
8. ultimate	h. abundantly
9. glowered	i. remove guilt from
10. frankly	j. turned white
11. dubious	k. concernedly

Answers to the Exercise

	9. e	6. b	3. k
11. f	8. c	5. h	2. g
10. a	7. h	4. d	1. j

Chapter 16

Report Card Jitters

. . . .

Words in This Chapter

▶ alleviate

▶ aversion

▶ cow

▶ dolorous

▶ enmity

▶ equable

▶ loath

▶ nadir

▶ nullify

▶ obsequies

▶ pate

▶ trepidation

▶ visage

. . . .

*A*s a teenager, you probably feel you don't have too much in common with your parents. While you may be right, there *is* one situation that your parents suffered through just as you are doing now: report-card day. The following story should strike a chord with people of all generations.

A Little Bedtime Reading

"I have an <u>aversion</u> to murder and mutilation, especially mine," said Buddy. "That's why, because you inquire, I'm <u>loath</u> to show my report card to my parents."

"Don't let them <u>cow</u> you," soothed his friend Tori. "Let's make a pact right now. You show your parents yours, and I'll show my parents mine. Or better yet, I'll show yours to my folks, and you show mine to yours!"

"Your kind words do nothing to <u>alleviate</u> my <u>trepidation</u>, especially because your grades are even worse than mine. I'm afraid there's no reprieve for me. I'm a dead man. Dead man walking!" Buddy shook his head, the picture of grief.

"You usually do much better than I do. Are your grades really that bad?" Tori asked.

Buddy's normally <u>equable</u> <u>visage</u> turned <u>dolorous</u>. "Horrible. The <u>nadir</u>, to use just one of the gazillion vocab words I missed on the last test. I got an F in vocab. But it's not my fault. For some reason, the teacher has a lot of <u>enmity</u> for me. I can't figure out why."

Tori laughed. "You can't figure out why! Get real! You took his toupee, put it on Jane's desk, and yelled, 'Eek! A hairy rat!' By the time Jane got done stomping on it, it was as flat as a pancake. And as vain as Mr. Blubnut is, he was completely embarrassed, totally mortified."

Buddy reached around and patted himself on the back. "Yeah, that was a good one, wasn't it? Old Blubberbutt was really furious. But is his bald <u>pate</u> reason enough to destroy my future? If I get another F next semester, my chances of getting into a good college will be <u>nullified</u>."

"Your life will be nullified, if I know your parents. You'll be grounded until you have grandchildren. But you know, I really empathize with you. I think Old Blubberbutt has antipathy for me, too. I laughed when you pulled your prank, and he was convinced we were co-conspirators."

Buddy was preoccupied with his own concerns and didn't listen to his friend's rambling. "If I try to exculpate myself by telling my parents the truth, I'll just exacerbate matters, making them even worse. There's no hope at all. It's futile. Will you attend the <u>obsequies</u> for me?"

"Absolutely," Tori assured him. "I'll even deliver the eulogy. After all, what are friends for?"

Defining Vocab from the Word Go

If the whole concept of grades and report cards didn't make you too nervous to concentrate, you probably recognized a lot of good vocabulary in the context of the story. Check your definitions against those given in this section.

alleviate (uh *leave* he ate): lessen, relieve. An aspirin or other painkiller (like the medication Aleve) can alleviate your headache. Studying vocabulary until you are confident you've mastered all the words in this book can alleviate much of your anxiety over the SAT.

aversion (a *vers*ion): disliking for. You have an aversion to getting up at the crack of dawn on the weekends, your one chance to sleep in.

The prefix *a*– means not or without. You would rather not have, or rather be without, something to which you have an aversion.

cow (rhymes with, *now*): intimidate. Don't let the neighborhood bully cow you; instead, stand up to him.

It's easy to see the relationship between the verb cow and the noun coward. A coward is one who is easily cowed. What does a coward do when he cowers? He shrinks and cringes, as from fear. You cower when you see that bully coming toward you.

dolorous (rhymes with, *soul* her us): sad, mournful. If the professor has a dolorous expression as she passes back the tests, you can predict that no one did very well.

enmity (*en* mitty): hostility. You have enmity toward your enemies.

You probably noticed from the example sentence that enmity and enemies are similar in form. They do, in fact, come from the same root, meaning "not friend."

equable (*ek* wah bull): not readily upset, tranquil, serene. A person who is laid-back, mellow, not at all hyper would be equable. Think of an equable person as being on an equal level: not too high (hyper), not too low (depressed).

loath (*low*-th): reluctant. You're loath to open the letter from your former beau, unsure whether you are over him or her enough to read what he or she has to say.

Don't confuse loath, the adjective, with loathe (note the e), the verb. To loathe is to dislike, detest, hate. The words do come from the same root, but loath is a milder form.

nadir (rhymes with, fade *dear*): lowest point. If you practice for years to go to the Olympics, then are ill and can't participate the day of the big event, that day is probably the nadir of your life.

You probably know that the zenith is the highest point, as the zenith of the sun is at noon. The nadir is the opposite of the zenith. I've always thought Zenith and Nadir would be good names for twin characters who are good (Zenith) and evil (Nadir).

nullify (rhymes with, *dull* if try): make of no value, negate. You've heard the expression "null and void," right? To nullify is to make null, to void. When you have a marriage annulled (ended, cancelled), you nullify it.

obsequies (rhymes with, *blobs* he keys): funeral services. Many workers, on the first day of fishing season, pretend that they have to attend a family member's obsequies and call in for the day off.

Do you know the word obsequious? An *obsequious* person is overly willing to serve or obey. Someone who always says, "Yes, of course, absolutely, whatever you want, whatever you say!" is obsequious.

pate (rhymes with, *date*): crown of the head. Pate is a humorous word, often used to make fun of someone, especially someone bald. Before you walk out the door, go over to your dad and teasing ask whether you can rub his pate for good luck on your date.

trepidation (rhymes with, step bid *nation*): fear, apprehension. You have trepidation about going to the top of a tall building when you have *acrophobia,* fear of heights.

The root *trep* means fear. What, then, do you suppose you are when you're intrepid? Given that the prefix *in–* can mean not, an intrepid person is "not fear," or brave.

visage (rhymes with, *his* age): face. You look at the police officer's visage when you are pulled over to see whether you can charm your way out of a speeding ticket or whether he or she has that stubborn expression that tells you you're out of luck.

Practicing Until You're Perfect

Directions: Match the definition to the word.

1. pate	a. funeral services
2. obsequies	b. hostility
3. dolorous	c. face
4. nadir	d. fear, apprehension
5. cow	e. lessen, relieve
6. equable	f. crown of the head
7. nullified	g. sad, mournful
8. loath	h. intimidate
9. alleviate	i. reluctant
10. trepidation	j. not easily upset
11. enmity	k. made of no value, negated
12. visage	l. lowest point
13. aversion	m. disliking for

Answers to the Exercise

1. f	4. l	7. k	10. d	13. m
2. a	5. h	8. i	11. b	
3. g	6. j	9. e	12. c	

Chapter 17

The Boy Who Barfed on Me

• •

Words in This Chapter

▶ ardent

▶ dour

▶ gargantuan

▶ glutton

▶ lumbering

▶ mortified

▶ olfactory

▶ piscine

▶ raucous

▶ recuperate

▶ sallow

▶ vile

• •

The life of an SAT tutor is never dull. There are some times, however, when I could do with a little less excitement, as you'll see in the following story.

Spinning a Tale

Jake, normally my most <u>ardent</u> student, dragged himself into my office Monday morning with all the enthusiasm of Custer greeting the Native Americans.

"Wow, you look terrible!" I said to him. "Your face is so pale and <u>sallow</u> you look like a ghost. That must have been some weekend you had!"

Jake dropped his books on the table, and put his head on them. "Oooh, I don't feel so great. I think I ate my body weight in pizza last night. A few of us were listening to music at Mark's, and we killed three extra-large pizzas with the works. No one else liked anchovies, so they kept putting them on my plate, and I kept eating them. I feel as if they are swimming around in my stomach right now. Why was I such a <u>glutton</u> last night?" He gave a <u>gargantuan</u> belch, and muttered a perfunctory, "Sorry."

I teasingly shook a finger at him. "Leave it to you to overdo it on the <u>piscine</u> pizza. Can I get you something, like an aspirin or antacid? How about a soda, to settle your stomach?"

Jake shook his head, a <u>dour</u> expression on his face. "I can't drink a thing. If I even think about food, I feel as if my stomach is going to —".

Suddenly, his eyes got big, and he jumped up. It looked as if he were going to make a run for the bathroom, but before he could stop himself, he threw up . . . all over his books, all over the desk, and all over me! I was inundated with the most <u>vile,</u> noisome insult to my <u>olfactory</u> nerves that I'd ever encountered. "Oh, Jake!" I looked down and almost got sick myself.

Poor Jake was <u>mortified,</u> so embarrassed that his formerly pale face turned red. "Sorry, sorry, sorry. Oh no, here it comes again! Back off, Suzee, quick!"

I grabbed him and shoved him in the direction of the bathroom. For the next several minutes all I heard were the <u>raucous</u> sounds of Jake being sick in the toilet. He finally came <u>lumbering</u> out, his heavy steps echoing in the hallway. He picked up his SAT books (which I had cleaned off) and said, "Maybe I should just reschedule for another time when I'm feeling better."

I nodded. "Go home and <u>recuperate</u>. Eat something more <u>salubrious</u> than sardines before the next time you come see me, okay?"

Jake looked at me. "Oh no, did you have to say 'sardines!' Ooooh." The last I saw of Jake, he was making a dash for his car, his hand over his mouth, his SAT papers flying all over the place.

Getting a (Vocab) Word in Edgewise

I hope you weren't too grossed out from the story to pay attention to the good vocabulary introduced there. Check the definitions in this section to make sure you understood the words correctly.

ardent (*are* dent): intensely enthusiastic or devoted. If you have an ardent desire to play varsity sports, you're are willing to practice for hours every day. An ardent suitor passionately and enthusiastically pursues the object of his or her desire.

dour (rhymes with, sewer): gloomy, sullen. You wear a dour expression when you lose an argument with your parents and have to spend the weekend at home instead of going on a road trip with your friends.

Note that dour does not rhyme with "sour." The word is not dow-er, but doo-er.

gargantuan (gar *gant* you an): enormous, gigantic. A football player who is six and a half feet tall and weighs 300 pounds may be described as gargantuan.

glutton (rhymes with, *but*ton): someone who overindulges (a pig, in other words!). You may have heard the cliché "a glutton for punishment," meaning someone who keeps going back even though he knows he's going to get hurt (get punished) again. A guy who asks out a girl three times, gets rejected three times, and goes back to ask a fourth time, is a glutton for punishment.

lumbering (*lum*-ber ing): moving heavily, clumsily, and noisily. If you're *slumbering* (sleeping), you don't want to woken up by someone lumbering around the house.

mortified (rhymes with, *sport* if try): embarrassed. The root *mor* means death. When you're so embarrassed you "just wanna die," you're mortified.

It may help you to remember this word if you associate it with two other *mort* words: mortuary (where dead bodies are displayed for funeral services) and mortician (the person working at the mortuary).

olfactory (ah'll *fact*ory): of the sense of smell. I once heard a particularly stinky cologne described as "an olfactory insult." Your olfactory nerves are responsible for your sense of smell.

piscine (rhymes with, *fly* seen): like or having do with fish (you probably know the Zodiac sign of the fish, Pisces). The sentence is trying to be humorous, referring to the anchovies — fish — on the pizza.

raucous (*raw* cuss): harsh-sounding, unpleasant-sounding. The sounds of someone puking his guts out in the toilet are not too pleasant.

recuperate (rhymes with, the *soup* her ate): be restored to health, get well, and recover. You tell your parents on Sunday after the SAT that while you'd love to do your chores around the house, you need to stay in bed all day and recuperate from the test.

sallow (rhymes with, *shallow*): of a sickly pale-yellow hue. When you eat your way around the county fair and then get on the roller coaster, your face looks sallow by the end of the ride.

vile (rhymes with, *trial*): offensive to the senses, repulsive, or disgusting. A vile vial in chemistry class may be a smoking beaker of something stinky that you can smell throughout the school.

There is another meaning of vile: morally base or evil, wicked, depraved. You *vilify* (use abusive language about) someone who is vile.

Exercising without Taking a Step

Directions: Match the definition to the word.

1. lumbering   a. huge

2. ardent   b. fishlike

3. sallow   c. gain health

4. mortified   d. harsh-sounding

5. dour   e. enthusiastic

6. raucous   f. embarrassed

7. glutton   g. healthful

8. recuperate   h. moving clumsily and noisily

9. olfactory   i. of a sickly yellow hue

10. piscine   j. disgusting

11. gargantuan   k. pertaining to the sense of smell

12. vile   l. gloomy

Answers to the Exercise

1. h	4. f	7. c	10. b
2. e	5. l	8. g	11. a
3. i	6. d	9. k	12. j

Chapter 18

King of the (Tongue) Studs

● ●

Words in This Chapter

▶ aesthetic

▶ articulate

▶ chaff

▶ emulate

▶ gingerly

▶ haberdashery

▶ pedant

▶ resplendent

▶ saunter

▶ scintillation

▶ talisman

▶ virile

● ●

*B*ecause I tutor in Southern California, I see students at their most casual, in shorts and T-shirts. Every now and then, however, I'll get a fashion plate, a student who wants to stand out in a crowd. He or she usually does so with clothing, but I can always count on a few (as the following story shows) who let their jewelry do the talking.

Once Upon a Time

"Thooothee, I finthed all the homework you gave me." Greg, usually the most <u>articulate</u> of my students, sat down at the desk and casually wiped off the little trickle of drool that had run down on his T-shirt. "What'th the matter?"

I stared at him, and he gave me a big grin. There was a <u>scintillation</u> in his smile . . . and I suddenly saw why: He had pierced his tongue! He was wearing a big silver tongue stud!

I had been working with Greg for three months, and thought I had seen everything. There was the day when he looked as if a <u>haberdashery</u> had blown up and sent mismatched items his way: a red jacket, an orange T-shirt, and lime green jeans. I remember well another day during which he <u>sauntered</u> in, even more <u>resplendent</u> in a banana yellow shirt with day-glo pink surfboard stickers on it. No one could ever accuse Greg of being the fade-into-the-background type.

"Greg, Greg, Greg." I shook my head and laughed. "What on earth have you done to yourself now? Are you trying to <u>emulate</u> some Australian aborigine tribe, look like a New Zealand Maori warrior, or what? You look just like some of the pictures I've seen in the travel magazines and history books."

My student shook his head. "I juth like it, okay? I think it lookth great. And more importantly, my girlfriend thinkth it'th <u>virile</u> — maketh me look more manly."

I chuckled. "A piece of metal in your tongue makes you look more manly? You're kidding, right? You just want to put me in a good mood with your banter and <u>chaff</u>. As far as I can tell, all the stud does is raise your recycling value, if the price of silver goes up! Maybe your decision makes fiscal sense, not physical sense!"

I continued. "Let's figure this out as a math problem. If the price of silver is currently —"

Greg interrupted me. "Thop being such a <u>pedant</u>, pleath! Can't you talk about anything without having to turn it into a teaching lethon?"

I laughed, and changed the subject. "Okay, okay, you win. No more discussions of your <u>aesthetic</u> qualities. From now on, you and I will stick to the matter at hand, increasing your SAT sagacity." And we did just that.

I thought nothing more of the matter, until about three months later. I got a package in the mail. It was a note from Greg, telling me his SAT score had gone up nearly 200 points, and thanking me for my help. At the end of the note was a P.S. "I got early admission to my first choice college, so I don't need my <u>talisman</u> anymore. I can think of no one who deserves it more than you." I <u>gingerly</u> picked up something that was wrapped in tissue paper: It was a candy wax tongue with a silver stud sticking through it!

Going Back on Your (Vocabulary) Words

Don't worry; none of the words Greg said with a lisp are among the tested vocabulary! In this section, you find definitions of the words you find in the not-star-studded but vocabulary-studded story.

aesthetic (rhymes with, yes *bet* ick): pertaining to beauty. These days, women who do makeup don't call themselves beauticians, but the more elegant-sounding "aestheticians."

articulate (are *tick* you late): able to speak clearly and express thoughts well. An articulate person gets his or her point across without saying, "Uh, well, it's like, you know" every other sentence.

chaff (rhymes with, *laugh*): good-natured teasing or joking. You hear a lot of chaff at the lunch table with your friends. Chaff can also be a verb. You chaff your buddy when you give him a hard time over his new outfit.

Be sure to use chaff in a cheerful, fun way. You chaff someone you like, not someone you're slamming or insulting.

Did you notice the bonus word in the passage, *banter*? It also means good-natured teasing or joking.

emulate (rhymes with, *them* you late): imitate. When you're standing in front of the mirror in your bedroom, holding the deodorant bottle as if it's a microphone and belting out songs, you're trying to emulate your favorite singers.

gingerly (rhymes with, *hinge* her lee): carefully, cautiously. If you have a sprained foot, you would step on it very gingerly, not wanting to put all your weight on it and make things worse.

haberdashery (*hab* er dash her ree): store selling gentleman's clothing, such as shirts and neckties. The next time you go to the mall to buy a T-shirt for yourself or a male friend, show some class and tell your mom you're "preparing to visit the neighborhood haberdashery."

pedant (rhymes with, *said* ant): a narrow-minded teacher, especially one who stresses minor points of learning. Once — only once — I made the mistake of correcting the grammar in my boyfriend's letters to me. He called me a pedant for the rest of our relationship (and I guess I deserved that).

resplendent (re *splen* dent): dazzling, shining brightly. If you dye your hair traffic-cone orange for a party, you have a resplendent head.

saunter (rhymes with, *lawn* ter): stroll, walk leisurely. On a Sunday afternoon when you're hanging out with your friends, you don't power walk around the neighborhood, you saunter.

scintillation (rhymes with, *win* till nation): sparkle, flash. When a lady gets a diamond ring, the first thing she does is put it on her finger and move her hand back and forth, watching the ring scintillate.

talisman (rhymes with, *pal* is man): a magic charm, a good luck charm. The people on TV who spin the Big Wheel to win a lottery are often clutching numerous talismans, like rabbits' feet, four-leaf clovers, and Beanie babies.

virile (rhymes with, *here* while): manly. Advertisements for gyms show brawny, virile guys pumping iron and being admired by all the girls.

Stepping Up to the Plate: An Exercise

Directions: Match the definition to the word.

1. talisman	a. pertaining to beauty
2. chaff	b. manly
3. gingerly	c. a narrow-minded teacher
4. emulate	d. dazzling
5. articulate	e. strolled
6. scintillation	f. gentlemen's clothing store
7. aesthetic	g. carefully, cautiously
8. resplendent	h. sparkle, flash
9. virile	i. able to speak clearly
10. sauntered	j. imitate
11. pedant	k. good-natured teasing
12. haberdashery	l. a magic charm

Answers to the Exercise

3. g	6. h	9. b	12. f
2. k	5. i	8. d	11. c
1. l	4. j	7. a	10. e

Chapter 19

The Girl Who Yelled, "You Stink!"

*U*sually, when I pick up the telephone at my office, it's to explain to parents about my tutorial services or to answer a question for a student. However, every now and then, something much more dramatic happens, as you see in this chapter's story.

The Story of My Life

"You stink!" The <u>strident</u> voice on the telephone opened with those words. I stood there, too <u>stupefied</u> to say anything. It isn't every day, after all, that I pick up the phone to hear myself yelled at by a teenager! The girl continued. "You totally, completely stink!"

I recovered myself enough to ask, "Who is this?"

"This is Jessica, your student from yesterday."

Ah, now I placed the voice. Jessica had come for the first time the day before. I liked her. She was an ebullient, bubbly cheerleader, an enthusiastic student who learned quickly. I thought we'd had a good session. She seemed to learn the material well, understand my lecture, and even laugh at my lame jokes. She left happy . . . or so I thought. Therefore, I was doubly surprised when she continued, "I want my money back!"

I had to find out what was wrong. It's one thing to be <u>remonstrated</u> by students who complain that I need to get better jokes (I hear that all the time), but it's another to be screamed at and <u>berated</u> at top volume.

"Why do you want your money back? What's the matter?" I tried to <u>placate</u> my caller, to calm her down so she would at least talk to me rather than just yell at me. My ear was already getting sore.

"I just finished reading the homework assignment you gave me. You remember, you said to read the math lectures in the Dummies book."

"Yes, Jessica, I remember the assignment. Didn't you like the material?"

"I liked it all right, but it wasn't anything new. It was almost exactly the same as the lecture! You don't know what you're talking about," she said <u>contemptuously,</u> her voice full of <u>disdain</u> and disgust. "All you did was read some book and then work up a lecture saying almost exactly the same thing! You stole someone else's lecture!"

Students have called me many things in my time, but no one has ever accused me of being a <u>plagiarist,</u> of taking someone else's work. And never before have I been asked to return my <u>compensation.</u> I tried to break into the diatribe, but Jessica was still talking, still in the middle of her hissy fit.

"Jessica —"

"I could have gotten the same stuff myself just reading the book!

"Jessica —"

"I want my money back, every penny of it!" Jessica was completely <u>unambiguous</u> in her demands, making it clear exactly what she wanted from me. I certainly couldn't accuse her of not stating her case <u>lucidly.</u>

Finally, I was able to get a word in edgewise. "Jessica. Do me a favor. Check out the front cover of the book. Look down and see the author's name. Read it to me, please."

I heard papers rustle as Jessica reached for her book. "*The SAT I For Dummies* by Suzee J. Vlk."

"Yes, Jessica. The reason I lectured just like the book is that I wrote the book. I didn't steal it from someone else and didn't plagiarize it; I wrote it myself."

Jessica was silent, then I heard a very soft whisper, "Never mind," and the phone was ever so gently put down.

Jessica came for her second session the next week and neither of us ever said another word about the whole incident.

Being True to Your (Vocab) Words

No, this story isn't told so you'd feel free to call up and harass me the way Jessica did. The purpose of the story is to introduce new vocabulary to use, as defined in this section. (And if you ever do call me up, at least use these words to show me that you've mastered them!)

berate (rhymes with, she *ate*): scold, rebuke. I think of berate as "give a B rating." When someone has been mean to you, you berate or scold her. Remember this as she no longer has an "A rating" with you but a "*B rate*-ing."

compensation (com pen *say* shun): payment for services, wages, remuneration. When you receive a paycheck for the work you've done, that's your compensation.

Compensation can also mean something given to make amends for a loss or damages. For example, if your friend borrows your new sweater and loses it, she may give you her new leather jacket in compensation. If your parents accuse you of breaking the window and ground you, and then later find out someone else did the damage, they may extend your curfew by way of compensating you for the pain and suffering you endured (after all, you missed a great party!).

contemptuously (con *temp* chew us lee): scornfully, disrespectfully. When you treat someone with contempt, you have a very low opinion of him or her. You may have heard the expression "contempt of court." If the judge feels you're not showing the court the proper respect, he or she may cite for contempt of court and fine or even throw you in jail.

disdain (rhymes with, this *pain*): scorn, contempt. When you've reached the exalted level of sophomore, you may look at a mere freshman with disdain.

lucidly (rhymes with, *who* sid lee): clearly. The root *luc* means light or clear. A lucid explanation is a clear, understandable explanation. You may also know the word ***elucidate,*** which means to clarify, to make clear.

placate (rhymes with, *say* date): to calm down, pacify, appease. Placate is to make peace or to calm down. (You may be more familiar with another form of this word: ***placid.***)

plagiarist (*play* jur ist): one who steals the work of another without giving proper credit. If you copy passages from the Internet, a book, or someone else's term paper without footnoting correctly, you're committing plagiarism.

remonstrated (re *mahn* stray ted): said in protest or complaint. When you remonstrate with someone, you disagree with or gripe about what she's doing. For example, your folks may remonstrate with you about the way you prioritize your time, spending too much (they think) with your friends and too little on your homework.

strident (rhymes with, *try* dent): loud, harsh, shrill. When you were a little kid and you heard your mom call you in a strident voice, you knew you were in big trouble!

stupefied (*stoop* if fyed): stunned with amazement; astounded. If you find out that you won the Grand Prize of a gazillion dollars in a sweepstakes, you would likely be stupefied.

unambiguous (un am *big* you us): clear. Something *ambiguous* (the opposite of this word) is capable of being interpreted two different ways, or is unclear. The root *ambi* means both; the suffix *–ous* means full of, so ambiguous means full of both or having both (or two different) meanings. For example, if you ask me whether I like your new sweater and I respond, "Oh, it's so <u>you</u>!" that's ambiguous. You don't know whether your sweater (and you) have been complimented or insulted. You could interpret my comment either way.

Giving it Your Best Shot: A Practice Exercise

Directions: Match the definition to the word.

1. remonstrate
2. contemptuous
3. unambiguous
4. compensation
5. lucid
6. strident
7. disdain
8. plagiarist
9. placate
10. berate
11. stupefy

a. loud, harsh, shrill
b. calm down, pacify
c. scorn, contempt
d. one who steals the work of another
e. clear
f. find fault with
g. crystal clear
h. payment for services
i. scold
j. stun with amazement, astounded
k. scornful, disrespectful

Answers to the Exercise

1. f
2. k
3. g
4. h
5. e
6. a
7. c
8. d
9. b
10. i
11. j

Chapter 20

Banned from the Bash

● ●

Words in This Chapter

▶ expatriate

▶ forlorn

▶ galvanized

▶ gratuitous

▶ humdrum

▶ pilgrimage

▶ rhetorically

▶ stultifying

▶ stymied

▶ wheedled

● ●

*I*s there anything better than going to a really great party? Is there anything worse than not being invited to that really great party? In this story, you see how one girl plotted to be included.

The Life of the Party: A Story

"Why so gloomy and glum?" asked Gwenette, noting the <u>forlorn</u> expression on her friend's face. "You look just like you did when the history teacher flunked you for saying that the first female Supreme Court justice was Diana Ross."

Barb shot a malicious glance at the redhead sitting across the room. "I just found out Tiffany is giving a party, probably *the* party of the year, and I'm not invited."

Gwenette shrugged. "Tiffany's ostracized you ever since you flirted with John. Her not liking you shouldn't exactly be front-page news. Besides, you are always saying how you hate, loathe, abominate, despise, and abhor Tiffany, so what do you care? You wouldn't go even if you were invited."

"Wrong. All the cutest guys are going to be there. You know Jude, who always has such great stories about his dad's <u>expatriate</u> days in Paris? He told me yesterday that he was definitely going."

"Big deal. I've heard those <u>humdrum</u> stories so often I could recite them in my sleep."

Barb rolled her eyes at her friend and asked <u>rhetorically</u>, "What am I going to do with you? You're so jaded that nothing impresses you anymore. But me, I'm full of wanderlust. I love hearing travel stories and can't wait to have some of my own to tell. I want to go everywhere, all around the world. I want to make a <u>pilgrimage</u> to the Czech Republic and see the town my grandparents grew up in. I want to take an excursion to Africa and photograph the animals. I love to hear how Grandpa Homer trekked to Nepal — wait, wait, I'm digressing. Let's stick to the topic of Tiffany and her party. How can I ingratiate myself enough with that witch to be invited to her bash? I'm open and amenable to some suggestions here."

Gwenette scratched her head and looked <u>stymied</u>. "I'm clueless. I have no ideas at all. Maybe we can solicit Colleen's help. She's really close to Tiffany and owes you a favor because of all the algebra homework you've helped her with."

"Yeah, right," scoffed Barb, "Just catch Colleen helping out someone else. She's a taker. All she ever gives are <u>gratuitous</u> slams and insults, totally uncalled-for trash talk. Even after everything I did for her, she saw me in the hall with some friends and said, 'Watch out everyone, make way — here comes the pod!'"

Gwenette cracked up. "A pod, as in a group of whales? I never thought Colleen was erudite enough to know a word like that. Well, scratch Colleen. How about Kristin? She seems to get along with Tiffany."

"Great idea!" exclaimed Barb, <u>galvanized</u> into action. "Kristin wants to go out with my dolt of a brother — though heaven knows why, he's such a loser — so maybe she'll help. I'll play matchmaker for her if she'll get me an invite to the party."

"And me, too," <u>wheedled</u> her friend.

"I thought you didn't care about the party, especially with all those <u>stultifying</u> men and their stories you've heard too many times," teased Barb.

"Are you kidding?" said Gwenette. "This is going to be *the* party of the year!"

Hanging on Every (Vocab) Word

No one is saying that a better vocab is going to get you invited to the best parties (although you never know!). However, by learning the words in this section, you get the reputation of being smart, are able to help people with their homework, and can call in the favors you're owed when it's time for the party invitations to go out. It's a win-win situation!

expatriate (rhymes with, hex *late* tree hut): a person who has left his homeland. If you marry a dashing Dane and go live in Copenhagen, leaving the United States behind, you become an expatriate. Note the root *ex* meaning out of or away from. *Patria* means fatherland. If you are away from the fatherland, you are away from your native country.

forlorn (for *lorn*): sad, unhappy, without hope. When you leave home, your dogs sit at the door staring at you with forlorn expressions on their faces; sad because you're going without them.

galvanized (*gal* van ized): stimulated, roused, or spurred into action. You're galvanized into studying when you get your midterm grade and find that it's a D, not the B you thought you'd have.

In biology class, you may have done an experiment in which an electric current galvanizes or rouses an item. When you are galvanized, you get a shock (metaphorically): The light bulb comes on in your brain, and you're rarin' to go.

gratuitous (grah *two* it us): uncalled for; without cause or justification. A gratuitous insult is one that came out of the blue, one you didn't deserve. People are always talking about "gratuitous sex and violence" on television; they mean unnecessary sex and violence. Note that gratuitous can also mean free. A gratuity is a tip you give to a waiter freely, money you're not obligated to give.

humdrum (*hum* drum): lacking variety, dull, monotonous, or boring. A humdrum story is one that you've heard a hundred times, one that you could easily sleep through.

pilgrimage (*pill* grim age): any long journey, especially to a religious site or a place of historical interest. A religious person makes a pilgrimage to a special church, mosque, or temple. A Civil War buff makes a pilgrimage to Gettysburg to see the battle site there.

You have heard about and studied the Pilgrims all of your life, but did you ever make the connection with the word pilgrimage? Here's something similar. You know what a hermit is, right, a person who likes to live alone? What do you suppose a *hermitage* is? It's a secluded retreat, a place where you can live away from other people, like a hermit.

rhetorically (ret *tore* ick lee): in a showy or artificial manner. A rhetorical question is one that is asked only for effect, with no answer required. When you try telling your dad a whopping big story and he looks at you saying, "What am I, an idiot?" you'd better not answer that question. It's rhetorical.

stultifying (rhymes with, *cult* if trying): foolish, stupid, dull, useless. Someone stultifying is so dull that you just stand there in a stupor, listening to him, too bored to move, praying he'll be done talking soon.

stymied (rhymes with, *fly* mead): frustrated by being blocked, obstructed, hindered. Ever catch reruns of the show *Murder She Wrote?* In the opening title, the star, Angela Lansbury, is reading a newspaper with the headline, "Murder Stymies Cops." The cops were frustrated because they were blocked in their efforts to catch the bad guys.

wheedled (rhymes with, needled): to get something by coaxing or flattering. You wheedle a later curfew out of your father when you tell him what a good job he's done being a father, such that he's raised a responsible child who wants to be just like him. Interestingly, this word originated from a German term meaning to wag, as in wagging the tail. When a dog wags his tail, he is trying to wheedle an extra treat out of you.

Putting These Words into Practice

Directions: Match each word to its definition.

1. stymied
2. gratuitous
3. expatriate
4. stultifying
5. forlorn
6. rhetorically
7. wheedle
8. humdrum
9. pilgrimage
10. galvanized

a. to get by coaxing or flattering
b. a long journey
c. lacking variety; boring
d. roused or spurred into action
e. a person who has left his or her homeland
f. sad, unhappy, without hope
g. foolish, stupid, dull
h. said for effect only
i. obstructed, hindered
j. uncalled for

Answers to the Exercise

1. i   3. e   5. f   7. a   9. b
2. j   4. g   6. h   8. c   10. d

Chapter 21

Kid Klepto, the Boy Who Robbed Me Blind

● ●

Words in This Chapter

▶ cached

▶ candid

▶ capacious

▶ disingenuously

▶ interminable

▶ larcenous

▶ peccadillo

▶ perjury

▶ pilfer

▶ riddled

▶ stealthily

▶ tangible

● ●

*U*sually when my tutorial sessions are over, I find items the students left behind, such as books, pencils, and calculators. However, in the case of one student, I had just the opposite problem, as you read in this chapter's tale.

More to the Story than Meets the Eye

"Jerome," I said, smiling at the student across the desk from me, "It's a mere peccadillo, but you happen to be stealing my calculator."

Jerome pulled out the calculator he had cached into his backpack. "Oh, is this yours?" he asked disingenuously, looking as innocent as it was possible for a boy wearing a heavy-metal-band T-shirt and a leather dog collar with silver studs to look. "I could have sworn it was mine."

"Then you would have committed perjury," I said, looking at my calculator, which I had covered in bright pink nail polish so that no student accidentally mistook it for his own. "You put the shocking pink on the calculator buttons to match the pink on your toenails, no doubt!" I bent over and pretended to look under the table at Jerome's sandalled feet.

Jerome blushed just a little, then shrugged and got down to work. A few minutes later, I noticed that the teen had knocked my extra SAT book off the table and was <u>stealthily</u> nudging it with his foot toward his backpack. I walked around the table and picked up the text, holding its cover in front of Jerome's face. "Before you say this is your book, see the <u>riddled</u> cover? My doggie nibbled on the book one afternoon, providing <u>tangible</u> proof of ownership. I can match the dog's teeth to the marks. Think of this cover as a doggie dental record."

I tried to keep an eye on Jerome after that, but I got lax for a minute, and the next thing you know, my reading glasses were in his pocket. The <u>larcenous</u> lad was stealing me blind! I was afraid even to leave the room to go to the bathroom, worried that he'd rummage through the desk while I was gone and <u>pilfer</u> something else. At that stage, it wouldn't have surprised me to come back to a dark office and the still-hot light bulbs in Jerome's pack!

It was an <u>interminable</u> two-hour session, but Jerome finally left. Before he took off, I laughingly but adamantly insisted that he let me go through his backpack. Sure enough, a little careful checking disclosed two pencils, a pen, two dog toys, and my stapler!

I was sufficiently concerned about this kleptomaniac to call Jerome's mother. She insisted on coming to my office to talk about the matter. She was frank and <u>candid,</u> telling me Jerome had always had this same sort of filching fetish — this pilfering problem — and was getting therapy. Mrs. Bilk and I had a good talk, after which I felt much better. It wasn't until an hour after she left that I looked around and couldn't find the silver candy bowl I keep by the door. The mother must have slipped the bowl into her <u>capacious</u> purse while I wasn't looking!

Putting in a Good (Vocab) Word

Unless the preceding story has robbed (!) you of your desire to master more vocabulary, go through the definitions and explanations in this section.

cached (*cashed*): hidden or stored. The way I've always remembered this word is to say, "I've cached my cash in the back of my drawer." A *cache* is a secret store of something. You may have a cache of candy bars hidden waaaaay back in the corner of your closet where your little brother can't find them.

candid (rhymes with, *Dan* did): honest, frank. A candid response to a question is straightforward and honest. People can easily get into trouble if they give a truly candid answer to a question such as, "Do these jeans make my butt look big?"

capacious (rhymes with, snap *hay* shuss): roomy, spacious, able to contain or hold much. A capacious brain can hold enough vocabulary to ensure your getting a good score on your test. A capacious suitcase can hold enough clothing to keep you in fresh togs for a three-week trip.

You may remember this word more easily in another form: capacity. A capacious suitcase has the capacity to hold a lot of clothing.

Bonus: Did you notice the bonus word, togs? *Togs* is an informal word for clothing or outfits, such as tennis togs. The word, interestingly enough, comes from the Latin term, *toga*.

disingenuously (dis in *jenn* you us lee): not straightforwardly, insincerely, with a pretence of innocence and sincerity. When a small child with jelly on her face looks you in the eye and tries to seem totally innocent while saying, "*What* jelly doughnut?" she is acting disingenuously.

interminable (in *term* in able): without end, seeming to last forever. As you watch the second hand slooooowly go around on the clock on the wall of your history class, you may think the day is interminable and will never end.

You know this word in another form: terminate. To terminate is to end. The bell finally rings, terminating what had seemed an interminable class.

larcenous (rhymes with, *sparse* hen us): thieving. A larcenous person comes to your home and takes everything that isn't nailed down. *Petty larceny* is the crime of taking items under a certain value, such as $50.00. *Grand larceny* is — you guessed it — the crime of taking items above a certain value. If someone swipes a cup holder for a car, that's petty larceny. If he steals the entire car, that's grand larceny.

peccadillo (rhymes with, *heck* a dill oh): a minor or petty sin; a slight fault. You love your best friend despite her peccadilloes, such as her habit of always being late or wanting to copy your homework at the last minute.

The suffix –*illo* means little. A peccadillo isn't a serious crime that will get you grounded for life, just a small fault that gets on your parents' nerves.

perjury (rhymes with, *fur* jury): telling a lie while under oath. A person in court swears to tell the truth, the whole truth, and nothing but the truth. If she then lies, she has committed perjury.

pilfer (rhymes with, *hill* fur): steal, filch, take small amounts. A person may pilfer candy from the dish on your counter or a pencil from the stash in your desk. You use the word pilfer to refer to a small theft, not to a large theft.

riddled (rhymes with, *fid*dled): having many holes; punctured. Ever hear on a police show the expression, "bullet-riddled car?" That means the car was full of bullet holes.

Riddled also has a secondary meaning of spread throughout. You may have heard your teacher say, "This report was riddled with errors," meaning it had errors in every part of it.

stealthily (rhymes with, *health* hill lee): secretively, furtively, in a sly manner. A cat may stealthily stalk a mouse, sneaking up behind it. The stealth bomber, one of the large military airplanes, is called that because it can avoid being detected on radar and, thus, function in secret.

tangible (rhymes with, *fan* jib bull): able to be touched; having form and substance. While an idea is intangible (can't be touched), the paper on which you write down your idea is tangible; you can feel and touch it.

Tangible also has a more common usage of definite or unmistakable. A tangible result of your studying all this vocabulary is a higher SAT score.

No Sweat! A Practice Exercise

Directions: Match the term to the definition.

1. pilfer	a. steal, filch, take small amounts
2. cached	b. roomy, spacious, able to contain much
3. stealthily	c. a minor or petty sin
4. capacious	d. hidden or stored
5. peccadillo	e. telling a lie while under oath
6. larcenous	f. without end, seeming to last forever
7. riddled	g. honest, frank
8. candid	h. able to be touched
9. disingenuously	i. thieving
10. interminable	j. having many holes, punctured
11. tangible	k. insincerely, with an air of false innocence
12. perjury	l. secretly, clandestinely

Answers to the Exercise

3. l	6. i	9. k	12. e
2. d	5. c	8. g	11. h
1. a	4. b	7. j	10. f

Chapter 22

A Jewel of a House

Words in This Chapter

- burnish
- chimerical
- ensconce
- foolhardy
- inconsolable
- invigorated

- minuscule
- superfluity
- sweltering
- unremitting
- uproarious
- wary

*E*ver been too busy to go shopping for something you want, then suddenly get it as a gift? That happened to Renee in this chapter's story, but things didn't turn out *exactly* the way she hoped.

. . . And They Lived Happily Ever After

Mick dragged himself into Renee's house, lifted his face into the stream of cool air coming from the air conditioner, and said, "Wow, it's good to be out of that sweltering heat. And I'm glad to find you at home, instead of at the office. You put in longer hours at that business of yours than anyone else I know. Given how hard *you* work, *I* feel guilty complaining, but I won't let that stop me." He groaned and stretched. "It has been a very long morning, but I have a surprise for you; a little payback for that great stock tip you gave me a few months back. I found the perfect house, and the boys are going to love it!"

Renee gave Mick a cool glass of lemonade and a hug. "A house? Really? Wonderful! That is a surprise! I've been meaning to go house-hunting myself, but I haven't had the time. Tell me all about this place. What style is it? Is it expensive?"

"It's actually a log cabin, a little on the <u>minuscule</u> side, but certainly large enough for your sons. Dillon and Cody are going to love it, and you are, too. It has plenty of room for their stuff and a great floor plan that will allow them to zoom around with their toys from place to place. Maybe I was a bit <u>foolhardy</u>, but I've taken a chance and already said we'd take it, just because I'm so sure they'll love it

"Your <u>unremitting</u> munificence always amazes me. You are so generous with your time and effort. I know the boys will love it. Tell me more!

"Well, there's a lot of copper throughout, like the roof over the patio. It's a little dull, but we can <u>burnish</u> it and make it gleam like new. There are four bedrooms and an oversized living room with a stone fireplace. There are smaller fireplaces in each of the bedrooms, as well as one in the kitchen."

Renee couldn't believe what she was hearing. "Six fireplaces? If you had told me you were trying to find a house with six fireplaces, I would have said that was a <u>chimerical</u> goal, totally unrealistic. Go on, what's the rest of the place like? Where can we put the home office?"

Mick looked at her quizzically. "I doubt the boys will care much about the home office, but okay. The place has wooden floors and a <u>superfluity</u> of storage space. There are drawers and cabinets and cubbyholes everywhere. I just know Dillon is going to go into his stealth stasher mode, stuffing all his toys everywhere, such that months later we find his little toy bear comfortably <u>ensconced</u> in the cushions of the living room chair. And remember the time Cody put a piece of his peanut butter and jelly sandwich in the junk drawer? We had ants for a month after that. Oh, and I even took the liberty of putting a little something green in the kitchen for you."

"Green? You mean broccoli, asparagus, something like that? You're already stocking the kitchen?" Suddenly Renee looked <u>wary</u>. "Mickey, I swear, if you put a frog in there ready to jump out at me —"

Mick laughed <u>uproariously</u>. "No, no, no frog. I love not only you but my head and limbs far too much. I know that I'd be missing one or more of them were you to have an agile amphibian leaping out at you. But it's an idea." He smiled mischievously and pretended to jot down a reminder on his notepad, then dodged the sofa cushion Renee hurled at him.

"So stop teasing me already!" she said, standing up and getting ready to go. "When can I go see the house? Are you <u>invigorated</u> enough from that lemonade to go take me?"

Mick shook his head. "What do you mean, take you? I brought the house here with me to show you, see what you think."

Renee stopped dead in her tracks. "What? You brought the house here? I don't understand." She watched as Mick went out to the garage, then came in staggering under the weight of a large log cabin playhouse.

"A playhouse?" Renee's face fell. "A playhouse," she repeated lugubriously. "I thought you meant a real house, a home we could all live in." She looked <u>inconsolable,</u> but Mick had a plan to cheer her up.

"Honey, remember I said there was something for you in the kitchen? I meant it. Go ahead and open the fridge." He pointed at a small plastic box in the corner of the "kitchen." Renee opened the door, and screamed in elation.

"An emerald ring? My birthstone! ! Oh Mick, this is wonderful, thank you so much." She put it on, then gave Mick a sideways glance. "And one more thing. As you yourself pointed out, I did give you that stock tip, which gave you the cash to fill up some of the other storage space here. I can label the cabinets: diamond, ruby, pearl . . . ."

Mick sat down heavily and grabbed his lemonade again. "I guess I deserved that: It would have been cheaper to buy a real house after all!"

Having the Last (Vocab) Word

Is your brain big enough to house (!) all the words you heard in this story? The definitions and example sentences are given in this section.

burnish (rhymes with, *fur*nish): polish by rubbing. You burnish the trophies you have on your shelf, joking that you want them so shiny they attract the attention of pilots who fly by at 30,000 feet.

Don't confuse burnish with burn. The SAT is notorious for giving you answers that would fit a "trap" definition. Unless you polish something so hard it ignites, burnishing is not burning.

chimerical (ki *mer* ic al): imaginary, fanciful. A kindergartner may draw a chimerical animal, giving it the head of his puppy, the body of his best friend, and the feet of a monster. Chimerical is often used as the opposite of realistic.

ensconced (en *scons*'d): placed or settled snugly or securely. You are ensconced in bed on a cold, rainy night, a good book (this one?) in hand, munchies on the nightstand.

foolhardy (rhymes with, *school* party): foolishly bold, reckless. It's foolhardy to make a rude digital gesture at a Hells Angels' motorcyclist as he or she goes by you.

inconsolable (in con *sole* able): unable to be comforted. When you miss what would have been the winning shot just as the buzzer sounds, you may be inconsolable, moping around the rest of the week.

invigorated (rhymes with, win *fig* or ated): full of life and energy. A good work-out, instead of making you exhausted, actually leaves you invigorated, ready to face the day.

minuscule (rhymes with, *win* us cool): extremely small. When you are given a minuscule diamond ring, it's not polite to pull out your magnifying glass and exclaim, "I know there's a stone here somewhere!"

superfluity (soup her *flew* itty): excess, overabundance. When you have a superfluity of clothing to the point where you can't shut your closet doors, it's time to take some of that stuff to charity.

sweltering (rhymes with, *shel*-ter-ring): uncomfortably, oppressively hot. When the temperature is over 100 degrees for five days in a row here in sweltering southern California, I start fantasizing about moving to northern Michigan and getting snowed in for months in a row.

unremitting (un re *mitt* ting): non-stopping, persistent, incessant. An unremitting gift-giver just keeps on giving and giving and giving (like this book, which presents you with word after word after word!). An unremitting headache just persists, won't stop. You no longer need fear an unremitting headache during the SAT, because you will know sooooo many words, you won't suffer brain strain.

The word *remit* is interesting. It means two different things. One common meaning is to slacken or decrease. When your headache remits, it decreases, becomes less painful. A second meaning is to send money in payment. Do you have your own credit card yet, or do you pay your own cell phone bill? If so, you may see the expression, "Please remit payment with this form" on the bill that comes in the mail.

uproarious (up *roar* he us): noisy, loud, boisterous. When a comedian is having a good night, he hears uproarious laughter after every joke he tells.

wary (rhymes with, *fairy*): cautious, careful, circumspect. You're wary when you tell your parents exactly what went on at summer camp, leaving out some details that they don't really need to know.

Exercising Your Right to Practice

Directions: Match the definition to the term.

1. burnish
2. superfluity
3. wary
4. foolhardy
5. chimerical
6. uproarious
7. inconsolable
8. minuscule
9. ensconced
10. invigorated
11. sweltering
12. unremitting

a. persistent, incessant
b. cautious
c. noisy
d. excess
e. uncomfortably hot
f. filled with energy
g. settled in securely
h. unrealistic
i. extremely small
j. unable to be comforted
k. polish by rubbing
l. recklessly bold

Answers to the Exercise

3. b	6. c	9. g	12. a
2. d	5. h	8. i	11. e
1. k	4. l	7. j	10. f

Part IV
Putting You to the (Practice) Tests

"That 'Analogies' section was a snap. It was like taking candy from a fish."

In this part . . .

*J*ust when you're sure your cranial cavity can't cram in one more piece of prattle, relief is at hand. You finally get to download the vocabulary you mastered by reviewing this entire book.

This part has five practice exams featuring the vocabulary you've mastered, with answer explanations following each exam. (If you thirst for yet more knowledge and need a refresher on the rest of the answer choice words, check out the glossary in Appendix B. Everything's there.)

The fifth and final challenge in this part is appropriately labeled the Genius Test. It tests words that were snuck into the nooks and crannies of the chapters, into the sidebars, into even the trivia and jokes. If you've mastered these, you've truly paid attention, gotten your money's worth from this book, and earned the appellation "genius."

Note: I don't include Analogy questions in these practice exams because they can be easy to answer even when you don't know what the tested words mean. So, instead, I focus in these exams on Sentence Completion questions (just like those on the SAT), which do require a strong vocabulary. Don't worry: If you can do these, Analogies really will be like taking candy from a fish!

Chapter 23

Practice Test #1

• •

*Y*ou say you can't take a test because you have a headache? Your head may be throbbing all right, but not from pain. All that knowledge you've acquired throughout the book is eager to be let out. Taking the following exam (under actual exam conditions, in a quiet room, without any interruptions) will give you the mental release you need to feel better.

Popping the Questions

Directions: Choose the best word to complete the sentence.

1. The sun filtering through the bedroom curtain had a - - - - effect on Janelle, who decided to go back to sleep.

    (A) dapper

    (B) soporific

    (C) disparaging

    (D) glib

    (E) newfangled

2. The - - - - contribution to his charity so overwhelmed the director that he couldn't stop stammering out his thanks to the millionaire donor and shaking her hand over and over again.

    (A) sluggish

    (B) munificent

    (C) archaic

    (D) hackneyed

    (E) noisome

3. The judge chastised the - - - - attorney, saying that her excessive chatter was alienating the jury and hurting her client's chances for acquittal.

    (A) halcyon

    (B) froward

    (C) prolix

    (D) corpulent

    (E) choleric

4. Glancing at the clock and seeing that time was about to run out, Ms. Howard was forced to - - - - her lecture, leaving out the last third of the material.

    (A) quibble

    (B) acclaim

    (C) dawdle

    (D) curtail

    (E) befuddle

5. Trying to - - - - their favorite rock star, the little girls dressed in navel-baring clothes and practiced their dance moves.

    (A) denigrate

    (B) adjure

    (C) resolve

    (D) attenuate

    (E) emulate

6. After hiking for the entire summer, living mostly on energy bars and water, LeVar returned so - - - - that all his clothes were much too big for him.

    (A) swarthy

    (B) immature

    (C) indolent

    (D) gaunt

    (E) frenzied

7. Armando's wife always carried snacks for him in her purse, knowing how - - - - her husband got if he left home without having breakfast.

    (A) ebullient

    (B) adamant

(C) peckish

(D) pliable

(E) stout

8. Guido was shocked at how - - - - he looked after spending all winter inside, with pneumonia, never getting any sunshine or exercise.

   (A) sartorial

   (B) pallid

   (C) opulent

   (D) grandiloquent

   (E) hoary

9. After executing a good run down the most difficult ski slope, Mr. Ludwig was in a - - - - mood, telling funny stories and laughing at his children's jokes.

   (A) lethargic

   (B) veteran

   (C) resourceful

   (D) hidebound

   (E) jocular

10. Bob blushed as he sat at the dais hearing the - - - - and judos of grateful clients who thanked him for saving them so much on their taxes over the years.

   (A) plaudits

   (B) turpitude

   (C) folly

   (D) vituperation

   (E) avarice

11. Dr. Weiss was so experienced in his field that even a - - - - glance at a patient was usually sufficient for him to make an accurate diagnosis.

   (A) lachrymose

   (B) garrulous

   (C) stentorian

   (D) profligate

   (E) perfunctory

12. It was obvious from the - - - - expression on the diver's face that he hadn't been able to find the expensive ring that had slipped off his wife's finger into the lake and would have to buy her another.

    (A) laconic

    (B) Brobningnagian

    (C) lugubrious

    (D) svelte

    (E) risible

13. Alice continued to - - - - over her vacation spot, one minute certain she wanted to go to Bhutan, the next minute thinking Yosemite would be more fun.

    (A) lament

    (B) fawn

    (C) expedite

    (D) vacillate

    (E) inundate

14. Kendra was - - - - about her chances of being on the reality TV show, sure that she had all the qualities the producers were seeking.

    (A) recalcitrant

    (B) salubrious

    (C) soignée

    (D) droll

    (E) sanguine

15. Fifi the miniature poodle approached Bruno the Great Dane with - - - -, concerned that he might either intentionally attack her or accidentally step on her.

    (A) pulchritude

    (B) badinage

    (C) avarice

    (D) trepidation

    (E) pedantry

16. A pedestrian bridge was erected over the busy intersection, hoping to - - - - some of the congestion by separating the strollers from the SUVs.

    (A) precipitate

    (B) alleviate

    (C) animate

    (D) disparage

    (E) dawdle

17. The bull became - - - - when teased in the ring, stomping, roaring, and finally charging in fury.

    (A) hackneyed

    (B) incensed

    (C) servile

    (D) lanky

    (E) doleful

18. The boss earned his employees' - - - - by docking their paychecks for matters out of their control, such as being late on account of traffic jams.

    (A) encomium

    (B) acumen

    (C) vim

    (D) enmity

    (E) juvenescence

19. The generous man was disgusted by his friend's - - - -, saying that he had never met anyone so greedy, grasping, and avaricious.

    (A) procrastination

    (B) candor

    (C) perspicacity

    (D) cupidity

    (E) docility

20. Realizing that Renee was a ---- at racing, Mick gave her several driving and safety lessons before allowing her on the track.

    (A) fop

    (B) neophyte

    (C) mendicant

    (D) chatterbox

    (E) plutocrat

21. The car salesman assured the irate buyer that the vehicle's horrible repair record was a(n) ---- because nearly all cars of that model and make and year had flawless performance.

    (A) encomium

    (B) dirge

    (C) polymath

    (D) aberration

    (E) pundit

22. The movie reviewer said that Rich, the ---- leading man, was so attractive that the females in the audience couldn't take their eyes off him.

    (A) virile

    (B) omniscient

    (C) abstemious

    (D) intractable

    (E) lugubrious

23. The young girl's happiness at getting a pony was obvious from her ----, which sported a non-stop grin.

    (A) torpor

    (B) pertinacity

    (C) visage

    (D) solvency

    (E) dolt

24. The investigating officer gave the suspected criminal every opportunity to - - - - himself, but he was unable to provide an alibi.

   (A) harangue

   (B) rebuke

   (C) pontificate

   (D) exculpate

   (E) befuddle

25. Opera star Stephanie Weiss said the orchestra played what should be an upbeat, lighthearted song as if it were a(n) - - - - and refused to sing the piece.

   (A) dirge

   (B) folly

   (C) acme

   (D) ingénue

   (E) dandy

Answering for Yourself

Check your answers in this section.

1. **B.** Soporific means sleep-inducing, putting Janelle back to sleep. The root *sop* means sleep.

   If you chose A, you probably confused dapper, meaning very well-dressed, almost over-dressed, with dappled. Sunlight may be dappled, meaning in spots or polka-dotted, but it wouldn't be dapper.

2. **B.** Munificent means generous. The director was overwhelmed by the generous contribution. Think of "muni" as "money." Someone muni-ficent is money-magnificent!

3. **C.** Someone prolix is excessively talkative. The root *pro* means outward, forth; *lix* means speech. A prolix person speaks out and holds nothing back.

4. **D.** To curtail is to shorten, to "cut the tail" off of something.

5. **E.** To emulate is to imitate. The girls were trying to be just like their favorite star by emulating or imitating her.

6. **D.** Gaunt means thin, often excessively thin to the point of looking ill.

7. **C.** Peckish means irritable from hunger. When a wife knows her husband is going to turn cranky and grouchy if he doesn't eat, she's smart to carry a supply of snacks for him.

8. **B.** Someone pallid is pale, as a person would be after being indoors ill all winter.

9. **E.** Someone jocular is cheerful, happy, in a joking sort of mood.

10. **A.** Plaudits (and kudos) are praises. Bob was blushing over hearing the praises from all his grateful clients.

11. **E.** Perfunctory means automatic, dutiful, without much effort. A perfunctory glance would be a quick once-over.

12. **C.** Lugubrious means sad, woeful. A diver who doesn't succeed in finding a ring and has to dish out cash for another is most likely sad.

13. **D.** To vacillate is to waiver, to be indecisive, unable to make up your mind.

14. **E.** Sanguine means cheerfully optimistic. Kendra was optimistic, or thinking positively, about her chances.

15. **D.** Trepidation is fear.

    The root *trep* means fear. While Fifi had trepidation, Bruno most likely was intrepid, not fearful. (The prefix *in–* means not.)

16. **B.** To alleviate is to make less intense, to make better. A bridge would reroute some of the foot traffic, making the intersection easier for both foot and car traffic.

17. **B.** Incensed means furious or burning mad (think of burning incense).

18. **D.** Enmity is hatred; dislike. You have enmity for an enemy.

19. **D.** Cupidity is greed, the love of money.

20. **B.** A neophyte is a novice, a beginner, someone new. *Neo* means new.

21. **D.** An aberration is an abnormality, something not usual.

    The prefix *ab–* means away from. An aberration is away from what you'd expect.

22. **A.** Virile means masculine or attractively manly. A virile actor captures the attention of the female audience.

23. **C.** A visage is a countenance, a face. The girl's joy was obvious from her appearance, the look on her face. Something on your *visage* is *visible* for everyone to see.

24. **D.** To exculpate is to release from blame, to get off the hook.

    Ex– means away from; *culp* means guilt; *–ate* means to make. To exculpate yourself is to make yourself "away from guilt" or show your innocence.

25. **A.** A dirge is a funeral hymn, a slow, sad song.

Chapter 24

Practice Test #2

• •

*N*ow that your brain is all warmed up (perhaps overheated!) from having gone through this book, you're ready for the next challenge. Take this test as seriously as you can, please, by sitting quietly and going through all the questions at one time. In other words, don't answer a few questions, then take a call, answer a few more questions, watch a TV show, and so on.

Calling These Questions into Question

Directions: Choose the best word to complete the sentence.

1. When the levee broke, the surrounding fields were - - - -, leaving the entire year's crops under six feet of water.

   (A) abjured

   (B) submissive

   (C) inundated

   (D) emaciated

   (E) upbraided

2. Mr. McKee had a(n) - - - - to computers, preferring, instead, to use an old-fashioned typewriter whenever possible.

   (A) aversion

   (B) accolade

   (C) lassitude

   (D) yielding

   (E) aberration

3. The actor always said that the horror movie he made was the ---- of his career and wanted to be remembered for his later, much better, movies.

   (A) dolt

   (B) senescence

   (C) serendipity

   (D) nadir

   (E) acclaim

4. When Regina lost her purse, she temporarily became a(n) ----, spending the afternoon begging for quarters to take the bus home.

   (A) fop

   (B) dandy

   (C) polymath

   (D) mendicant

   (E) tyro

5. The young girl used all her charms to ---- a new sound system out of her grandfather, telling him how she knew he had the money for one because he had been so incredibly successful and smart in his business.

   (A) upbraid

   (B) antiquate

   (C) carp

   (D) wheedle

   (E) squander

6. The ---- expression on the listener's face showed he didn't understand a word the speaker was saying.

   (A) preposterous

   (B) vacuous

   (C) peripatetic

   (D) frowzy

   (E) discerning

7. The play was hysterically funny, mostly due to the good-natured - - - - between the two leads who enjoyed insulting and teasing each other.

   (A) badinage

   (B) lamentation

   (C) panegyric

   (D) parsimony

   (E) cupidity

8. The parents were shocked by the - - - - violence in the movie, which had no connection to the plot and seemed totally unnecessary.

   (A) gratuitous

   (B) mercenary

   (C) verbose

   (D) insolvent

   (E) funereal

9. The cosmetic surgeon said that making women more - - - - or at least making them feel they were more beautiful was extremely rewarding.

   (A) prodigal

   (B) peevish

   (C) obtuse

   (D) indigent

   (E) pulchritudinous

10. Given the instructor's reputation for being - - - - in academic matters, no one was surprised when he stubbornly refused to allow make-up exams, despite a school policy encouraging professors to do so.

    (A) languid

    (B) precocious

    (C) fatuous

    (D) froward

    (E) insolvent

11. The job interviewer felt that if an applicant would ---- his former employer, he'd speak badly of his next boss as well, and thus refused to hire anyone who insulted previous superiors.

    (A) denigrate

    (B) laud

    (C) fawn

    (D) befuddle

    (E) vacillate

12. Roy said that even a ---- could perform the task, as it required no intelligence.

    (A) dandy

    (B) parvenu

    (C) chatterbox

    (D) sycophant

    (E) dolt

13. The grandmother claimed not to recognize the ---- young man in front of her, saying he'd both grown up and slimmed down since last she saw him.

    (A) taciturn

    (B) affluent

    (C) disgruntled

    (D) discursive

    (E) lanky

14. The headmaster never lost an opportunity to make his point, lecturing his students in a bombastic, ---- way.

    (A) despondent

    (B) miserly

    (C) pontificating

    (D) perfunctory

    (E) hapless

15. The girl cared for her grandfather, planning ---- meals that were nutritious, appealing, and tasty.

    (A) salubrious

    (B) noisome

    (C) noxious

    (D) unruly

    (E) rotund

16. The painter showed the saint with a(n) ---- smile on her face as she ascended to heaven on a golden cloud.

    (A) obese

    (B) prolific

    (C) disconsolate

    (D) parsimonious

    (E) beatific

17. The hammock company advertised its product as perfect for a stress-free, ---- day spent napping in the yard.

    (A) magnanimous

    (B) taciturn

    (C) vociferous

    (D) placid

    (E) acute

18. The husband told his wife that even after all these years he loved her more every day, going into a ---- about her virtue and intelligence and beauty.

    (A) panegyric

    (B) dirge

    (C) rebuke

    (D) diatribe

    (E) torpor

19. Although eager to be self-employed, Ixchel was - - - - to give up her company benefits, especially retirement and health care.

    (A) sanguine

    (B) loath

    (C) ludicrous

    (D) loquacious

    (E) somnolent

20. Ralph - - - - at his friend who had just asked out the same woman who Ralph himself had hoped to date.

    (A) glowered

    (B) expedited

    (C) yielded

    (D) placated

    (E) precipitated

21. The athlete assured the coach that while he had made mistakes in his - - - - youth, he was no longer a beginner but had matured and learned his lessons.

    (A) woebegone

    (B) comely

    (C) callow

    (D) soporific

    (E) destitute

22. The father told his daughter to be more - - - - in choosing her dates, to select wisely and not accept every offer.

    (A) precocious

    (B) vivacious

    (C) effervescent

    (D) discerning

    (E) malleable

23. The army officer was ---- in his dress uniform, medals shined, pants creased, shoes polished to a high gloss.

    (A) acquiescent

    (B) dapper

    (C) fractious

    (D) carping

    (E) terse

24. The child's ---- face alerted us that she had gotten socks for her birthday, not the puppy she had requested.

    (A) opulent

    (B) beatific

    (C) inaudible

    (D) succinct

    (E) funereal

25. The traveler sought advice from the ---- head of the youth hostel who had seen, heard, and done it all.

    (A) lachrymose

    (B) sagacious

    (C) laggard

    (D) tenacious

    (E) irresolute

Not Taking No for an Answer

Check your answers in this section.

1. **C.** To inundate is to flood. Think of the "und" in inundate as being und-erwater.

2. **A.** An aversion to something is a dislike.

   The prefix *a*– means not or without. You want not to have, or to be without, something to which you have an aversion.

3. **D.** A nadir is the lowest point, either literally or, as in this case, metaphorically. The worst movie of his career is the actor's lowest point.

4. **D.** A mendicant is a beggar, a panhandler.

5. **D.** To wheedle is to charm, especially with flattery and sweet talk.

6. **E.** Vacuous means stupid or showing a lack of intelligence.

Vac means empty. An "empty" expression shows you just don't get what's going on.

7. **A.** Badinage is good-natured joking and teasing. You and your friends indulge in a little badinage at the lunch table every day.

8. **A.** Gratuitous means unearned, extra, unnecessary. The phrase "gratu-itous sex and violence in the movie" has become a cliché, meaning too much, or unnecessary, sex and violence.

9. **E.** Pulchritudinous means beautiful. The job of a plastic surgeon was to make the women more beautiful, or at least to make them feel more beautiful.

10. **D.** Froward means stubborn, obstinate, refusing to change, or disobedient.

11. **A.** To denigrate is to speak badly of, to insult, to put down.

The root *de–* means down from.

12. **E.** A dolt is an unintelligent, unsophisticated person.

13. **E.** Lanky means tall and thin, especially with long limbs that a person hasn't gotten used to yet, like a young man who trips over his own long legs.

14. **C.** To pontificate is to speak in a pompous or dogmatic way.

15. **A.** Salubrious means healthful.

Salu means health; *–ous* means full of. A salubrious meal is "full of health," good for you.

16. **E.** Beatific literally means saint-like, but it can also mean happy. A saint has a happy, saint-like smile as she ascends to heaven.

17. **D.** Placid is tranquil, calm, mellow, laid-back, and relaxed; just the type of attitude you'd have when kicking back in a hammock.

18. **A.** A panegyric is a speech or song of high praise.

19. **B.** Loath means reluctant, not eager or willing.

20. **A.** To glower at is to glare at, to look at angrily.

21. **C.** Callow means young and immature.

22. **D.** To be discerning is to show good judgment.

23. **B.** Dapper means neat, trim, and attractive in appearance.

24. **E.** Funereal means gloomy, dismal, and appropriate for a funeral.

25. **B.** Sagacious means intelligent, full of wisdom.

Chapter 25

Practice Test #3

• •

*H*ere's yet another practice exam to test your skills (see Chapters 23, 24, and 26 for three others). Sit down in a quiet room, turn off the TV and cell phone, and put that incredibly expanded brain of yours to work.

Begging the Questions

Directions: Choose the best word to complete each sentence.

1. Lisa was voted Most - - - - Student in school, with everyone agreeing that she out-talked the rest of the kids ten to one.

   (A) garrulous

   (B) svelte

   (C) maligned

   (D) destitute

   (E) callow

2. The wedding planner jokingly agreed to guarantee everything, even a(n) - - - - day, free of rain, sleet, or snow, June through August.

   (A) effervescent

   (B) halcyon

   (C) antiquated

   (D) polymath

   (E) Brobdingnagian

3. The author was dismayed at how her book was changed into a movie, ---- about everything from poor casting to ugly backdrops.

   (A) docile

   (B) carping

   (C) frowzy

   (D) lauding

   (E) solvent

4. The college admissions officer was impressed by the ---- and obviously well-thought-out comments made by the student and approved his application.

   (A) mercenary

   (B) peckish

   (C) astute

   (D) despondent

   (E) homely

5. After having chemotherapy treatments, Brent was ----, spending most of his day lying on the couch watching TV or playing video games.

   (A) vociferous

   (B) magnanimous

   (C) querulous

   (D) languid

   (E) loquacious

6. The writer's essay was marked down for being full of cliches, trite comments, and ---- expressions.

   (A) parvenu

   (B) laconic

   (C) dynamic

   (D) hackneyed

   (E) venerable

7. The movie star told his agent not to be such a ---- and flatterer, but to give him an honest appraisal of the state of his acting career.

    (A) sage

    (B) tyro

    (C) pedant

    (D) reviler

    (E) toady

8. The reporter won a Pulitzer Prize for his insightful, shrewd, and ---- reporting on corruption in government.

    (A) comely

    (B) incisive

    (C) jocular

    (D) froward

    (E) affluent

9. The Senate voted to ---- their fellow politician for behavior that was unethical, immoral and quite possibly criminal.

    (A) censure

    (B) fawn

    (C) dawdle

    (D) vacillate

    (E) expedite

10. The energetic, cheerful, ---- French teacher was an excellent selection for the position of cheerleading coach.

    (A) frivolous

    (B) lethargic

    (C) ebullient

    (D) unkempt

    (E) pallid

11. Phillipa went to the electrologist to have - - - - body hair removed from her legs so that she wouldn't have to keep shaving them.

    (A) rangy

    (B) comely

    (C) surly

    (D) taciturn

    (E) superfluous

12. Because our dog, Thor, was so dominant, we knew that if we got a second dog, she'd have to be - - - - and submissive to him.

    (A) profligate

    (B) mellifluous

    (C) lachrymose

    (D) servile

    (E) antediluvian

13. Craig considered his perfect SAT score to be the - - - - of his senior year, saying that nothing else he did was more exciting or rewarding to him.

    (A) acme

    (B) turpitude

    (C) candor

    (D) dandy

    (E) plaudits

14. The workers soon learned that although their boss was a - - - - who seemed to care more about his clothing and his appearance than his job, he was actually highly skilled and hard working.

    (A) toady

    (B) dolt

    (C) miser

    (D) parvenu

    (E) fop

15. John scored the winning water polo goal and enjoyed the congratulations and - - - - of his teammates.

    (A) diatribes

    (B) avarice

    (C) kudos

    (D) vituperation

    (E) harangues

16. The - - - - woman's friends said that if she were paid by the word, she'd be the wealthiest woman in town.

    (A) doleful

    (B) terse

    (C) voluble

    (D) frenzied

    (E) senescent

17. The scout said that the ball player's - - - - performance showed he was too slow and lazy to do well in major league baseball.

    (A) acclaimed

    (B) insolvent

    (C) pithy

    (D) sluggish

    (E) superannuated

18. The business owner, realizing many of his laborers were - - - -, set up a no-interest loan program to help the men afford to pay for emergencies, such as medical problems.

    (A) juvenescent

    (B) indigent

    (C) perspicuous

    (D) stout

    (E) choleric

19. The girl was embarrassed at being caught looking ---- when her boyfriend came over unannounced and vowed she would be better groomed from then on.

    (A) stout

    (B) voluble

    (C) unkempt

    (D) glib

    (E) resourceful

20. Everyone tried to avoid the ---- neighbor who complained constantly about everything from the road noise to the neighborhood dogs.

    (A) noisome

    (B) unruly

    (C) swarthy

    (D) querulous

    (E) parsimonious

21. After his morning workout, Eddie was full of ---- and vigor, reenergized, and ready to have a productive day at the office.

    (A) vim

    (B) opulence

    (C) wrath

    (D) paean

    (E) serendipity

22. The ---- professor was highly respected for his scholarly research and well-written articles in academic journals.

    (A) abstemious

    (B) refractory

    (C) erudite

    (D) archaic

    (E) felicitous

23. The handyman was fired not for being incompetent but for being ----, because he was capable of doing anything, but too lazy to begin.

    (A) perspicuous

    (B) indolent

    (C) hidebound

    (D) salubrious

    (E) perfunctory

24. When the high school student was given a credit card, he immediately got into trouble for his ---- spending and buying thousands of dollars' worth of clothes and sports equipment.

    (A) acquiescent

    (B) adamant

    (C) noxious

    (D) prodigal

    (E) soignée

25. The newspaper editorial ---- the mayor, calling him irresponsible, incompetent, and corrupt.

    (A) attenuated

    (B) quibbled

    (C) eulogized

    (D) maligned

    (E) enervated

Explaining the Answers Away

Check your answers in this section.

1. **A.** Someone garrulous is extremely talkative.

2. **B.** A halcyon day is calm and tranquil; a beautiful day for a wedding.

3. **B.** To carp is to complain, to grouse, or to nit-pick.

4. **C.** Astute comments are insightful, shrewd, perspicacious, or in the know.

5. **D.** Languid means drooping, weak, or sluggish.

6. **D.** Hackneyed expressions are overused. They're too common, just like clichés and trite comments.

7. **E.** A toady is a kiss-up, a sycophant, a brown-noser, someone who flatters to excess.

8. **B.** Something incisive is sharp, keen, astute.

9. **A.** To censure is to punish severely. The word is often used in an official sense; Congress may censure a politician.

10. **C.** An ebullient person is energetic, upbeat, vivacious.

11. **E.** Superfluous means excessive an unnecessary. Many hair removers actually say on the tube "for removal of superfluous body hair."

12. **D.** Servile means slavish, very submissive and compliant. A servile dog submits to a dominant dog.

13. **A.** The acme is the top point, the best part.

14. **E.** A fop is a clothes-horse, a person overly concerned with his appearance and his dress.

15. **C.** Kudos are praises, congratulations.

16. **C.** Voluble means very talkative.

17. **D.** A sluggish performance is slow and uninspired.

18. **B.** An indigent person is poor, living in poverty.

19. **C.** Unkempt means untidy, having a neglected appearance.

20. **D.** Someone querulous is complaining all the time.

21. **A.** Vim is life, energy.

    The root *vi* means life.

22. **C.** Erudite means scholarly or well learned.

23. **B.** Someone indolent is lazy, not energetic.

24. **D.** Prodigal means recklessly extravagant.

25. **D.** To malign is to speak badly about.

Chapter 26
Practice Test #4

* *

*I*f you've done the practice exam chapters in order (Chapters 23 through 25 before getting to this one), you're now a veteran of vocabulary. Take the following exam (under actual test conditions, of course, in a quiet site with no interruptions) and see whether you've saved your best for last.

Giving this Test the Acid Test

Directions: Choose the best word to complete the sentence.

1. The mother claimed her child was ----, able to read and write when he was two years old, an age when other children were just learning their ABCs.

    (A) fatuous

    (B) precocious

    (C) somnolent

    (D) wishy-washy

    (E) hapless

2. The ---- teacher refused to let her students take make-up exams, stubbornly insisting that any child who wasn't present the day of the exam would receive a zero score.

    (A) hackneyed

    (B) pulchritudinous

    (C) vituperative

    (D) intractable

    (E) woebegone

3. The players were afraid to enter the locker room at half time, knowing the coach would be there ready to ---- them for their horrible performance on the field.

    (A) rail at

    (B) fawn over

    (C) extol

    (D) effervesce

    (E) dilly-dally

4. The ---- boy realized he was not experienced enough to perform the tasks alone and began looking for an older partner who had more maturity and experience.

    (A) venerable

    (B) callow

    (C) peripatetic

    (D) halcyon

    (E) dogmatic

5. Lucy was annoyed at her father's ---- pronouncements, which assumed that he was always correct and that no one else's opinion should even be considered.

    (A) aberrant

    (B) hapless

    (C) malleable

    (D) wan

    (E) dogmatic

6. The teenage girls ---- through the mall, not shopping for anything in particular, but stopping to look at whatever caught their fancy.

    (A) vituperated

    (B) reviled

    (C) squandered

    (D) sauntered

    (E) hectored

7. The normally gorgeous girl said she wanted to look - - - - for Halloween, so she chose a costume that made her appear old, fat, and unattractive.

   (A) svelte

   (B) stentorian

   (C) judicious

   (D) ingenious

   (E) homely

8. When the mother bellowed her son's name in a(n) - - - - voice, everyone in the neighborhood heard her call.

   (A) stentorian

   (B) sycophantic

   (C) choleric

   (D) terse

   (E) erudite

9. Patrick became - - - - when he walked into the parking lot and saw some-one had dented his brand new car and taken off without leaving a note.

   (A) gaunt

   (B) insolvent

   (C) choleric

   (D) froward

   (E) munificent

10. It was merely a lucky chance, pure - - - - that my class ring happened to be found by a former teacher at my school who knew how to get the ring back to me.

    (A) pulchritude

    (B) parsimony

    (C) inanity

    (D) omniscience

    (E) serendipity

11. The drama coach had to make a ---- assessment of the qualities of those who auditioned for the play, deciding who would make the best leading man.

    (A) sartorial

    (B) judicious

    (C) doleful

    (D) hidebound

    (E) perfunctory

12. We hardly recognized the ---- woman in front of us, because she had lost 50 pounds in the year since we'd last seen her.

    (A) dogged

    (B) coeval

    (C) antediluvian

    (D) svelte

    (E) acute

13. The ---- wit of the comedian allowed him to answer the questions of the audience and overcome the jabs of the hecklers.

    (A) wishy-washy

    (B) surly

    (C) coruscating

    (D) discursive

    (E) nescient

14. On vacation, Elle was content to be ----, rarely washing her hair or putting on makeup.

    (A) peripatetic

    (B) frowzy

    (C) hoary

    (D) rangy

    (E) peckish

15. The newscaster hired a beauty and wardrobe consultant to help her develop a more ---- appearance, knowing that when she went on national television, millions of people would be judging her on her looks.

    (A) soignée

    (B) lugubrious

    (C) vociferous

    (D) impecunious

    (E) profligate

16. The preacher urged his congregation to be charitable, telling them that giving help to the ---- asking for quarters on the street is the right thing to do.

    (A) toady

    (B) mendicant

    (C) plutocrat

    (D) chatterbox

    (E) pedant

17. Brenda said that even though she and Dorothy Parker were not ---- but from different times, she felt a type of kinship with the poet.

    (A) obese

    (B) halcyon

    (C) prolific

    (D) coeval

    (E) fatuous

18. Ethan was rejected by the fraternity, whose president said the frat was looking for people from old, established families who'd had money for many generations, not ---- whose money was newly earned.

    (A) slatterns

    (B) pedants

    (C) parvenus

    (D) pundits

    (E) laggards

19. Knowing he was - - - -, the reporter went to the library to get background materials on the subject so that he could be informed and knowledge-able when he did his interview.

    (A) perspicacious

    (B) mellifluous

    (C) superannuated

    (D) nescient

    (E) irresolute

20. Calvin was noted for his - - - - responses, often answering a long question with just one word.

    (A) pithy

    (B) wan

    (C) superfluous

    (D) fatuous

    (E) puerile

21. The surgeon was respected for his diagnostic - - - -, his ability to recog-nize possible ramifications of very complicated and difficult situations.

    (A) folly

    (B) acumen

    (C) swarthiness

    (D) indigence

    (E) senescence

22. The members of the golf club chose - - - - to head their board, men and women of wealth and position who had grown up used to privileges.

    (A) polymaths

    (B) sycophants

    (C) slatterns

    (D) tyros

    (E) plutocrats

23. The student newspaper - - - - the food in the cafeteria, saying that it was the best-tasting lunch in any school in the city, rivaling even the fast-food restaurants' offerings.

    (A) vilified

    (B) extolled

    (C) squandered

    (D) carped

    (E) railed at

24. The teenager accused her father of having - - - - standards that hadn't changed in the 40 years since he had been a teen himself.

    (A) precocious

    (B) enervated

    (C) malleable

    (D) antediluvian

    (E) vacuous

25. When she found out her favorite student had earned a perfect score on his SAT, Mrs. Laughlin broke into a - - - -, saying she always knew he was intelligent and capable.

    (A) paean

    (B) dirge

    (C) torpor

    (D) candor

    (E) turpitude

Making the Grade: Answers

Check your answers in this section.

1. **B.** Someone precocious is advanced for his age, ahead of his peers.

2. **D.** Someone intractable is stubborn, unwilling to change. The root *tract* means to draw or pull. Someone intractable cannot be pulled away from his position.

3. **A.** To rail at is to yell at, to scold, or speak badly about.

4. **B.** Someone callow is youthful and inexperienced.

5. **E.** Dogmatic means stubbornly opinionated, narrow-minded.

6. **D.** To saunter is to meander, to wander aimlessly.

7. **E.** Homely means plain and unattractive.

8. **A.** A stentorian voice is a very, very loud voice.

9. **C.** Choleric means hot-tempered, angry, wrathful.

10. **E.** Serendipity is luck or good fortune, especially in finding something accidentally.

11. **B.** Judicious means wise and careful, showing sound judgment.

12. **D.** Svelte means fashionably slender.

   Choice E, acute, means keen or quick of mind, shrewd. It has nothing to do with being "a cute" woman.

13. **C.** Coruscating means suddenly displaying brilliance and wit.

14. **B.** Someone frowzy is dirty, neglected, and untidy in appearance.

15. **A.** Soignée means meticulously dressed and well-groomed.

16. **B.** A mendicant is a beggar, one who asks for help.

17. **D.** Coeval means of the same age or period, contemporary.

18. **C.** A parvenu is a person of humble origins who has gained wealth and position.

19. **D.** Someone nescient is ignorant, lacking knowledge.

   The root *scien* means knowledge; *ne–* is a negative prefix. Nescient is literally not knowing or without knowledge.

20. **A.** Pithy means concise, terse, and full of meaning. A pithy response is short and to the point.

21. **B.** Acumen is shrewdness, keenness, and quickness in understanding and dealing with a situation.

22. **E.** A plutocrat is a person exercising power or influence over others by right of wealth or position.

23. **B.** To extol is to praise highly.

24. **D.** Antediluvian means very old, old-fashioned, primitive.

   Ante– means before.

25. **A.** A paean is a song of praise.

Chapter 27

Genius Test

● ●

So, you think you're the King of Craniums, the Baron of Brainiacs, the Sultan of Sesquipedalianism? Here's your chance to prove your theory!

This Genius Test is just for fun and bragging rights. Very few of these words will actually show up on standardized tests (thank goodness!). However, the words in this test have all shown up previously in this book. The vast majority of words weren't part of the regular word lists, but were bonuses (bonusii?) tucked away in the nooks and crannies. Some words are from sidebars. Some words are from answer explanations. Some words are even from the bonus trivia/joke asides. All words were defined in the text (and of course, are in the glossary, should you give up and have to go there to get the definitions). Just how carefully have you been paying attention?

Just to give you a sporting chance, I've narrowed the answer choices down to four instead of the usual five. Good luck, and have fun!

Without Question: Answering the Toughest Questions

Directions: Grab a four-leaf clover in one hand and a parachute in the other to catch your ego as it plunges as you attempt to answer the following questions.

1. If your ex-boyfriend is trying to traduce you, he's most likely to succeed by calling you which of the following?

   (A) the most beautiful woman he's ever met

   (B) the biggest cheater in school

   (C) the least talkative person in school

   (D) the best athlete in the city

2. You have a horse named Dastard. When he encounters another member of the equine persuasion (another horse), if he lives up to his name, he's most likely to

   (A) bite the other horse

   (B) try to establish an intimate relationship with the other horse

   (C) run away from the other horse

   (D) call it mean, nasty, hurtful horse names

3. Your best buddy tells you he had a sternutative episode on Saturday night. You

   (A) feel jealous that he has a better social life than you do

   (B) offer him a box of tissues and the name of your allergist

   (C) feel sorry for him but ask to copy his homework; no sense in both of you doing all that work

   (D) try to borrow the videotape

4. Your Sweetie asks you to come over to her place for what she terms "an evening of gustatory delights." You can do your part by bringing along

   (A) your workout clothes

   (B) a bottle of good wine

   (C) a CD of romantic music

   (D) three more buddies to form a study group

5. You read an ad for a housing complex called Aquiline Acres and deduce the neighborhood has many

   (A) waterfalls

   (B) eagles

   (C) gemstones

   (D) fruit trees

6. Your fiancée returns the gift you gave her, calling it pinchbeck. It most likely was

   (A) clothing that was much too tight

   (B) food she was allergic to

   (C) cheap, fake jewelry

   (D) a video that contained objectionable material

7. You are most likely to Bowdlerize which of the following?

   (A) hot love letters you think your snoopy mom is going to find sooner
   or later

   (B) your car just before setting off on a cross-country trip

   (C) a man in a ridiculous-looking hat

   (D) a term paper you bought off the Web

8. A sculptor asks whether he can make a stone carving of your callipygian
   feature. You will be modeling which of the following?

   (A) your smile

   (B) your legs

   (C) your butt

   (D) your chest

9. You're going out to meet someone who describes himself as an epicure.
   You're most likely to find him in which of the following places?

   (A) a swimming pool

   (B) a pharmacy

   (C) a library

   (D) a restaurant

10. Your grandmother has what you consider an abnormal obsession with
    your being punctilious, and so she lectures you whenever you

    (A) are late for an appointment

    (B) let your grades slip

    (C) show poor manners

    (D) display your belly button

11. Which of the following would you use to cover your opisthenar?

    (A) a helmet

    (B) a glove

    (C) plastic wrap

    (D) an insurance policy

12. An animal described as xanthous is headed your way. You look up, expecting to see which of the following critters?

    (A) a cardinal

    (B) a raven

    (C) an albino rhino

    (D) a tiger

13. You have a new job that pays you one dollar every femtosecond. How many dollars do you have in one second?

    (A) a quadrillion

    (B) a billion

    (C) a quadrillionth

    (D) a billionth

14. Your little sister has acute pogophobia. She's most likely to start screaming in fear when she sees

    (A) a poodle

    (B) a Popsicle

    (C) a beard

    (D) a banjo

15. A character in a book is described as turdine. You expect her to spend most of her time

    (A) in the bathroom

    (B) in a birdhouse

    (C) at the dentist's office

    (D) talking

16. If Mr. Wonderful offers you "a night of funambulism!" you're most likely to end up

    (A) at the circus

    (B) in the principal's office

    (C) hiding from the police

    (D) bald

17. Your brother's best friend tells you he considers himself muliebrose. Which of the following should you do?

    (A) call 911

    (B) ask him to lend you money

    (C) introduce him to your sister

    (D) run, run, run!

18. If you hear something described as esculent,

    (A) it makes your toes tap

    (B) it makes your armpits sweat

    (C) it makes your ears burn

    (D) it makes your mouth water

19. Entering the gates of the amusement park, you hear a rumor that the antepenultimate guest of the day gets a Lifetime Free Pass. You run around trying to change your position so that you are in which place in line?

    (A) third to last

    (B) second to last

    (C) third from the front

    (D) second from the front

20. Your father, hurrying you into the car, tells you not to be facetious at Great Aunt Griselda's place this afternoon. Which of the following should you leave at home?

    (A) your little brother

    (B) your exercise equipment

    (C) your appetite

    (D) your sense of humor

21. A rather unusual-looking man approaches you and tells you he was sent from Up There to be your nemesis. You should

    (A) hug him because he's your One True Love

    (B) run because he's an agent of retribution, seeking revenge for a past wrongdoing

    (C) tell him your troubles, because he's a licensed psychiatrist

    (D) show him your trick knee so he can operate on it later

22. When the professor asks you a question, you give him a flippant response. He

    (A) laughs at your pun

    (B) marks you down for being a smart-aleck

    (C) tells you he's impressed with your creativity

    (D) repeats the question

23. You offer to fustigate someone on behalf of a friend and begin looking around for

    (A) a stick to wallop him upside the head

    (B) your car keys to give him a ride

    (C) a pan to cook him dinner

    (D) your class notes to share with him

24. Rather than lie about someone in a letter, you merely say that he is feckless, counting on the fact that your reader probably won't know the word. You've just called the person

    (A) reckless

    (B) mentally challenged

    (C) overweight

    (D) weak

25. Your dad tells you that for Father's Day, he wants something from a nearby haberdashery. He's asking for

    (A) computer supplies

    (B) golf equipment

    (C) car accessories

    (D) clothing

26. Your brother calls, says he's coming home for Spring Break, and asks you to warn the parents that he's now hirsute. You break the news to them that Junior is

    (A) tattooed

    (B) bearded

    (C) engaged to be married

    (D) in trouble with the law

27. At his retirement dinner, the man heard himself called "someone with amazing probity." He knows that

    (A) his intelligence is being questioned

    (B) his character is being praised

    (C) he's being teased about having fathered eight children

    (D) he's being congratulated on his good luck

28. You offer to fix up your friend with a man you know. She says okay "as long as he's not superannuated; I can go out with nearly anyone but I draw the line at someone superannuated." She doesn't want to date a man who is

    (A) hairy

    (B) annoying

    (C) old

    (D) stupid

29. Your kitty, Fearless Feline, suffers from brontophobia. The poor thing cowers in terror under the bed

    (A) at the sight of men

    (B) at the sight of mice

    (C) at the sound of bathwater being run

    (D) at the sound of thunder

30. You're looking for someone to help you titivate. You put an ad in the paper for a

    (A) SAT tutor

    (B) chauffeur

    (C) wardrobe consultant

    (D) babysitter

31. You assure your date's parents that you're a good person, saying that you carefully eschew which of the following?

    (A) love

    (B) meat

    (C) drinking and driving

    (D) your parents

32. Your neighbor asks you to help him search for his pied pooch. You're scouring the vicinity for a dog that is

    (A) huge and fat

    (B) very old and gray

    (C) lame

    (D) black and white

33. You are known as the Professor of Pandiculation. You received your nickname because of your habit of

    (A) yawning

    (B) scratching your nose

    (C) flirting

    (D) snatching food from other people's plates

34. Your mother tells you to clean up your doggerel. You

    (A) wash the graffiti off the wall

    (B) toss your clothes in the laundry

    (C) jump in the shower to scrub your back

    (D) chase Fido the Filthy, pooper scooper in hand

35. You're looking for horripilation. You're most likely to find it

    (A) in the garage

    (B) in your kitty's litter

    (C) on your arms

    (D) in the fridge

36. Your friend tells you she's just finished a pangram. Which class has she most likely been in?

    (A) home economics

    (B) Calculus

    (C) world history

    (D) typing

37. If you are bibulous, you are most likely to get into trouble with which of the following?

    (A) a clergyman

    (B) a highway patrol officer

    (C) a pediatrician

    (D) a basketball coach

38. You're looking for someone to help you with your orthography. Whom should you ask?

    (A) a mattress salesman

    (B) a dental hygienist

    (C) an English teacher

    (D) a travel agent

39. A store named Various Viands most likely sells

    (A) shoes

    (B) watches

    (C) video games

    (D) groceries

40. You refuse to pay for a professional photograph you had taken of you, saying it makes you look "positively piscine." You think you look

    (A) as dumb as an ox

    (B) fish-faced

    (C) fat as a pig

    (D) as if you're snarling

41. Who is most likely to use the word brummagem to describe something of yours?

    (A) a professional chef you had over to sample your cooking

    (B) an antiques appraiser looking at your jewelry

    (C) your father reading your report card

    (D) a mechanic looking at your car engine

42. Which of the following would be a dream job for a philogynist?

    (A) football coach

    (B) movie critic

    (C) harem-keeper

    (D) mountain climber

43. Your friend, trying to fix you up with a date, tells you he (or she) has a dearth of dentistry. You know that your date

    (A) has extremely white teeth

    (B) has braces

    (C) has no teeth

    (D) has career plans of becoming a dentist

44. If you are a plenipotentiary, you have

    (A) the best social life of anyone you know

    (B) a lot of power

    (C) an amazing number of jokes in your head

    (D) excellent grades in school

45. You complain to your parents about the swim coach's high-handed behavior. You're griping that he

    (A) is too competitive

    (B) encourages cheating

    (C) favors girls over boys

    (D) is overbearing and doesn't care about your feelings

46. You get back a paper on which the teacher has written, "You did a desultory job." Which grade are you most likely to receive on the paper?

    (A) A

    (B) B

    (C) C

    (D) F

47. You are known as someone with a lot of mettle. You're most likely to do which of the following?

    (A) go sky-diving

    (B) talk non-stop

    (C) save every penny you've ever earned

    (D) get a bad reputation at school

48. Students in horology class have what spread all over their desks when doing their homework?

    (A) Halloween masks

    (B) dictionaries

    (C) watches

    (D) gardening tools

49. Your mother's mother is coming over for a visit, and you feel the need to frequent a tonsorial establishment. Where are you going?

    (A) to a saloon

    (B) to a shoe store

    (C) to a barber shop

    (D) to a psychiatrist's office

50. When someone asks you to describe this test, you tell him, "It was, like, totally abecedarian!" You are saying you considered the test to be

    (A) elementary, very easy

    (B) mind-boggling, very difficult

    (C) rude and crude

    (D) full of lame jokes

Standing Corrected: Answers to the Test

That was fun, wasn't it? Check your answers against those in this section. No, getting half of the problems correct doesn't mean you're a half-wit, it means you're a vocabulary virtuoso! The test had some extremely difficult words in it. If you answered even a third of them correctly, congratulations!

1. **B.** To traduce is to slander, to say bad things about. Your ex traduces you by calling you a big cheater.

   If you chose A, you fell for the trap. You may be seduced by sweet talk, but you're traduced by cheat talk.

2. **C.** A dastard is a coward. If you chose A or D, you confused dastard with a similar-sounding word that you and I are too refined to mention.

3. **B.** Sternutation is sneezing. Your buddy spent Saturday night sneezing, not squeezing, poor guy.

4. **B.** Gustatory means pertaining to the sense of taste. An evening of gustatory delights would be one with good food.

5. **B.** Aquiline means like or pertaining to an eagle.

   If you chose A, you got trapped thinking of "aqua" like the water; if you chose C, you probably got trapped thinking of "aquamarines."

6. **C.** Pinchbeck is counterfeit, cheap, fake jewelry. Your fiancée found out about that cubic zirconium you were trying to pass off as diamonds, and is returning the piece.

7. **A.** To Bowdlerize is to take out the dirty parts, to clean up. If your love letter is too hot for your mom's comfort, you Bowdlerize it before she discovers it in your supposedly secret place.

8. **C.** Callipygian means having beautiful buttocks. Now, isn't that word alone worth the price of this book?

9. **D.** An epicure is one who enjoys fine food and drink.

   I hope you didn't fall for the cheezy trap, choice B. An epicure has nothing to do with a cure.

10. **C.** A punctilious person is careful with matters of etiquette and good manners. Choice A was too obvious for a question in a "genius" test, don'tcha think? Being punctilious is not the same as being punctual.

11. **B.** Your opisthenar is the back of your hand. When your mother asks you whether you've studied your material, you can tell her the answers are on your opisthenar.

12. **D.** Xanthous means yellowish-brown, tawny. Cardinals are red, ravens are black, albinos are white, and tigers are xanthous.

13. **C.** Femto is a prefix meaning quadrillionth. A femtosecond is one-quadrillionth second.

14. **C.** Pogophobia is the fear of beards. As for D, well, there may be a word that means "fear of banjos," but I haven't learned it yet. If you come across such a term, please let me know.

15. **B.** Turdine means like a thrush, a type of bird. If you chose A, I want you to know that this isn't that type of book!

16. **A.** Funambulism is tightrope walking, something you're most likely to see at the circus. Of course, choice C could conceivably be correct, as well, should you walk a tightrope yourself between two buildings and get caught by the cops.

17. **C.** Someone muliebrose likes women. Play matchmaker by introducing a muliebrose man to your older sister.

18. **D.** Something esculent is edible, tasty. Of course, if that esculent something is hot chili peppers, B and C may also be correct!

19. **A.** The ultimate position is the last position. The penultimate position is the second to last position. The antepenultimate position is the third to last position.

20. **D.** Someone facetious is funny, but in an inappropriate sort of way. A facetious person makes a wise crack, then immediately says, "Just kidding!"

21. **B.** Nemesis was the Greek goddess of vengeance. A nemesis is anyone who's out to get you, or more specifically, who's out to get you back for something.

22. **B.** Someone flippant is a smart-aleck, always cracking wise. A flippant answer is usually disrespectful, saucy and impertinent.

23. **A.** To fustigate someone is to beat him with a stick. Can you imagine a police detective using that word to a criminal? "Now, now, didn't your mother teach you not to fustigate others?"

24. **D.** Feckless is just a high class way of saying ineffective, irresponsible, a loser.

25. **D.** A haberdashery is a gentleman's clothing store. Hmm . . . I don't know of any equivalent word on the distaff side. Is there a term that means a ladies' clothing store? Maybe boutique would work, but it seems to me I've seen men's clothes in boutiques, too.

26. **B.** Hirsute means hairy, shaggy, or bristly. Think of the Smith Brothers (on the cough drop box), the men of ZZ Top (the singers), and Rip Van Winkle after his 20-year snooze as hirsute dudes.

27. **B.** Probity is good character, morality, integrity. In the 1960s, when people were calling police officers pigs, some cops responded by wearing badges saying (P)robity—(I)ntegrity—(G)uts.

28. **D.** Superannuated means old. To a teenager, anyone over 30 seems superannuated, right?

29. **D.** Brontophobia is the fear of thunder.

30. **C.** To titivate is to spruce up, to dress up. However, I strongly advice you not to run an ad saying you're looking for a titivator. The world is full of a lot of strange people, and very few of them know the proper meaning of titivate.

31. **C.** To eschew is to avoid, to shun. Good people avoid drinking and driving. Choice B was just too, too obvious, don't you think? Eschew does not mean chew.

32. **D.** Pied means covered with splotches of different colors, such as black-and-white spotted. A Dalmatian is a pied pooch.

33. **A.** Pandiculation is the act of yawning and stretching. I've often thought that exercises classes, along with aerobics hours, should have pandiculation periods. I'd volunteer to lead those.

34. **A.** Doggerel is verse, especially silly or crude verse, just the type you see as graffiti on walls.

35. **C.** Horripilation is what you call it when the hair on your body, especially on your arms, stands up. When you're so scared you get goose bumps and your hair rises, that's horripilation.

36. **D.** A pangram is a sentence, usually used as a typing exercise, with all the letters in it. You use a pangram to teach you how to hit all the keys on the keyboard.

37. **B.** Someone bibulous customarily drinks a lot. If you've had a few beers, that highway patrol officer is not going to be your best buddy.

38. **C.** Orthography is correct spelling.

    If you chose A, you fell for the trap of thinking of Ortho mattresses. If you chose B, you fell for the trap of thinking of orthodontics.

39. **D.** Viands are foodstuffs, things to eat.

40. **B.** Piscine means fish-like. If you pucker up and make a fish-face when giving your granny a little smooch on the cheek, that's a piscine peck.

41. **B.** Brummagem means fake and artificial, and usually refers to jewelry. When you find out that supposedly 24-karat gold bracelet your friend gave you is actually just gold tone, the piece is brummagem.

42. **C.** A philogynist loves women. If he could be in a harem all day, he'd be in seventh heaven.

43. **C.** A dearth is a lack of. A dearth of dentistry means either he never went to the dentist or has no teeth (and the former situation could certainly lead to the latter situation). You may want to rethink asking this friend to fix you up in the future.

44. **B.** A plenipotentiary has much power. Of course, if you have a good social life, good grades, and a lot of jokes, you may have power as a result of those things!

45. **D.** A high-handed person thinks only of himself and bulldozes over everyone else. He doesn't care about your feelings.

46. **C.** A desultory job is one that was not methodical, but done in an aimless way. The paper wasn't bad enough for an F or a D, but not good enough for an A. It was just so-so.

47. **A.** Mettle is courage. If you are willing to jump out of a perfectly functional plane, chances are you're pretty brave.

48. **C.** Horology is the science of making watches, clocks, and other time-keeping devices. Why, what did you think it meant? (Tsk, tsk!)

49. **C.** Tonsorial means pertaining to hair. A tonsorial establishment is a barbershop, a hair dresser, or the like.

50. **A.** Abecedarian has two meanings: in alphabetic order, and "easy as A-B-C;" elementary. Someone as brilliant as you undoubtedly considers this exam super-easy!

Part V
The Part of Tens

The 5th Wave   By Rich Tennant

TRAGICALLY DOUG HAD JUST COMPLETED THE VOCABULARY PORTION OF HIS SAT EXAM BEFORE SETTING SAIL THAT DAY.

AMELIORATE!! AMELIORATE!!

Anyone here know what "ameliorate" means?

In this part . . .

*H*ere's your chance for once in your life to be surrounded by a bunch of perfect tens! Sit back, doff your thinking cap, don your party hat, and enjoy!

This part has no new word lists, no practice exams — nothing to boggle, baffle, or bewilder you. These chapters are just for fun, but they do provide valuable information. For example, where else but in this part can you find out how to use the perfect vocabulary to talk your way out of gym class, a traffic ticket, and even a dental appointment? Where else can you find great quotes about vocabulary? And where but here can you find out how to master SAT vocab even if English isn't your first language?

Chapter 28

Ten Ways to Put a Good Vocabulary to Use in the Real World

. . . .

In This Chapter

▶ Using the right vocabulary to dodge a dilemma

▶ Employing the right vocabulary to achieve your ambition

▶ Enjoying the right vocabulary to tease or please others

. . . .

*R*ight now, you may not care about the real world. All you care about is getting through your test. But given that you've been sweating and fretting your way through mastering all these words, why not use them in every day activities and make all that pain and suffering — um, I mean, joy and pleasure — really pay off for you? This chapter gives you ten techniques for getting double your value from these words.

Titivate (Spruce Up, Enhance, Embellish) Your Love Letters

Tell your dearly beloved that the very *seraphim* and *cherubim* (angels) sing of your love, and that you are *sanguine* (cheerfully optimistic) your relationship will last forever.

For guys: Anyone can call a woman beautiful, but you'll always be remembered if you call her *pulchritudinous.*

For girls: Anyone can tell a man that he's a real man, but it takes a real woman to tell him he's *virile.*

Get Out of Gym Class

If you're trying to con the gym teacher, for heaven's sake, don't give him or her a *prosaic* (commonplace, humdrum) note saying you have a backache and can't participate in class that day. Instead, pen an *epistle* (letter) saying that you're a *bungling* (clumsy) *maladroit* (clumsy, bungling) *dolt* (blockhead) and can't participate. Chances are, the teacher won't have a clue what the letter means, but won't want to admit his or her *nescience* (ignorance) and will let you go rather than lose face.

Intimidate a Mechanic

Perhaps you're the rare mechanically gifted person who can tell your mechanic exactly what's wrong with your car and not be intimidated that he or she knows more than you do. But most people walk in and say, "Well, you know, it's like this klunk-thunk noise when I slow down . . . ." The *supercilious* (stuck-up) mechanic looks down his nose at you, pats your shoulder *condescendingly* (in a manner as if he's better than you) and says, "Don't worry, we'll find the problem and fix it." The next thing you know, you're given a bill for an *exorbitant* (excessive, extravagant) amount. You have no idea whether to *impugn* (question, challenge as false) or respect his *veracity* (truthfulness). Ah, but if you were to face said mechanic and *mellifluously* (in a honeyed, sweet voice) say *grandiloquently* (in a grand manner): "There's a *Stentorian* (loud) knocking that is *exacerbated* (made worse) upon *deceleration* (slowing down)," he'll be too intimidated to rip you off.

Compliment the Cook

When the meal was sheer delight and you want to make sure that you're invited back for another one, tell the cook how much you enjoyed his or her *delectable* (delicious) *repast* (meal) or *savory* (delicious) and *succulent* (juicy) *collation* (light meal). Not only will your host or hostess be flattered that you took the time to learn such words to compliment the cooking, the cook will be eager to find out more and thus invite you back for seconds. (Be sure to brush up on your vocab before the return engagement!)

Get Out of Doing Chores

You say you just can't face getting up early on a Saturday morning to vacuum the carpet or mow the lawn? Inform your parents that you are too *sluggish* (slow), *somnolent* (sleepy), and just plain *indolent* (lazy) to complete the task today, that you'd rather *procrastinate* (put off, postpone) until tomorrow or better yet, *eschew* (avoid) it entirely. Of course, if your parents were *savvy* (smart, shrewd) enough to *peruse* (examine) this book themselves, they will know to accuse you of *malingering* (shirking your duties, pretending to be ill to get out of work) and insist you immediately become full of *vim* (life, liveliness) and get to work.

Placate (Calm Down) an Irate (Furious) Parent Over a Heinous (Really, Really Bad) Grade

Your parents are *incensed* (furious) because your grades took a *precipitous* (steep) drop this semester? *Pacify* (calm down) them with a sentence such as, "Of course, *venerable* (honorable) parents, I *acquiesce* (consent, yield to without protest) to your proposed punishment, but plead *extenuating* (lessening the seriousness of, excusing) circumstances: I was so *industrious* (hardworking) with my *logomachy* (word games, arguments and discussion about words) that there was a *dearth* (lack of) of time for more *prosaic* (commonplace, everyday) activities, such as studying for that chemistry test."

Refuse a Date without Crushing an Ego

You really, really don't want to go out with someone, but you don't want to hurt his or her feelings. Use your vocabulary to *mitigate* (make less severe or painful) your rejection. "While normally I would accept with *alacrity* (eager haste) such an offer, I *lugubriously* (sadly) must say no as I have to *toil* (work) in my father's *noisome* (smelly, malodorous) *piscine* (pertaining to fish) palace, helping him on the boat this weekend."

Bamboozle (Confuse, Discombobulate) a Traffic Officer

When the officer pulls you over, smile *ingenuously* (innocently) and *susurrate* (whisper), "Why, Sir, Officer Sir, did you think my *celerity* (speed) excessive? I have nothing but *deference* (respect) for the law, of course, but in this case, I must *dolorously* (sadly) and with the utmost *reverence* (respect) for your badge, *dispute* (argue with) your statement." He'll be so busy working that one out that he'll forget about the ticket and let you off with an *admonition* (warning).

Frustrate Your Dentist

Dentists are uncommonly *proficient* (skilled) at interpreting what you say, even when your tongue is numb and your mouth full of instruments. "Th uh ore?" she knows means, "Is there much more?" Why not have a little fun and instead say, "I *proffer* (offer) a *paean* (song of praise) to your *meticulous* (detailed, pain-staking) dental *opus* (grand work)?" Watch her head explode as she tries to figure that one out!

Leave a Classy Legacy in Your Yearbook

Don't you *loathe* (hate) it when everyone signs the same *trite, hackneyed* (overly common, overused) phrases like, "Stay as sweet as you are" and "You'll go far, big guy!" in your yearbook? Show some style and try instead, "Don't be *protean* (changing) when it comes to your *dulcet* (sweet) status!" and, "You're a potential *potentate* (powerful person), *Brobdingnagian* (big) guy!"

Chapter 29

Ten Great Quotes about Words

- -

In This Chapter

▶ Telling about talking

▶ Speaking about squawking

▶ Venerating verbalizing

- -

*O*h sure, when you show off your new and improved vocabulary — and you will want to, believe me — you'll sound *erudite* and *sagacious* (smart). But if you want to sound really, truly *scintillating* (brilliant), go one step further. Enlighten your listeners with what other people have to say on the subject of talking and vocabulary. The following ten (er, nine!) quotes are great ones to toss into a conversation.

"Words are the physicians of a mind diseased."

— Aeschylus

"The question is," said Alice, "whether you can make words mean so many different things."

"The question is," said Humpty Dumpty, "which is to be master — that's all."

— Lewis Carroll

"When I feel inclined to read poetry, I take down my dictionary. The poetry of words is quite as beautiful as the poetry of sentences."

— Oliver Wendell Holmes

"I am a bear of very little brain, and long words bother me."

— Winnie-the-Pooh (A. A. Milne)

"Like golden apples in silver settings are words spoken at the proper time."

— Proverbs 25:11

"If you can teach me a new word, I'll walk all the way to China to get it."

— Turkish proverb

"The difference between the right word and the almost right word is the difference between lightning and the lightning bug."

— Mark Twain

"One great use of words is to hide our thoughts."

— Voltaire

"Choice word and measured phrase above the reach
Of ordinary men."

— William Wordsworth

Chapter 30

Ten Ways to Master Words When English Is a Foreign Tongue

*I*n English, when you don't understand something, you say, "It's Greek to me." At this stage, trying to master all the vocabulary in this book may prompt you to say in resignation, "Oh, I dunno; it's English to me." Never fear. You can and will become accustomed to all the words in this book and many, many more. In this chapter, you find ten suggestions for making learning both easy and fun. And always remind yourself when you're at your *nadir* (lowest point) that no matter how little English vocabulary you feel as if you know, you can be pretty sure that Americans know even less vocabulary in your native tongue!

Although these ten (actually, nine, but it's close enough!) tips were designed primarily to help non-native English speakers, they're good for everyone. Even if you grew up in Smalltown, USA, right in the heartland and have enunciated English since your first "mama," you can benefit from the suggestions in this chapter.

Look for Similarities with Words in Your Native Language

Many English words are derived from (okay, shamelessly stolen from!) words in other languages. Speak French? Then you know *ennui,* meaning boredom. That's an easy word for you, but a difficult word for native English speakers.

Speak Spanish? You're familiar with the prefix *biblio,* meaning book (think of a library: biblioteca). In English, therefore, you can figure out that a bibliophile is a book-lover (*biblio* means book; *phil* means love). Speak German? *Weltschmerz* is an astonishingly hard word for English speakers, but you know it means sentimental melancholy or pessimism over the state of the world.

Localize As You Vocalize

Some people, myself included, are peripatetic learners. That is, you learn by walking around. You can remember that you learned the word *loquacious* (talkative) while sitting at your desk in your bedroom, but the word *taciturn* (not talkative) while at the kitchen table, driven out of your room by your sibling's loud music. Perhaps you learned *Brobdingnagian* (huge) while sitting in the waiting room of your doctor's office and *Lilliputian* (tiny) in the car on the way home. Try to recall the location where you learned the word; replay the study place and locale in your brain. You may be pleasantly surprised at how easily you can associate the two.

Bonus trivia: The Greek philosopher Aristotle used to lecture while walking around. His followers were called the Peripatetics. Now that's a piece of trivia you can use when you're moseying through the mall.

Associate Places Back Home with New Vocab

Did you come from a very sleepy small town? Think of it as *somnolent* (sleepy). Did you hail from a huge, bustling metropolis? Think of yourself as *cosmopolitan* (worldly, sophisticated). Do your parents have a store selling men's attire? They are *haberdashers* (a *haberdashery* is a gentleman's clothing store). Does your hometown have a statue hailing war heroes in the downtown square? It's celebrating the *intrepid* (brave) citizens. The key is to visualize points back home and use this vocabulary to describe them.

Memorize the Words in a Tactile (Touching, Tangible) Fashion

I had a teacher give me this hint when I was very young, and I've used it ever since. When you learn the words dealing with, for example, talk, touch your mouth. Put on lip gloss or brush your teeth when you're learning *chatterbox* (a talkative person) or *garrulous* (talkative) to remind yourself that those words have to do with the mouth. Put your shoes on while learning *perambulate* (walk) or *ambulatory* (able to move) to fix in your mind that those words have to do with getting up and moving. Eating a bit too much? When you open the fridge door, recall *obese* (fat), *corpulent* (overweight), and *rotund* (round, overweight). When you grab a healthy apple instead of a slice of chocolate cake, give yourself a verbal pat on the back with words like *svelte* (fashionably slim).

Associate Words with American TV Shows

Ever seen the sitcom *Friends?* Think of the people in that show as *amicable* and *amiable* (friendly). In the drama *ER,* the doctors are always *frenzied* and *frenetic* (wild and frantic, going in bursts of action). My favorite show, *Frasier,* is both *erudite* (learned, scholarly) and *risible* (causing laughter). As you're watching TV — something that also increases your vocabulary, especially if you watch the History, Discovery, or public broadcasting channels — try to associate words with both the shows and the stars.

Give Nicknames to Your Friends, Family, and Professors

Is your math teacher rather harsh in his grading, refusing to change your B+ to an A–? He's Mr. *Draconian* (extremely severe or cruel). You say your father is a sharp dresser, always in a suit and tie when he goes to work? He's *Dapper* Dad (well-dressed, natty). Your older brother is a little too fond of having wine with dinner? He's your *Bibulous* Brother (*bibulous* means addicted to or fond of alcoholic beverages).

String Words Together

When you were a child, did you ever play the game "Shopping?" Where I grew up, in Indiana, the shopping game had each person adding something to the list. The first person would say, "I'm going shopping and I'm going to buy a marble." The second person would say, "I'm going shopping and I'm going to buy a marble, and a puppet." The third person would say, "I'm going shopping and I'm going to buy a marble, a puppet, and a doorknob." The goal was to remember as many items as possible. The first person who forgot an item lost. The same technique can work with your vocab. When you walk to the dinner table, mutter to yourself, "I'm *ambling* (walking) to my *comestibles* (dinner), which I hope will be *salubrious* (healthful)." getting ready for a date, look in the mirror and say, "I'm *embellishing* (enhancing) my *comeliness* (attractiveness) for my date, who I hope will be *munificent* (generous) and pay for dinner at a nice restaurant, where we will offer *kudos* and *plaudits* (praises) to the chef for the meal."

Enlist the Help — and Harassment — of Your Friends and Family

People love to help when they're asked, especially if helping means they can hassle you at the same time! Give everyone you know a list of five to ten words, the ones you find the most difficult to remember, and ask them to bombard you with those words every single time they see you or talk to you. Assign your best friend the word frowzy, and she'll enjoy saying, "My, you're looking too *frowzy* (ill-groomed, sloppy) today; time to go get a haircut and some decent clothes." Your little brother could be given *lachrymose* (tearful), which he would use as, "If you don't give me five dollars to go see a matinee, I'll be lachrymose. I'll be even more lachrymose if you make me eat veggie pizza instead of sausage pizza."

Arrange for a Secret Word Dropper

My father used this technique for me when I was young. I wrote out my vocabulary words on slips of paper and gave them to Dad. He'd put them in all sorts of places for me to discover. I'd open my lunchbox and find *delectable* (delicious). I'd step into the shower and find taped to the shower curtain *noisome* (smelling bad). Have your friends and family do the same for you. Create as many slips of paper with words as you can and ask your buddies to spring them on you, putting them in places where you can't help but see them. You may find a word on the seat of your car, on your desk at school, or under your pillow. The unexpectedness of seeing the words helps to fix them in your mind.

Appendix A

Additional Resources

• •

Suppose you've read through this book three times and still can't get enough of this wonderful vocabulary? I hear you, my fellow *logophile* (word-lover). This appendix lists some of my favorite Dummies titles that can help you expand your *erudition* (learning, knowledge) even further, and also suggests a few Web sites to check out.

Do You Read Me? Books to Check Out

Some of the books listed have specific vocabulary lists; some simply use great (meaning "just may be found on that test you have to take") vocabulary in the body of the book. Either way, these books are worth checking out.

I've first listed the books I've written (you are eager to read more of my lame jokes, aren't you?); the other books I recommend are in alphabetical order.

The SAT I For Dummies, 5th Edition
by Suzee Vlk (Wiley Publishing, Inc.)

The GRE For Dummies, 4th Edition
by Suzee Vlk (Wiley Publishing, Inc.)

A Word A Day: A Romp Through Some of the Most Unusual and Intriguing Words in English
by Anu Garg and Stuti Garg (Wiley Publishing, Inc.)

Latin For Dummies
by Clifford A. Hull, Steven R. Perkins, and Tracy Barr (Wiley Publishing, Inc.)

Philosophy For Dummies
by Tom Morris (Wiley Publishing, Inc.)

Poetry For Dummies
by The Poetry Center, John Timpane, and Maureen Watts
(Wiley Publishing, Inc.)

Shakespeare For Dummies
by John Doyle and Ray Lischner (Wiley Publishing, Inc.)

Vocabulary For Dummies
by Laurie E. Rozakis (Wiley Publishing, Inc.)

If books aren't your thing, keep in mind that any reading is better than no reading, so consider magazines and newspapers as sources of new vocabulary. Two magazines — *Time* and *Newsweek* — are particularly noted for using the type of impressive vocabulary you're likely to see on the test.

Surfing Web Sites for More Vocab

If you're the type who would rather stare at a computer screen than a printed page, you may enjoy a few of my favorite vocabulary Web sites:

- www.M-W.com
- www.wordsmith.org/awad
- www.dictionary.com

Consider signing up for e-mail service at any of these three sites. After you sign up (see the instructions at each site), you receive daily e-mail messages, each with a new word. Each e-mail message not only introduces you to a word and defines it but also gives examples of how the word is used and often tells the origin of the word.

Appendix B

Glossary

● ●

*T*his isn't your everyday, run-of-the-mill glossary — no way! Sure, it gives you pronunciations and definitions of the words taught throughout this book just as any standard glossary would, but it's also a great study tool. The definitions are in a separate column from the words, which means you can cover the definition column and use this glossary as a self-test.

aberration (rhymes with, scab her *na*tion)	a departure or deviation from the norm
abeyance (rhymes with, uh *say* dunce)	temporary suspension
abhor (rhymes with, uh *bore*)	to hate or shrink from in disgust
abjure (rhymes with, scab *sure*)	to give up, renounce
abomination (uh bom in *na*tion)	anything hateful and disgusting
abstemious (rhymes with, crabs *them* he us)	moderate or temperate, especially in eating and drinking
acclaim (a *claim*)	approval, praise (also as a verb meaning to approve or to praise)
accolade (rhymes with, *back* coal aid)	a sign of approval
acme (rhymes with, *back* me)	the highest point, the peak
acquiescent (rhymes with, *back* we yes sent)	agreeing or consenting without protest
acumen (rhymes with, *back* you men)	shrewdness, keenness, and quickness in understanding and dealing with a situation

acute (rhymes with, a *suit*)	keen or quick of mind, shrewd
adage (rhymes with, *bad* smidge)	an old saying that has been popularly accepted as truth
adamant (*ad* uh mint)	unrelenting, unyielding
addendum (rhymes with, then *den* dumb)	something added, an appendix or supplement
addle (rhymes with, paddle)	to muddle or confuse
adjure (rhymes with, *bad* sure)	to command solemnly, often under oath, to entreat or appeal to
adroit (rhymes with, uh *boy't*)	skillful or expert
adulation (rhymes with, *sad* you nation)	intense admiration, excessive flattery
adulterate (a*dult* her eight)	to make inferior by adding a less valuable substance
adumbrate (rhymes with, a *dumb* date)	to foreshadow in a vague way, to sketch in an outline of, to give a sketchy idea of
aesthetic (rhymes with, yes *bet* ick)	pertaining to beauty
affable (rhymes with, *laugh* able)	friendly, pleasant, and easy to talk to
affluent (rhymes with, *laugh* you gent)	wealthy, having an abundance of money
agitate (rhymes with, *badge* it ate)	to upset or disturb
alacrity (rhymes with, a *black* city)	eager willingness or readiness
alleviate (uh *leave* he ate)	to lessen, relieve
ambience (*ahm* bee unce) (also spelled ambiance)	the environment, the atmosphere, the milieu
amble (rhymes with, *gamble*)	to walk in a leisurely manner
ambulatory (*am* byoo lah tory)	able to walk, moving from one pace to another

animated (rhymes with, *ban* him wait Ed)	lively, vigorous, spirited
animosity (an nim *mas* itty)	strong feeling of hatred or dislike
antediluvian (ant tea dill *loo* vee un)	very old, old-fashioned, or primitive
antiquated (*ant* tick waited)	old-fashioned, out of date, obsolete, or old
aquiline (rhymes with, *talk* will line)	like an eagle
arbitration (are bit *tray* shun)	the settlement of a dispute by a person selected to hear both sides and come to a decision
archaic (ark *hay* ick)	ancient, antiquated, old-fashioned
ardent (*are* dent)	intensely enthusiastic or devoted
articulate (are *tick* you late)	able to speak clearly and express thoughts well
asterisk (rhymes with, *pasture* risk)	starlike sign
astral (rhymes with, *pass* trull)	of, from, or like the stars
astute (rhymes with, us *toot*)	having or showing a clever or shrewd mind, or cunning
attenuated (at *ten* you waited)	slender, thin
audacious (rhymes with, clawed *a* shuss)	bold, daring, or fearless
avarice (rhymes with, *have* a hiss)	greed, desire to get something
aversion (a *version*)	disliking for
Bacchanalia (back uh *nail* yuh)	drunken party
badinage (rhymes with, *sad* in midge)	humorous banter or ridicule
banal (rhymes with, men *pal*)	commonplace, dull, or stale
beatific (be uh *tiff* ick)	serenely happy, or blissful
befuddle (rhymes with, wee *pud*-dle)	to confuse

belittle (be *little*)	to make seem little or less important, to speak slightingly of
bemoan (rhymes with, he *groan*)	weep, lament, or express sorrow for
bequeath (rhymes with, be*neath*)	to leave by Last Will and Testament, to hand down to another
berate (rhymes with, she *ate*)	to scold, rebuke
beseech (rhymes with, she *peach*)	to ask for earnestly, to beg for
besmirch (rhymes with, she *perch*)	to besmirch is to bring dishonor to, to sully
bete noire (bet no *wah*)	a person or thing that's disliked or feared, and thus avoided
bilk (rhymes with, *milk*)	to cheat or defraud
blanch (rhymes with, *ranch*)	to make white, to take the color out
blench (rhymes with, *clench*)	to whiten, to bleach, to become pale
bogus (rhymes with, *go* Gus)	not genuine
bombastic (bomb *bass* tick)	using high-sounding language, pompous
bon mot (bone *moe*)	an apt, clever, or witty remark
bourgeois (boo *zwah*)	of the middle class, conventional
bourgeoisie (boor zwah *zee*)	the middle class
bovine (rhymes with, so *fine*)	like an ox
bowdlerize (rhymes with, *loud* her eyes)	to remove passages considered offensive, to expurgate
brawny (rhymes with, *scrawny*)	strong and muscular
Brobdingnagian (rhymes with, Bob din *nag* he un)	giant

brontophobia (brahn toe *foe* be uh)	fear of thunder
brummagem (rhymes with, *come* a gem)	cheap and gaudy substitute for the real thing
bungle (rhymes with, *jungle*)	to do or make things clumsily
burly (rhymes with, *curly*)	big and strong, heavy and muscular
burnish (rhymes with, *fur*nish)	to polish by rubbing
cached (*cashed*)	hidden or stored
cadge (*cage*)	to get by begging or scrounging
cajole (rhymes with, the *hole*)	to persuade or prevail upon, to coax
callipygian (calluh *pige*-ee un)	having shapely buttocks
callow (rhymes with, *shallow*)	young and inexperienced, immature
calumny (rhymes with, *gal* yum knee)	false and malicious statement meant to hurt someone's reputation
candid (rhymes with, *Dan* did)	honest, frank
candor (rhymes with, *grand* or)	fairness, honesty, or frankness
canine (rhymes with, *say* fine)	like a dog
capacious (rhymes with, snap *hay* shuss)	roomy, spacious, able to contain or hold much
carp (rhymes with, *harp*)	to find fault with, take exception to
castigate (rhymes with, *pass* the gate)	to punish by giving public criticism
celerity (rhymes with, so *there* kitty)	speed, swiftness
celestial (sell *less* tea ull)	of the universe, of the planets or stars
censure (rhymes with, *then* sure)	strong disapproval, a formal expression of disapproval

cessation (rhymes with, yes *nation*)	stopping, ceasing
chaff (rhymes with, *laugh*)	good-natured teasing or joking
chatterbox (rhymes with, *fatter* fox)	a person who talks incessantly
chimerical (ki *mer* ic al)	imaginary, fanciful
choleric (rhymes with, go *there* ick)	hot-tempered, angry, wrathful
cliché (rhymes with, we *play*)	an expression or idea that has become overused
closefisted (*cloze* fist ed)	tightfisted, stingy, closing your hand on money
coeval (rhymes with, no *evil*)	all of the same age or period, contemporary
comely (rhymes with, *some* he)	attractive
comestible (rhymes with, home *best* nibble)	food
compensation (com pen *say* shun)	payment for services, wages, remuneration
compliant (rhymes with, Mom *try* ant)	yielding, submissive
constellation (rhymes with, John's tell *lay* shun)	group of stars in the sky
consternation (cons stir *na*tion)	great fear or shock that leaves one feeling helpless or bewildered
contemptuously (con *temp* chew us lee)	scornfully, disrespectfully
convivial (rhymes with, one *give* he uh)	having to do with a feast or festive activity
copiously (rhymes with, *hope* he us lee)	abundantly, a lot
corpulent (*corp* you lent)	fat, fleshy
corroborating (core *rob* burr rating)	confirming, bolstering, supporting
coruscation (rhymes with, chorus *say* shun)	a sudden brilliant display of wit
cow (rhymes with, *now*)	to intimidate, to make afraid or submissive

craven (rhymes with, *rav*en)	so cowardly, abjectly afraid
cupidity (rhymes with, stu*pid*ity)	greed for gain, inordinate desire to appropriate another's wealth or possessions
curtail (rhymes with, *shirt* tail)	shorten
cygnet (rhymes with, *pig* net)	a young swan
dandy (rhymes with, *can*dy)	a man whose style of dress is ostentatiously elegant or fashionable
dapper (rhymes with, *tap* her)	neat, trim, smart in dress or appearance
dastard (rhymes with, *bas*tard)	cowardly evildoer
daunt (rhymes with, *haunt*)	to make afraid, to intimidate, to dishearten
dawdle (rhymes with, *paw* dull)	to waste time by being slow or idle
declaim (rhymes with, re*claim*)	to speak in a dramatic, pompous way
defalcate (rhymes with, the *tall* Kate)	to steal or misuse funds, to embezzle
demean (rhymes with, see *teen*)	to treat badly
denigrate (rhymes with, *then* pig great)	to blacken the reputation of someone, defame, decry
denounce (rhymes with, the *ounce*)	to condemn strongly
derogatory (rhymes with, her *jog* a story)	disparaging, belittling, lessening someone's good name
desist (rhymes with, he *twist*)	to stop, abstain, cease from
despondent (rhymes with, yes *pond* dent)	dejected, losing hope, losing heart
destitute (rhymes with, *yes* bit toot)	without resources, in poverty

deter (rhymes with, he *fur*)	to stop or discourage a person from doing something
detest (rhymes with, he *best*)	to hate, abhor
diatribe (rhymes with, *try* a bribe)	a lengthy bitter, abusive criticism
dilatory (rhymes with, *thrill* a story)	causing delay, slow or late in doing things
diligent (rhymes with, *pill* he gent)	persevering and careful in work, painstaking
dirge (rhymes with, *purge*)	a song of mourning, sung at a funeral, also the wake itself
disaster (rhymes with, this *past* her)	sudden misfortune, calamity
discerning (rhymes with, this *turn*ing)	having or showing good judgment or understanding
disconsolate (rhymes with, this *con* soul yet)	unhappy, forlorn, unable to be comforted
discursive (rhymes with, this *purse* give)	rambling, wandering from one topic to another
disdain (rhymes with, this *pain*)	scorn, contempt
disgruntled (dis *grunt* tulled)	discontented, in a bad mood or bad humor
disingenuously (dis in *jenn* you us lee)	not straightforwardly, insincerely, with a pretence of innocence and sincerity
disparage (rhymes with, this *carriage*)	to show disrespect for
dissertation (dis ser *tay* shun)	a formal and lengthy treatise on a subject
dither (rhymes with, *with* her)	to be indecisive, vacillate, waver
docile (rhymes with, *floss* while)	submissive, easy to manage
dogged (rhymes with, *frog* Ed)	persistent, stubborn

doggerel (*dog* er ull)	trivial, awkward, often comically bad verse
dogmatic (rhymes with, frog *mat* pick)	stating opinions in a positive or arrogant manner
doleful (rhymes with, *soul*ful)	sorrowful, mournful, discontent
dolorous (rhymes with, *soul* her us)	sad, mournful
dolt (rhymes with, *bolt*)	a stupid, slow-witted person, a blockhead
doughty (rhymes with, *doubt* he)	brave
dour (rhymes with, sewer)	gloomy, sullen
droll (rhymes with, *troll*)	amusing, especially in an odd or surprising way
dubious (rhymes with, *cube* he us)	doubtful
dynamic (rhymes with, try *ham* ick)	energetic, vigorous
ebullient (ih *bull* yent)	bubbling over with enthusiasm, exuberant
effervescent (rhymes with, deaf fur *yes* sent)	lively, vivacious, high-spirited
elephantine (*elephant* tine)	huge, heavy, slow, clumsy, or like an elephant
ellipsis (rhymes with, he *lips* kiss)	the omission of a word or words necessary for complete grammatical construction but understood in the context
emaciated (rhymes with, he *may* she waited)	abnormally thin or wasted
emulate (rhymes with, *them* you late)	to imitate
encomium (in *comb* he um)	a formal expression of praise
enervated (rhymes with, *when* her dated)	weakened, devitalized
enmity (*en* mitty)	hostility
ennui (on *we*)	boredom

ensconced (en *scons*'d)	placed or settled snugly or securely
entreat (rhymes with, when *beat*)	to plead for
epicure (rhymes with, *pep* pick cure)	a person who enjoys and has a discriminating taste for fine foods and drinks
equable (*ek* wah bull)	not readily upset, tranquil, serene
equine (rhymes with, *heck* fine)	like a horse
ersatz (rhymes with, *her* flats)	a synthetic (fake) version of a product meant to replace something else
erstwhile (rhymes with, *first* while)	former
erudite (rhymes with, *there* you bite)	learned, scholarly
esculent (rhymes with, *yes* you'll lent)	fit to be used for food, edible
eulogy (rhymes with, *you* low gee)	high praise
exculpate (*ex* culp ate)	to remove guilt or blame from, get off the hook
execrable (rhymes with, *hex* bubble)	detestable, abominable
exemplary (ex *semp* lury)	serving as a model or example, worth imitating
expatriate (rhymes with, hex *late* tree hut)	a person who has left his homeland
expedite (rhymes with, *hex* speed height)	to speed up, hasten, facilitate
expurgate (rhymes with, *hex* berg gate)	to remove obscene or objectionable passages
extol (rhymes with, necks *pole*)	to praise highly
fait accompli (fate ah comb *plea*)	something already done or in effect, making opposition or argument useless
fatuous (rhymes with, *that* you us)	silly, foolish, complacently stupid, or inane

fawn (rhymes with, *yawn*)	to act servilely, to cringe and flatter
fawning (rhymes with, *yaw*ning)	flattering, showing servile deference
febrile (rhymes with, *feeble*)	feverish
feckless (rhymes with, *reck*less)	weak and ineffective, careless and irresponsible
felicitous (rhymes with, so *this* it us)	very happy
fiat (rhymes with, *me* hot)	an order issued by legal authority
filch (*fill*-ch)	to steal something small or petty
fiscal (rhymes with, *this* gull)	pertaining to money
fledgling (rhymes with, *pledge* wing)	a young bird
flippant (rhymes with, *hip* ant)	disrespectful, saucy, or impertinent
fodder (rhymes with, *nod*der)	coarse food, the kind used to feed cattle and horses, such as straw, hay, and so on
folly (rhymes with, *trolly*)	a lack of understanding or sense, foolishness
foolhardy (rhymes with, *school* party)	foolishly bold, reckless
footless (*foot* less)	not efficient, clumsy, or inept
foozle (rhymes with, whose'll)	to make or do something awkwardly, to bungle
fop (rhymes with, *cop*)	a dandy, someone who is excessively concerned with being fashionable
forlorn (for *lorn*)	sad, unhappy, without hope
fractious (rhymes with, *back* shuss)	hard to manage, unruly, rebellious
frank (rhymes with, *thank*)	openly, honestly, candidly

frenzied (*friends* heed)	hyperactive, upset, running around like a chicken with its head cut off
froward (rhymes with, *throw* word)	stubbornly willful, not easily controlled
frowzy (rhymes with, *lou*sy)	dirty, untidy, neglected in appearance
frugal (rhymes with, *who* gull)	economical, careful in the use of goods
funereal (few *near* he ull)	gloomy, dismal, appropriate to a funeral
galvanized (*gal* van ized)	stimulated, roused, or spurred into action
gambol (rhymes with, *ramble*)	to jump and skip about in play, to frolic
gargantuan (gar *gant* you an)	enormous, gigantic
garrulous (rhymes with, *bar*rel us)	talking too much
gauche (*go* shhhh)	lacking grace, especially social grace, awkward, tactless
gaunt (rhymes with, *haunt*)	abnormally slim, especially from lack of nourishment
gawky (rhymes with, squawky)	awkward, often from being disproportionately tall
gingerly (rhymes with, *hinge* her lee)	carefully, cautiously
glib (rhymes with, *bib*)	speaking in a smooth, easy manner
glower (rhymes with, *shower*)	glare, look angrily
glutton (rhymes with, *but*-ton)	a person who eats too much
gourmand (rhymes with, your *pond*)	one who pigs out or someone who eats to excess, a gourmet, one who is an epicure and is an excellent judge of fine food and drinks

graffiti (rhymes with, laugh *he* tea)	inscriptions, slogans, and so on scratched or drawn on a wall or other public surface
grandiloquent (rhymes with, hand *brillo* went)	using pompous, bombastic words
graphologist (rhymes with, laugh *all* oh gist)	a handwriting expert, one who studies handwriting
gratuitous (grah *two* it us)	uncalled for, without cause or justification
gustatory (rhymes with, *bust* a story)	having to do with the sense of taste
haberdashery (*hab* er dash her ree)	store selling gentleman's clothing
hackneyed (rhymes with, *black* weed)	overused or trite
halcyon (rhymes with, *pals* he on)	happy, tranquil, or idyllic
hapless (rhymes with, *cap* less)	unfortunate, unlucky
harangue (ha *rang*)	a loud, noisy, or scolding speech, a tirade
hector (rhymes with, *vector*)	to bully or browbeat
hedonism (rhymes with, *she* phone ism)	pursuit of pleasure as a way of life
hiatus (rhymes with, why *hate* us)	a break or a gap
hidebound (rhymes with, *side* hound)	obstinately conservative and narrow-minded
highhanded (*high* handed)	overbearing, arbitrary
hoary (rhymes with, *story*)	grayish white or having gray hair, old
homely (rhymes with, *Rome* Lee)	plain or unattractive in appearance
horology (rhymes with, sore *all* oh gee)	the art or science of making timepieces
horripilation (rhymes with, sore uh pill *ay* shun)	the state of having your hair standing on end

humdrum (*hum* drum)	lacking variety, dull, monotonous, boring
hydrophobia (high droe *foe* bee uh)	fear of water
hypochondriac (high poe *con* dree ack)	person abnormally anxious over health, especially an imagined illness
illegible (ill *ledge* ible)	difficult or impossible to read
immature (rhymes with, *him* that sure)	not completely grown, not finished
impecunious (im peck *you* knee us)	poor, penniless
implicit (rhymes with, him *this* it)	not plainly express what you're talking about
implore (rhymes with, him *sore*)	to beg earnestly
importune (rhymes with, him sore *goon*)	to urge, ask or beg for persistently
inane (rhymes with, in-*sane*)	lacking sense, foolish, silly
inaudible (rhymes with, in *clawed* drib bowl)	not loud enough to be heard
incensed (in *sensed*)	angry, enraged, exasperated
incisive (rhymes with, we *sighs* give)	sharp, keen, or acute
inconsolable (in con *sole* able)	unable to be comforted
indigent (rhymes with, *in* smidge gent)	poor, needy
indolent (rhymes with, *win* dough lent)	lazy, idle
industrious (in *duss* tree us)	steady and hard-working
inept (rhymes with, win *slept*)	clumsy or bungling, inefficient
ingenious (rhymes with, in *gene* ee us)	clever, resourceful
ingénue (*on* gin oooh)	an innocent, inexperienced, unworldly young woman
inkling (rhymes with, twinkling)	an indirect suggestion, a slight indication, a hint

innuendo (rhymes with, win you *friend* dough)	an indirect remark, especially one derogatory
insinuate (in *sin* you ate)	to work something into a conversation indirectly and artfully, suggest or hint indirectly
interminable (in *term* in able)	without end, seeming to last forever
intestate (rhymes with, in*vest* eight)	without a will
intimation (rhymes with, win *Tim* nation)	a hint, an indirect suggestion
intractable (in *track* table)	hard to manage, stubborn
intransigent (in *trans* sig gent)	refuses to compromise
intrepid (rhymes with, in *step* hid)	bold, fearless, very brave
inundate (*in* uhn date)	to flood or deluge, to overwhelm with a great amount of anything
invigorate (rhymes with, win *fig* or ate)	full of life and energy
ironhanded (iron *handed*)	in a rigorous, severely controlling manner
irony (rhymes with, *hi* Ronnie)	a circumstance that's the opposite of what may be expected
irresolute (ear rez so *loot*)	indecisive, wavering, vacillating
jaded (rhymes with, *faded*)	tired, worn out, wearied, or satiated as from overindulgence
jejune (rhymes with, duh *spoon*)	not mature, childish
jocular (rhymes with, *clock* you'll er)	speaking or acting in jest or merriment, jokingly
joey (rhymes with, *showy*)	a baby kangaroo
judicious (rhymes with, you'd *dish* us)	wise and careful, showing sound judgment
jurisprudence (jur is *prew* dence)	the science or philosophy of law

juvenescent (rhymes with, you've an *ess* sent)	becoming young, growing youthful
kleptomaniac (rhymes with, *slept* toe maniac)	a person with an abnormal, persistent impulse to steal, not prompted by need
kudos (rhymes with, *you* doze)	praise, glory, fame
lachrymose (rhymes with, *back* him gross)	tearful, sad, mournful
laconic (la *con* nick)	using few words, terse
laggard (rhymes with, *haggard*)	a slow person, one who falls behind
lamentation (lam men *tay* shun)	bewailing, mourning, regret
lampoon (rhymes with, cram *soon*)	to ridicule or attack
languid (rhymes with, *bang* wid)	drooping, weak, sluggish
languish (rhymes with, *anguish*)	to fail in health, become weak
lanky (rhymes with, *crank*y)	awkwardly or ungracefully lean or long
larcenous (rhymes with, *sparse* hen us)	thieving
lassitude (rhymes with, *gas* it, Dude)	weariness, languor, listlessness
laud (rhymes with, *clawed*)	to praise
lethargic (rhymes with, Beth *barge* it)	drowsy, dull, sluggish
lissome (rhymes with, *this* some)	limber, moving gracefully and easily
listless (*list* less)	weary, spiritless, languid
lithe (*lie*-th)	flexible, limber, bending easily
loath (*low*-th)	reluctant
lobbyist (rhymes with, *hobby* ist)	a person acting for a special interest who tries to influence decisions
loquacious (rhymes with, no *play* she us)	very talkative
lucidly (rhymes with, *who* sid lee)	clearly

lugubrious (loo *gyoo* bree us)	mournful, doleful, dismal
lumbering (*lum*-ber ing)	moving heavily, clumsily, and noisily
lupine (*lou* pine)	like a wolf
maladroit (rhymes with, pal uh *boy't*)	awkward, clumsy, bungling
malaise (mal *lays*)	physical discomfort early in an illness
malign (rhymes with, the *sign*)	to speak evil of, to defame
malleable (rhymes with, *gal* he able)	capable of being changed or trained
mediate (rhymes with, *bed* it eight)	to bring about a conciliation or settlement
mellifluous (rhymes with, sell *if* flu us)	sounding sweet and smooth, honeyed
mendicant (rhymes with, *when* Dick can't)	a beggar
mercenary (rhymes with, *purse* in dairy)	serving merely for pay
meticulous (rhymes with, ri*dic*ulous)	detail-oriented, very careful, even finicky
mettle (rhymes with, *ket*tle)	courage, spirit, and a high quality of character
minatory (*min* uh tory)	threatening or menacing
minuscule (rhymes with, *win* us cool)	extremely small
miserly (rhymes with, *wiser* Lee)	stingy, hoarding wealth
mortified (rhymes with, *sport* if try)	embarrassed
mot juste (rhymes with, go *shoes*)	exactly the right word
mundane (rhymes with, fun *gain*)	commonplace and ordinary
munificent (rhymes with, spoon *if* is sent)	splendidly generous
nadir (rhymes with, fade *dear*)	lowest point
narcissism (rhymes with, *are* sis ism)	excessive interest in one's own appearance
narcolepsy (*nark* oh lep see)	medical condition marked by a frequent and uncontrollable desire for sleep

neophyte (rhymes with, *see* oh fight)	beginner, novice
nescient (rhymes with, *mesh* cent)	ignorant, lacking knowledge
newfangled (rhymes with, too *tangled*)	new, novel
nocuous (*knock* you us)	harmful, poisonous, noxious
noisome (rhymes with, *boys* some)	having a bad odor, foul-smelling, injurious to the health, harmful
novice (*nah* viss)	a beginner, an apprentice
noxious (rhymes with, *box* shuss)	injurious, harmful to the health, or unwholesome
nullify (rhymes with, *dull* if try)	make of no value, negate
obdurate (rhymes with, *blob* fur ate)	stubborn, not giving in readily
obese (rhymes with, go *peace*)	very overweight
obsequies (rhymes with, *blobs* he keys)	funeral services
obstinate (rhymes with, *blobs* tin ate)	stubborn, dogged, mulish, not yielding to reason or plea
obtuse (rhymes with, blob *loose*)	slow to understand, dull
odious (*oh* dee us)	arousing or deserving hatred, disgusting (don't confuse odious with odorous, meaning having a pronounced odor or smell)
olfactory (ah'll *factory*)	of the sense of smell
omniscient (ahm *nish* ent)	knowing all things
openhanded (open *handed*)	generous, giving or sharing freely
opisthenar (oh *piss* then are)	the back of your hand
opprobrium (oh *pro* bree um)	the disgrace attached to conduct that's viewed as grossly shameful
opulent (rhymes with, *pop* you lent)	rich, wealthy, affluent

orthography (rhymes with, North *hog* graph he)	spelling in accord with common usage, the study of spelling
oscillate (rhymes with, *ahs* till late)	to move back and forth
osculate (rhymes with, *ahs* que late)	to kiss
ossify (rhymes with, *ahs* if try)	to develop into bone
ossuary (rhymes with, *ahs* you airy)	a container, like an urn, for the bones of the dead
ostensibly (rhymes with, ahs *ten* sib lee)	seemingly, apparently (with the strong implication that the truth is otherwise)
ostentatious (rhymes with, ahs ten *played* us)	make a showy display of wealth, pretentious
osteopath (rhymes with, *ahs* we oh path)	a bone doctor, a physician who primarily works with the skeletal system
ostracize (rhymes with, *ahs* duh size)	to banish, bar, and exclude
ovine (rhymes with, *so* fine)	like a sheep
paean (*pi* uhn)	a song of praise
pallid (rhymes with, *gal* hid)	pale, especially from illness or shock
pandiculation (pan dick you *lay* shun)	the act of stretching and yawning
panegyric (pan uh *jeer* ick)	speech expressing high praise
parasite (rhymes with, *hair* a sight)	a person who flatters in exchange for free meals or other items
parry (rhymes with, *hairy*)	to ward off or deflect
parsimonious (pars im *moan* he us)	stingy, sparing
parvenu (rhymes with, *far* when you)	a person of humble origins who has gained wealth and position and risen in society, especially one considered unfit for the position (an upstart)

pate (rhymes with, *date*)	crown of the head
peccadillo (rhymes with, *heck* a dill oh)	a minor or petty sin, a slight fault
peckish (rhymes with, *deck* fish)	irritable, touchy, often from hunger
peculate (rhymes with, *speculate*)	to steal or misuse funds, to embezzle
pedant (rhymes with, *said* ant)	a narrow-minded teacher, especially one who stresses minor points of learning
pedestrian (rhymes with, red *yes* tree un)	ordinary and dull, lacking interest or imagination
peevish (rhymes with, *heave* fish)	irritable, fretful, spiteful
perambulate (rhymes with, fur *am* byoo late)	to walk about, stroll
peregrinate (rhymes with, *there* rig grin ate)	to travel or walk
perfunctory (rhymes with, her *funk* tore he)	done merely as form or routine, superficial
peripatetic (pair uh pah *tet* ick)	walking or moving about, itinerant
perjury (rhymes with, *fur* jury)	the willful telling of a lie while under oath
perspicacious (purse pick *kay* shuss)	having keen judgment or understanding, acutely perceptive
pertinacious (rhymes with, fur tin *hay* shuss)	holding firmly and stubbornly to a purpose
pilfer (rhymes with, *hill* fur)	steal, filch, take small amounts
pilgrimage (*pill* grim age)	any long journey, especially to a religious site or a place of historical interest
pinchbeck (*pinch* beck)	sham, a cheap imitation
piscine (rhymes with, *fly* seen)	like or having do with fish
pithy (rhymes with, *with* he)	concise, terse, and full of meaning

placate (rhymes with, *say* date)	to calm down, to pacify, to appease
plagiarism (rhymes with, *sage* her ism)	to take another person's work and pass it off as your own
plagiarist (*play* jur ist)	one who steals the work of another without giving proper credit
platitude (rhymes with, *at*titude)	commonplace or trite remark, but one uttered as if it were fresh and original
plaudits (rhymes with, *clawed* its)	expressions of praise
pliable (rhymes with, *fry* able)	easily influenced or persuaded
plunder (rhymes with, *blun*-der)	to rob by force, especially in warfare
plutocrat (rhymes with, *you* toe brat)	a person exercising power or influence over others by right of wealth or position
pogophobia (go *foe* bee uh)	fear of beards
poltroon (rhymes with, whole *goon*)	not just a coward but a thorough coward
polymath (rhymes with, *trolly* path)	a person of great and diversified learning
pontificate (pahn *tiff* fi kate)	to speak in a pompous or dogmatic way
poult (rhymes with, *bolt*)	any young fowl
pragmatic (rhymes with, hag *matt* ick)	practical
precipitate (pre *sip* it tate)	acting, happening, or done very hastily or rashly
precocious (pre *coe* shuss)	developed or matured beyond what is normal for the age, prematurely developed
probity (rhymes with, *grow* bitty)	a person with integrity who is upright in her dealings

procrastinate (pro *crass* tin eight)	put off, postpone
procrastinator (pro *crass* tin eight her)	one who habitually postpones or puts off things
prodigal (rhymes with, *odd* dig gull)	recklessly wasteful, extravagant
prodigy (rhymes with, *rod* smidge he)	a child of highly unusual talent or genius
proffer (*proff* her)	to offer
proficient (rhymes with, know *fish* scent)	highly skilled, competent
profligate (rhymes with, *off* fig late)	recklessly extravagant (this word also refers to someone who has abandoned himself/herself to vice or indulgence)
prolific (rhymes with, go *jif* ick)	fruitful, abounding, producing many/much
prolix (rhymes with, *go* licks)	wordy, long-winded
promulgate (*prom* mull gate)	to publish or make known officially
prosaic (rhymes with, mo*saic*)	commonplace, dull, and ordinary
protocol (rhymes with, *photo* call)	the code of ceremonial forms and courtesies accepted as proper for dealings between officials
pseudo (rhymes with, *you* know)	counterfeit, pretended, or sham
puerile (rhymes with, *sure* while)	childish, silly, immature
pulchritudinous (rhymes with, hulk bit *two* din us)	beautiful
punctilious (punk *till* he us)	scrupulous about every detail of behavior
punctiliously (punk *till* he us lee)	very careful about every detail of behavior, very exact

pundit (rhymes with, *one* zit)	a person who has or professes to have great learning or authority
purloin (rhymes with, *sir*-loin)	to steal
pusillanimous (pew sill *an* im us)	timid, cowardly, or fainthearted
querulous (*k'were* you luss)	full of complaints
quotidian (rhymes with, pro *bid* he un)	daily, either in the sense of recurring every day or something everyday and common
rail (rhymes with, *sail*)	to speak bitterly, complain against
ramble (rhymes with, *gamble*)	to roam about, stroll idly without any particular goal
rancor (*rank* or)	continuing and bitter hate, deep spite or malice
rangy (rhymes with, *strange* he)	tall and thin
rash (rhymes with, *dash*)	too hasty, to the point of being reckless
raucous (*raw* cuss)	harsh-sounding, unpleasant-sounding
ravishing (rhymes with, *lavish* sing)	causing great joy or delight, entrancing
rebuke (rhymes with, see *duke*)	scold
recalcitrant (re *cal* sit trant)	stubbornly defiant, refusing to obey authority
recuperate (rhymes with, the *soup* her ate)	to be restored to heath, get well, and recover
refractory (rhymes with, she *back* story)	hard to manage, stubborn
refrain (rhymes with, she *train*)	to hold back, stop from doing
remonstrated (re *mahn* stray ted)	said in protest or complaint

rendezvous (rhymes with, *pond* they you)	a designated meeting place
resolved (re *zolved*)	determined, fixed in purpose
resourceful (re *source* full)	able to deal creatively and effectively with problems and difficulties
resplendent (re *splen* dent)	dazzling, shining brightly
revelry (*rev* uhl ree)	noisy merry-making, boisterous festivity
rhetorically (ret *tore* ick lee)	in a showy or artificial manner
riddled (rhymes with, *fid*dled)	having many holes or punctured, spread throughout
rifle (rhymes with, *trifle*)	to ransack and rob a place
risible (rhymes with, *visible*)	laughable, humorous
rotund (rhymes with, so *punned*)	round, plump
ruddy (rhymes with, *bud*dy)	red or reddish
sagacious (suh *gay* shuss)	showing keen perception and sound judgment
sallow (rhymes with, *shallow*)	of a sickly pale-yellow hue
salubrious (rhymes with, gal *lube* free us)	healthful, wholesome
sanguine (*sang* win)	cheerful, optimistic
sartorial (rhymes with, car *story* ull)	pertaining to clothing or to tailors
Saturnalia (sat turn *ale* yuh)	period of unrestrained revelry
saunter (rhymes with, *lawn* ter)	stroll, walk leisurely
savory (*save* or he)	appetizing, pleasing to the taste or smell
scintillation (rhymes with, *win* till nation)	sparkle, flash
scrupulous (*screw* pyew luss)	extremely careful to do things right

self-effacing (rhymes with, elf *erase* sing)	to be inconspicuous and withdraw yourself from notice
senescence (rhymes with, when *yes* sense)	growing old, aging
senile (rhymes with, *she* while)	showing deterioration from old age, especially mental impairment and confusion
serendipity (rhymes with, care in *dip* pity)	luck or good fortune, especially in finding something accidentally
servile (rhymes with, *curve* vile)	like a slave, yielding, submissive
sesquipedalian (rhymes with, yes we said *hale* he un)	using foot-and-a-half-long, or very long, words
sham (rhymes with, *ham*)	a counterfeit, a fake
sheepish (rhymes with, *keep* fish)	embarrassed, awkwardly shy or bashful
sidereal (rhymes with, bride *hear* he all)	of or pertaining to the stars
slattern (rhymes with, *pat*tern)	an untidy and slovenly woman
slovenly (rhymes with, *glove* hen lee)	untidy, dirty
sluggish (rhymes with, buggish)	lacking energy, slow-moving
soignée (for women), soigné (for men) (swan *yea*)	meticulously dressed, well-groomed
soiree (swah *ray*)	party or gathering in the evening
solicitously (sole *is* it us lee)	concernedly, showing care and compassion
solvent (rhymes with, *doll* vent)	able to pay one's debts, financially sound
somnambulism (som nam byou *lay* shun)	sleepwalking
somniloquist (som *nill* oh quist)	a person who talks in his or her sleep

somnolent (rhymes with, *Mom* no lent)	sleepy, drowsy
soporific (rhymes with, cop or *if* ick)	causing sleep
sotto voce (so toe *voh* chay)	in an undertone, so as not to be overheard
spurious (rhymes with, *fury* us)	false or counterfeit
squander (rhymes with, *wan*-der)	to spend recklessly, use in a wasteful manner
stealthily (rhymes with, *health* hill lee)	secretively, furtively, in a sly manner
stellar (rhymes with, *feller*)	of the stars, like a star in shape
stentorian (rhymes with, when *story* un)	very loud
stout (rhymes with, *out*)	fat, corpulent
strapping (rhymes with, *clapping*)	tall and well-built, robust
strident (rhymes with, *try* dent)	loud, harsh, shrill
stultifying (rhymes with, *cult* if trying)	foolish, stupid, dull, useless
stupefied (*stoop* if fyed)	stunned with amazement, astounded
stymied (rhymes with, *fly* mead)	frustrated by being blocked, obstructed, hindered
submissive (sub *miss* ive)	yielding, unresisting, docile
subtle (*sut* tull)	delicately suggestive, not grossly obvious
succinct (rhymes with, the *pinked*)	clearly and briefly stated, terse
superannuated (super *ann* you ated)	too old or worn for further work, old-fashioned, outdated
superfluity (soup her *flew* itty)	excess, overabundance
superfluous (sue *per* flew us)	surplus, excessive
supple (rhymes with, *coup*le)	limber, able to bend and move easily

supplicant (rhymes with, *yup* lick can't)	one who begs or asks humbly
surcease (sir *seize*)	an end or cessation
surly (rhymes with, early)	bad-tempered, unfriendly
sustenance (rhymes with, *bus* ten dense)	nourishment, food
svelte (rhymes with, *felt*)	slender, willowy, elegant, graceful
swagger (rhymes with, *stagger*)	to walk with a bold, arrogant stride
swarthy (*swore* thee)	dark-complexioned
sweltering (rhymes with, sheltering)	uncomfortably, oppressively hot
swindle (rhymes with, spin-dle)	to cheat, to get money or property from another by false pretences
sycophant (*sick* oh fant)	a flatterer
tacit (rhymes with, *lass* it)	not expressed or declared openly, but implied or understood
taciturn (rhymes with, *acid* turn)	not liking to talk, almost always silent
talisman (rhymes with, *pal* is man)	a magic charm, a good luck charm
tangible (rhymes with, *fan* jib bull)	able to be touched, having form and substance, definite or unmistakable
tenacious (rhymes with, when *play* shuss)	persistent, stubborn
terse (rhymes with, *verse*)	brief, concise, succinct, free of superfluous words
tightfisted (tight *fisted*)	stingy, holding tight to money
timorous (rhymes with, *him* or us)	timid or afraid
tinge (rhymes with, *hinge*)	to color slightly, to give a tint to

titivate (rhymes with, *sit* give eight)	to dress up or spruce up
tittup (rhymes with, *sit* up)	to move in a frolicsome or prancing way
toady (rhymes with, *road* he)	a yes-man, one who flatters to excess, a sycophant
tome (rhymes with, *home*)	a book, especially a large, scholarly, or ponderous one
torpor (*tore* pour)	sluggishness, inactivity
traduce (rhymes with, duh *goose*)	to say untrue or malicious things about, to slander
trepidation (rhymes with, step bid *nation*)	fear, apprehension
trite (rhymes with, *bite*)	stale, overused, and no longer fresh and original
trudge (rhymes with, *budge*)	to walk wearily or laboriously
turdine (rhymes with, *bird* dean)	of, like, or pertaining to a robin or a bluebird
turpitude (rhymes with, *burp* it rude)	vileness, depravity
tyro (rhymes with, *why* bro)	a novice, a beginner
ultimate (rhymes with, *cult* tim ate lee)	final, conclusive
unambiguous (un am *big* you us)	clear
underhanded (*under* handed)	secret, sly, deceitful
ungainly (un *gain* lee)	awkward, clumsy
unkempt (rhymes with, fun *them*'t)	untidy, having a neglected appearance
unremitting (un re *mitt* ting)	non-stopping, persistent, incessant
unruly (un *rule* he)	hard to control or restrain
untoward (un *toward*)	awkward, clumsy
upbraid (*up* braid)	to criticize or rebuke sharply
uproarious (up *roar* he us)	noisy, loud, boisterous

ursine (rhymes with, *fur* sign)	like a bear
vacillate (rhymes with, *gas* till eight)	to waiver in mind, show indecision
vacuous (rhymes with, *sack* you us)	stupid, showing lack of intelligence
valetudinarian (val uh tude din *air* ee un)	person in poor health
valiant (rhymes with, *gal* he sent)	brave
venerable (rhymes with, *when* her able)	worthy of respect by reason of age and dignity
veracity (rhymes with, her *gas* city)	truthfulness
verbose (rhymes with, sir *gross*)	wordy, long-winded
verdant (rhymes with, *fur* dent)	green
veteran (*vet* er un)	experienced, practiced
viands (rhymes with, *try* ands)	foods, especially choice dishes
victuals (rhymes with, *picked* you'lls)	food
vile (rhymes with, *trial*)	offensive to the senses, repulsive, or disgusting, morally base or evil, wicked, or depraved
vilify (rhymes with, *will* he try)	to use abusive language about
vim (rhymes with, *him*)	energy, vigor
virile (rhymes with, *here* while)	manly
virtuoso (rhymes with, *fur* chew oh so)	displaying great skill
visage (rhymes with, *his* age)	face
vituperate (rhymes with, my *group* her eight)	to find fault with, to vilify, revile, abuse
vivacious (rhymes with, try *play* bus)	lively, energetic
vociferous (rhymes with, go *dif*fer us)	loud, noisy, vehement
voluble (rhymes with, *doll* you pull)	talkative

vulgar (rhymes with, _gull_ grrrr)	common and popular, belonging to or characteristic of the common people
vulpine (rhymes with, _dull_ pine)	like a fox, foxy
wan (rhymes with, _on_)	unhealthily pale, of a grayish, sickly color
wanderlust (_wander_ lust)	an impulse, longing, or urge to wander or travel
wary (rhymes with, _fairy_)	cautious, careful, circumspect
wheedle (rhymes with, _need_-le)	to coax or persuade by flattery or endearments
whelp (rhymes with, _help_)	a young dog — or a young lion, tiger, leopard, bear, or wolf
wishy-washy (_wish_ he _wash_ he)	indecisive, vacillating
woebegone (_whoa_ be gone)	overwhelmed with grief, distress and sorrow
xanthous (_zan_ thus)	yellow, yellowish
xenophobia (zee no _foe_ bee uh)	fear of strangers
xerophobia (zero _foe_ bee uh)	fear of dryness and dry places
yegg (rhymes with, _egg_)	a criminal, especially a safecracker or burglar
yielding (rhymes with, _field_ ding)	giving up under pressure, surrendering, submitting

Index

• *B* •

• C •

FOR DUMMIES®

The easy way to get more done and have more fun

PERSONAL FINANCE

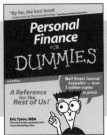

0-7645-5231-7

0-7645-2431-3

0-7645-5331-3

Also available:

Estate Planning For Dummies
(0-7645-5501-4)

401(k)s For Dummies
(0-7645-5468-9)

Frugal Living For Dummies
(0-7645-5403-4)

Microsoft Money "X" For
Dummies
(0-7645-1689-2)

Mutual Funds For Dummies
(0-7645-5329-1)

Personal Bankruptcy For
Dummies
(0-7645-5498-0)

Quicken "X" For Dummies
(0-7645-1666-3)

Stock Investing For Dummies
(0-7645-5411-5)

Taxes For Dummies 2003
(0-7645-5475-1)

BUSINESS & CAREERS

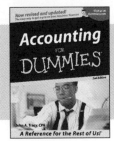

0-7645-5314-3

0-7645-5307-0

0-7645-5471-9

Also available:

Business Plans Kit For
Dummies
(0-7645-5365-8)

Consulting For Dummies
(0-7645-5034-9)

Cool Careers For Dummies
(0-7645-5345-3)

Human Resources Kit For
Dummies
(0-7645-5131-0)

Managing For Dummies
(1-5688-4858-7)

QuickBooks All-in-One Desk
Reference For Dummies
(0-7645-1963-8)

Selling For Dummies
(0-7645-5363-1)

Small Business Kit For
Dummies
(0-7645-5093-4)

Starting an eBay Business For
Dummies
(0-7645-1547-0)

HEALTH, SPORTS & FITNESS

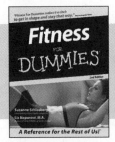

0-7645-5167-1

0-7645-5146-9

0-7645-5154-X

Also available:

Controlling Cholesterol For
Dummies
(0-7645-5440-9)

Dieting For Dummies
(0-7645-5126-4)

High Blood Pressure For
Dummies
(0-7645-5424-7)

Martial Arts For Dummies
(0-7645-5358-5)

Menopause For Dummies
(0-7645-5458-1)

Nutrition For Dummies
(0-7645-5180-9)

Power Yoga For Dummies
(0-7645-5342-9)

Thyroid For Dummies
(0-7645-5385-2)

Weight Training For Dummies
(0-7645-5168-X)

Yoga For Dummies
(0-7645-5117-5)

Available wherever books are sold.
Go to www.dummies.com or call 1-877-762-2974 to order direct.

FOR DUMMIES®

A world of resources to help you grow

HOME, GARDEN & HOBBIES

Feng Shui
0-7645-5295-3

Gardening
0-7645-5130-2

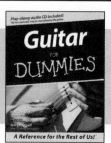

Guitar
0-7645-5106-X

Also available:

Auto Repair For Dummies
(0-7645-5089-6)

Chess For Dummies
(0-7645-5003-9)

Home Maintenance For
Dummies
(0-7645-5215-5)

Organizing For Dummies
(0-7645-5300-3)

Piano For Dummies
(0-7645-5105-1)

Poker For Dummies
(0-7645-5232-5)

Quilting For Dummies
(0-7645-5118-3)

Rock Guitar For Dummies
(0-7645-5356-9)

Roses For Dummies
(0-7645-5202-3)

Sewing For Dummies
(0-7645-5137-X)

FOOD & WINE

Cooking
0-7645-5250-3

Cookies
0-7645-5390-9

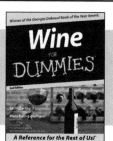

Wine
0-7645-5114-0

Also available:

Bartending For Dummies
(0-7645-5051-9)

Chinese Cooking For
Dummies
(0-7645-5247-3)

Christmas Cooking For
Dummies
(0-7645-5407-7)

Diabetes Cookbook For
Dummies
(0-7645-5230-9)

Grilling For Dummies
(0-7645-5076-4)

Low-Fat Cooking For
Dummies
(0-7645-5035-7)

Slow Cookers For Dummies
(0-7645-5240-6)

TRAVEL

Italy
0-7645-5453-0

Hawaii
0-7645-5438-7

Las Vegas
0-7645-5448-4

Also available:

America's National Parks For
Dummies
(0-7645-6204-5)

Caribbean For Dummies
(0-7645-5445-X)

Cruise Vacations For
Dummies 2003
(0-7645-5459-X)

Europe For Dummies
(0-7645-5456-5)

Ireland For Dummies
(0-7645-6199-5)

France For Dummies
(0-7645-6292-4)

London For Dummies
(0-7645-5416-6)

Mexico's Beach Resorts For
Dummies
(0-7645-6262-2)

Paris For Dummies
(0-7645-5494-8)

RV Vacations For Dummies
(0-7645-5443-3)

Walt Disney World & Orlando
For Dummies
(0-7645-5444-1)

Available wherever books are sold. Go to www.dummies.com or call 1-877-762-2974 to order direct.

FOR DUMMIES®

Plain-English solutions for everyday challenges

COMPUTER BASICS

0-7645-0838-5

0-7645-1663-9

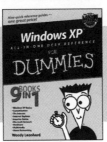

0-7645-1548-9

Also available:

PCs All-in-One Desk
Reference For Dummies
(0-7645-0791-5)

Pocket PC For Dummies
(0-7645-1640-X)

Treo and Visor For Dummies
(0-7645-1673-6)

Troubleshooting Your PC For
Dummies
(0-7645-1669-8)

Upgrading & Fixing PCs For
Dummies
(0-7645-1665-5)

Windows XP For Dummies
(0-7645-0893-8)

Windows XP For Dummies
Quick Reference
(0-7645-0897-0)

BUSINESS SOFTWARE

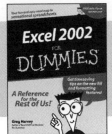

0-7645-0822-9

0-7645-0839-3

0-7645-0819-9

Also available:

Excel Data Analysis For
Dummies
(0-7645-1661-2)

Excel 2002 All-in-One Desk
Reference For Dummies
(0-7645-1794-5)

Excel 2002 For Dummies
Quick Reference
(0-7645-0829-6)

GoldMine "X" For Dummies
(0-7645-0845-8)

Microsoft CRM For Dummies
(0-7645-1698-1)

Microsoft Project 2002 For
Dummies
(0-7645-1628-0)

Office XP For Dummies
(0-7645-0830-X)

Outlook 2002 For Dummies
(0-7645-0828-8)

Get smart! Visit www.dummies.com

- **Find listings of even more *For Dummies* titles**

- **Browse online articles**

- **Sign up for Dummies eTips™**

- **Check out *For Dummies* fitness videos and other products**

- **Order from our online bookstore**

Available wherever books are sold. Go to www.dummies.com or call 1-877-762-2974 to order direct.

FOR DUMMIES®

Helping you expand your horizons and realize your potential

INTERNET

0-7645-0894-6

The Internet FOR DUMMIES

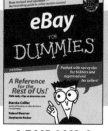

0-7645-1659-0

eBay FOR DUMMIES

0-7645-1642-6

Also available:

America Online 7.0 For Dummies
(0-7645-1624-8)

Genealogy Online For Dummies
(0-7645-0807-5)

The Internet All-in-One Desk Reference For Dummies
(0-7645-1659-0)

Internet Explorer 6 For Dummies
(0-7645-1344-3)

The Internet For Dummies Quick Reference
(0-7645-1645-0)

Internet Privacy For Dummies
(0-7645-0846-6)

Researching Online For Dummies
(0-7645-0546-7)

Starting an Online Business For Dummies
(0-7645-1655-8)

DIGITAL MEDIA

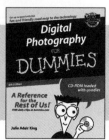

0-7645-1664-7

0-7645-1675-2

0-7645-0806-7

Also available:

CD and DVD Recording For Dummies
(0-7645-1627-2)

Digital Photography All-in-One Desk Reference For Dummies
(0-7645-1800-3)

Digital Photography For Dummies Quick Reference
(0-7645-0750-8)

Home Recording for Musicians For Dummies
(0-7645-1634-5)

MP3 For Dummies
(0-7645-0858-X)

Paint Shop Pro "X" For Dummies
(0-7645-2440-2)

Photo Retouching & Restoration For Dummies
(0-7645-1662-0)

Scanners For Dummies
(0-7645-0783-4)

GRAPHICS

0-7645-0817-2

0-7645-1651-5

0-7645-0895-4

Also available:

Adobe Acrobat 5 PDF For Dummies
(0-7645-1652-3)

Fireworks 4 For Dummies
(0-7645-0804-0)

Illustrator 10 For Dummies
(0-7645-3636-2)

QuarkXPress 5 For Dummies
(0-7645-0643-9)

Visio 2000 For Dummies
(0-7645-0635-8)

Available wherever books are sold. Go to www.dummies.com or call 1-877-762-2974 to order direct.

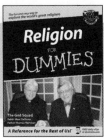
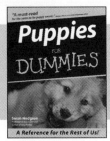